Accession no
919021

LG TELEPEN
01

D1424378

1-25

Africa's ibrary Three

Geoffrey Parrinder is Professor of the Comparative
Study of Religions in the University of London. After
ordination he spent twenty years teaching in West Africa
and studying African religions, and became the founder
member of the Department of Religious Studies in the
University College of Ibadan, Nigeria. He has travelled
widely in Africa, and in India, Pakistan, Sri Lanka,
Burma, Iran, Israel, Jordan and Turkey and has lectured
in Australia, America and India, and at Oxford. He is the
author of many books on world religions which have been
translated into eight languages.

By the same Author

West African Religion
Religion in an African City
African Mythology
African Traditional Religion
The Story of Ketu
Witchcraft, European and African
The Christian Approach to the Animist
The Christian Debate
Comparative Religion
Asian Religions
The World's Living Religions
What World Religions Teach
A Dictionary of Non-Christian Religions
A Book of World Religions
Jesus in the Qur'an
Avatar and Incarnation
Upanishads, Gita and Bible
The Bhagavad Gita: A Verse Translation
Worship in the World's Religions
Mysticism in the World's Religions
The Indestructible Soul
The Wisdom of the Forest

Africa's Three Religions

GEOFFREY PARRINDER

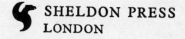

SHELDON PRESS
LONDON

ER COLLEGE
ACC. No.
91902101
DEPT.
CLASS No.
299.6 PAR
LIBRARY

First published in Great Britain in 1969 in Penguin's African Library
as *Religion in Africa*
Second edition published in 1976 by Sheldon Press, Marylebone Road, London NW1 4DU

Copyright © Geoffrey Parrinder, 1969

All rights reserved. No part of this book may be
reproduced or transmitted in any form or by any
means, electronic or mechanical, including
photocopying, recording or by any information
storage and retrieval system, without permission in
writing from the publisher.

Printed in Great Britain by
The Camelot Press Ltd, Southampton

ISBN 0 85969 096 2

Contents

Part Four: Conclusion

Introduction

The study of African religion is fairly new and not long ago it might have been doubted whether there was any African religion, at least in the tropics, just as some people queried whether there was any African history. But much research has been done in the present century into the religions of African peoples, and universities have come to include courses on African religion in their studies. In fact the pendulum has swung to the other extreme. When a great British university recently formulated a syllabus for study of different areas of the world, including most aspects of the cultures of Europe, Asia, America, and Africa, in the first draft the only area for which study of religion was proposed was Africa.

Many books have been written about cults and rituals in restricted areas, but few attempts have been made till now to consider the religions of Africa as a whole. It is important that this should be done, because the interactions of religions are significant facts of modern life, and the effect of religious belief and practice is felt in social and political spheres.

For the study of traditional African religious beliefs it has often been found convenient to limit attention to Africa south of the Sahara. But in a consideration of all religions this is clearly impossible. Islam, in particular, spread from North Africa into the western Sudan and thence into the tropics, and in doing so it affected the older tropical religion. Christianity in modern times went by sea round Africa, but in early centuries it extended from Egypt into Nubia and as far as Ethiopia. In this century Ethiopia has been prominent in African political affairs, and a church in Uganda is linked with the Orthodox Church in Egypt.

The one limitation that has been accepted in this book is that the only religions discussed are those that are still living. There is no examination of the ancient Egyptian religion of the Pharaohs and pyramids, as that was very complex and can be studied in any handbook of ancient Egyptian religion. As a system that religion has long been dead and is now the concern chiefly of archaeologists, though some traces of its influence may remain in a few popular practices in Christian, Muslim or traditional African religions.

The living religions of Africa fall into three natural groups: traditional religions, Christianity, and Islam, in order of appearance. The term 'traditional religions' is being increasingly used to denote what former writers called 'animism', 'fetishism' or 'polytheism'. All these labels can be justified, to some extent, but none is adequate as descriptive of the whole field, and all can be applied to many religious beliefs and practices in other parts of the world. Both Islam and Christianity are 'traditional religions' in Africa, in the sense that they have long traditions in the continent, and so it must be noted clearly that when the term 'traditional religions' is used in this book it means the older preliterate religions, mostly of tropical and southern Africa.

Since the traditional religion was preliterate it had no scriptures of its own, no ancient texts, and no old expressions of faith which could reveal what it was like to belong to such a religion in the past. This is a serious disadvantage to study, and it must be borne in mind when comparing the ancient faith with newer literate religions. In the present century many books have been written on the traditional religions of Africa, and in the main they are careful and impartial studies, but they are written by outsiders who have no experience of these religions as their own faith. Anthropologists, who have been most active in this field, some missionaries and administrators, and a few historians and others, have written books on African religion, but their differing points of view have to be taken into account. These writers are mostly Europeans and Americans, but growing numbers of Africans are making valuable studies in this field. They are generally theologians, such as C. G. Baëta, E. B. Idowu and J. S. Mbiti, with some sociologists like J. Kenyatta, J. B. Danquah and K. A. Busia. No doubt they are closer to the religion of their fathers than Europeans are, yet these modern academic Africans share little of the old faith and consider it largely from the outside. There cannot now appear a text from a convinced believer in the old religion who is not affected by modern ways.

The history of the traditional religion is unknown and few foreign descriptions were made before this century that merit close study, though there are a few hints in some of the more careful explorers' writings. This means that the development of religion can rarely be guessed, and when statements are made which claim that there is more witchcraft belief today or a higher incidence of neurosis due to the clatter of modern life, there is little scientific evidence for such assertions. There is hardly any knowledge of the incidence of religious practice in the past, which might show how far all society observed rituals, and suggest whether there were any nonconformists or unbelievers; judging from other continents there may have been some. But some idea of older religious attitudes can be gathered from artistic productions, which may be old or may continue old themes, from myths which relate ancient traditions, and from rituals which perpetuate earlier practice. By examining modern belief and custom the significance of religion can be estimated and some knowledge gathered of the philosophy which lies behind action.

This is a study of religion, considered as a subject in its own right, like law or language, despite its many ramifications and relationships. The fact that many studies of African religions have been made by anthropologists means that they have tended to concentrate on their special interests, the organization of society and patterns of kinship. Descriptions have been made of social customs, such as initiations, weddings or coronations. But these are not necessarily very religious phenomena, or they may have only marginal religious reference and shed little light on belief in spiritual things, so that they need not be considered at length here. Likewise ethical and political matters are not central to our concern, except where they have clear links with religious practice.

Further, although studies of African religion are usually impartial nowadays they often have a cold air, as if the writers were dissecting something dead. Partly this may come from the presuppositions of the student, tending to regard religious belief as superstitious. With an illiterate religion this temptation is greater, since there are no great philosophical systems or voluminous classical texts to daunt the investigator. And there is a tendency, in face of a religious phenomenon, to look for a theory that might explain it away, such as regarding belief in God as a symbol of a deified society as did Durkheim, or a projection of a father figure in the manner of Freud. So both the deeper philosophy and the inner life of religion can be missed, as a tone-deaf man would not appreciate a symphony, and even a critic may be unable to compose a line of music.

In some of the descriptions of African religion one is reminded of the Indian parable of the blind men and the elephant. One found its trunk and declared it was a pipe, another felt its legs and said it was a tree, a third touched its tail and claimed it was a brush, and a fourth got hold of a tusk and said it was a spear. None of these had any proper conception of the elephant, not even when they put together their knowledge of the pipe, tree, brush and spear. But if they had had a closer acquaintance with a more common animal, like a horse or even a dog, they might have made more sense of the elephant. Similarly the comparative study of religions in other continents, and comparative study of other religions in Africa, can be helpful in understanding the attitudes behind traditional religion. They may indicate some of the patterns of the past and prospects for the future. For example, the cults of Islamic saints in the Sudan, and the emergence of prophetic movements in the tropics among Christians, reveal important elements of African religious life.

Christianity is the oldest of the great living literary religions of Africa, following on ancient Egypt. The minor exception of Judaism will be dealt with briefly, because the numbers of Jews in Africa are very small today. Since Christianity is a historical religion it is important to sketch something of its history and growth in the African continent, although in a land of such size this must be done cursorily. There is a great deal of literature on the church in Egypt from early times till now, and rather less on its life in Ethiopia, while the fortunes of other churches in North Africa after the Arab conquest are still obscure. In tropical and southern regions the history of Christianity began with Portuguese navigators from the fifteenth century and only really emerged to importance from the nineteenth century. Even in this short period the history is a jigsaw puzzle of many missions and personalities, only some of whom can be mentioned. There is a vast missionary literature but much less material on life in the African churches. A four-volume study by C. P. Groves, *The Planting of Christianity in Africa*, is a mine of information but difficult reading, and it has emphases and conclusions that are debatable.

The extension of Christian churches over Africa in modern times is a remarkable event, with consequences that affect the whole continent in every aspect of life. They have been particularly occupied with education, finding it one of the most valuable weapons of advance, and to a lesser degree with health and politics. Here again restriction of study is needed to specifically religious elements. But special attention must be given to the many independent African church movements, which figure little in mission records but have produced a large literature of their own which is only now being revealed to a wider public.

As a historical, scriptural and international religion Christianity is rapidly replacing traditional religion in many places, and it is often rival or parallel to Islam. Its forms in tropical and southern Africa have been European, but many efforts towards naturalization into African forms have been made by translating the scriptures into hundreds of African languages, and by mission and independent churches adopting customary dress and music. That Christianity can become truly African is shown in the fact that for centuries it has been the state religion of Ethiopia, and this country shows interesting examples of ascetic as well as popular religion. Relationships of Christianity with Islam have not been easy, both under Muslim dominance in North Africa and European dominance of the tropics. But even before the end of imperialism there had begun peaceful inter-religious dialogue, which can develop and fit into the general religious tolerance that has marked much of African life.

Islam entered Africa within a few years of its foundation in Arabia, in the seventh century A.D., and it spread along the northern coastal lands with remarkable rapidity. But then its expansion slowed down and it was centuries before Islam reached the tropics. Even more surprising, in view of the proximity of Arabia and constant trading, was the small penetration of Islam into East Africa till quite modern times. It says much for the coherence of African traditional life and religion that it resisted pressures from east and west, until holy wars or imperialism forcibly broke up the old order of society. Even then the old world outlook has remained under much of Islam and Christianity.

The history of Islam in Africa is sketched briefly in the following pages, since its present extent cannot be understood without some history. For North Africa there is much literature in Arabic and a good deal in French from the period of colonialism. Less study has been made of Islam in the Sudan and tropics, but recent research has revealed unexpected reserves of work on West Africa in Arabic and in other languages which use an Arabic script. In English the magisterial studies by J. S. Trimingham on Islam in the Sudan, Ethiopia, East and West Africa are mines of information on the history, the life and prospects of Islam.

Although Islam seems to have a relative uniformity, and in Africa has spread almost entirely in its orthodox Sunni form, yet it is impressive to note the number of religious orders that have flourished in all areas of African Islam. Mystical experience and ascetic self-denial have made a strong appeal, and have helped to root Islam deeply into African life once it has been introduced. Despite holy wars and the rigidity of some law schools, Islam has tolerated a good deal of African custom. A proliferation of cults of holy men in North Africa and the Sudan demonstrates the power of Islam to provide for popular levels of religion and its ability to take over holy places from the older religion. In modern times the impact of Western culture on the Islamic world has been great and has caused many tensions. But in Africa this religion has made a powerful appeal because of its ancient traditions, literacy and international character, and it has made many advances into the tropical regions in this century.

Social and political changes have inevitably affected religion in Africa, as in every other continent. There is an outward decline of the traditional religion, observable in this century even if undocumented in the past. Islam and Christianity have profited by this decline and have hastened it in many places. They have their own internal problems and it will be seen in the future whether they can hold their gains, or whether one will progress at the expense of the other, or both suffer from growing secularism. But while external forms of the old religion decay, there are many traditional religious attitudes that will remain for a long time. It would be foolish to suppose that a convert throws off all his past beliefs at once or even over years. When efforts have been made to force a radical change, as in the creation of artificial villages of converts, they have usually broken down and in any case they have done little to change the faith of the rest of society.

Study of many of the traditional religious beliefs and customs will be undertaken first in this book, because even where cults are weakened and altars are neglected, the world outlook may be virtually untouched. Few, if any, Africans have been completely unaffected by modern ways, in trade and government, but many have clung to traditional rituals and beliefs. Others have formally left them but have not joined a church or Muslim community, though they may be potential converts and in census returns they may acknowledge that they come within the scope of church or mosque. Others are Christians from families with several generations of converts, or Muslims from centuries of Islamic history. The most thoroughly rooted in Islamic culture, of course, are the peoples of Egypt and North Africa, and among Christians the Copts of Egypt and Ethiopia.

Some suggestions of distinctive marks of African religion will be made at the end. But that there are particular emphases should not be allowed to obscure the fact that Africans of different religions are human beings who have shared in the universal religious quest for the meaning of life.

Part One: Traditional Religions

1 Literature and Art

The study of ancient traditional religious beliefs of Africa is doubly difficult. First, there is the great variety and multiplicity of peoples, the lack of a central tradition, especially in Africa south of the Sahara. This can be overcome, to some extent, by selecting beliefs of outstanding importance shared by different African peoples, while noting regional differences; but it must be recognized that this is only partial and many exceptions may remain unobserved. However the effort must be made, because the only alternative is to abandon the study altogether. The second difficulty is the complete lack of written documents from within the religion. Not only are there no summaries of doctrine in ancient African religion, but no written exposition of spiritual experience, and nothing to tell what it was like to be a believer in the old religion. In India and China, for example, there are many texts about religious belief and practice, compiled over centuries. There are many popular beliefs as well, in the religion of villagers or jungle tribesmen, which find little mention in the scriptures. But the importance of the texts is that they speak from within the tradition and they give their own interpretation of faith, uninfluenced by outside observers.

India and China were in the mainstream of literary development, not isolated but often linked with Mesopotamia, Palestine and Greece. The art of writing is a rare discovery, but it was shared by India with Phoenecia and the West. China developed its own syllabic forms. But Africa was cut in two by desert and tropical forest, with the sea not properly navigated till the fifteenth century. These provided effective barriers to the spread of literary culture, and there were only trickles of trade across the desert till the modern world crossed it by air; and it still sends trade round the coasts. Even Islam, with its powerful armies and dynamic culture, had to take the longest route round the western coastline. It arrived in North Africa in the seventh century but did not reach the western savannah till the thirteenth. Even then Islam was confined to the Sudan and did not enter the tropical regions till they were opened by Western trade in the nineteenth century. In the east, Christianity reached Ethiopia by the fourth century but went no further, and no significant advances were made in the tropics till the nineteenth century.

The lack of literature in tropical Africa is a result of isolation, not of African inability to express thoughts. The ancient north Europeans and Americans had no writing till it was brought to them by visitors from other countries. There was no literature for the ancient religions of these continents until well into the Christian era and knowledge of them was often preserved by Christian missionaries, as has happened in Africa too.

If there are no scriptures, however, there is a great deal of artistic expression, which is the indigenous language of African belief and thought. Neglected and despised for long, African art has been appreciated in this century all over the world. This is Africa's own visible and tangible self-expression, and a great deal of it is concerned with religion.

The effect of the discovery of African art upon Europeans and Americans has been great, and it has influenced the work of artists like Epstein, Moore and Picasso. The imagination displayed in African sculpture has stimulated those artists who were trying to get free from the materialistic naturalism of the last century, and the fact that African art expresses belief is a corrective to the notion of 'art for art's sake'. Abstract forms of some kinds of African art have been particularly appealing, though the discovery of the many bronzes and terracottas of Ifé and Nok has shown that there have been ancient forms of naturalism in Africa also.

There are many varieties of African art. Painting is known especially from rock paintings which are found all over the continent, and in this the Bushmen were expert. Unfortunately the Bushmen no longer paint and interpretation of the paintings that remain is uncertain, though hunting scenes cannot be simply representative since they contain religious and magical themes.

But painting is still done in many places, on walls of houses and temples, on tombstones and rock surfaces, and its patterns are both representational and symbolical.

The most important forms of plastic art are in sculpture. There is not much stone sculpture, and what exists is restricted mainly to Sierra Leone, Nigeria and the Congo, with some fragments remaining at Zimbabwe in Rhodesia. Soft stone is the chief material, though quartz and granite have also been used. Ivory has been carved with great delicacy, both in native forms and under Portuguese influence.

The oldest sculptures are the terracottas from the culture found at Nok in Northern Nigeria, which are over two thousand years old. These are mostly human and animal heads and figures, naturalistic and cylindrical. But it is not known who made them and the Nok culture and religion have vanished, unless they were developed by the Yoruba of Ifé later. The famous terracottas and bronzes of Ifé and district in Western Nigeria have been known to the West only in modern times but date from about the thirteenth century onwards. Many of the bronze heads are representations of sacred kings, some of them are crowned, and all the life-size bronze heads have a row of holes above the face in which probably bead veils were fixed. To this day Yoruba kings wear bead veils on special occasions and formerly it was the rule for all public appearances. Other sculptures represent Yoruba gods, such as Oduduwa the founder of the race, and Olokun the sea god whom the German explorer Frobenius not inappropriately called the Yoruba Poseidon. Many bronze heads are characterized by expressions of serenity, but there are others which show age, disease and suffering. Some of them depict animals that are common in life and mythology: chameleon, ram, dog, elephant, bull, monkey and owl. The related bronzes of Benin are derivative from Ifé, but are more stylized and are chiefly of royal and ancestral use.

Less known are the mud sculptures which abound in Africa, but which from the nature of their material cannot be moved or exported. This art is still practised without an eye on the souvenir trade, which has caused so much art to degenerate today. Gods, human beings and animals are represented in profusion in clay:

Olokun of the Yoruba, Legba the mischievous spirit of Dahomey, and Ala the great mother goddess of the Ibo. The liveliness of the artistic mind in mud sculpture is seen in that it freely mixes old and new, and Christian figures appear alongside the older gods, as they do in the life of the people. The clay is nearly always painted in bright primary colours.

Wood is the favourite material of all for sculpture. There are countless masks, figures, dolls, stools, headrests, drums, screens, doors, divining trays and gaming boards. The Yoruba are particularly noted in this field and as William Fagg says they have probably 'produced more sculptures per thousand persons than any other'. But all over West and Central Africa there is abundant wood carving. There is much less in East and South Africa, though some is found in Malagasy.

The innumerable wooden masks are some of the best known and collected specimens of African art. These are religious, whether they are naturalistic, formal or abstract. They represent the dead or attendant spirits in their rituals, or 'secret societies' connected with the dead or serving to suppress witchcraft. Impassive or terrifying, distorted or abstract, the masks powerfully demonstrate the awesomeness of the dead as well as the conviction that death is not the end. They are made to be worn by people who impersonate the dead, their bodies usually being covered with robes beneath the masks, and they must not be spoken of as human beings but as spirits.

The many different types of mask to be found all over Africa underline the great variety of African art. The variety may suggest confusion, but it comes from the fact that African art arises within tribal limits and expresses the beliefs of that limited society. However, such limitations need not be exaggerated. Although there were many tribal limitations in Africa in the past, there were also considerable empires which included smaller tribal units. In addition, there were migrations and displacements of population which involved mingling of cultures. The extent of Yoruba art, its influence on Benin, and possible links with Nok, illustrate this wider scope of art, not to mention its effect on Dahomey in the old days of Yoruba empire and later wars. Even within a narrow tribal limit the members of a tribe had little difficulty in understanding the art produced by specialists, for it was both popular and functional, not made in a secret language for artists. To the outsider this is little help, until it is realized that the art can be understood only within the context of the whole culture. Knowledge of religion therefore throws light upon the interpretation of art, and the art illuminates the religion. Hence it can be claimed that African art provides a kind of scripture of African religion, for it is its expression from within.

One of the most important African arts is music, both instrumental and accompanied by dance and song. Some of the drum songs, dirges and cult verses have been collected by R. S. Rattray, J. H. Nketia and P. Verger, but a great deal remains to be done. Many dances are religious and form part of cult dramas, and others may be distinguished as social. But a religious dance is social in the sense that it is performed by several dancers and fulfils social functions, and even an apparently secular jig done by workmen on the road or farmers in the fields can be related to the strength of the iron tools that are being used or the fertility of the seed that is planted.

Africa has taught dances to America and Europe, in rumbas and sambas, introducing new rhythms, steps and gestures. Some of these dances are expressions of the desire for fertility, which is the concern of many cults, but they are not necessarily obscene. Indeed the Western manner of dancing in couples on every occasion may have appeared obscene to Africans before they got used to it, for the couple together expressed only the fulfilment of the fertility dance. Even the secular dance cannot be separated from the religious, for both embody the life force or vital energy which is the supreme value of life, and the separation of sacred and profane cannot be made as it is in Europe. African music and dancing express, like other forms of art, the harmony of sense and form, of rhythm and meaning, in which the beautiful is also the good, and the ugly is bad.

This throws light also on a much debated question about the religious or humanistic nature of African plastic art. It is remarkable that such an authority as Fr Kevin Carroll, who has done a great deal to foster and develop Yoruba religious art, should conclude that traditionally 'it is a humanistic rather than a deeply religious art, even when directly concerned with the creation of religious objects'. He particularly objects to claims that African artists are inspired by the exalted religious function of their work, and set about it with great devotion and concentration.* But appearances can be deceptive. African rituals often have a casual air to the outside observer, and who can say what people feel when they carve a mask or pour a libation?

On the other hand Ulli Beier maintains that African art is 'deeply expressive' of the old religion, and the form of art is 'always the expression of the ideas that inspired it'. From this viewpoint he criticizes attempts that have been made, and in which Carroll is eminent with his school of carvers at Oyé Ekiti, to Christianize African art. He asks how it is possible for 'an art-form that was inspired by traditional Yoruba religion to be adapted to Christian ideas?' The church has provided the carvers with new work but not with new inspiration, their figures are dull, and in fact 'it is only the Christian carvings that give a profane impression'.†

At least it may be said that Carroll's carvers, working in traditional forms, have produced work that is often far superior to that of many modern African carvers and painters who merely imitate European styles, in a kind of *blanchitude*. The latter have no doubt demonstrated that Africans are quite capable of working in Western styles but, as William Fagg says, they have often given up their 'birthright for a mess of pottage'. And this leading authority agrees that Carroll 'has demonstrated the viability of a Christianized traditional art'. He even suggests that there are more affinities between Christianity and the 'pagan' religions than are usually admitted. One of the most significant is the similarity between fundamental African philosophical concepts of 'force' and the Christian concept of grace. A search for such affinities is essential for the naturalization of Christianity into the African background and to help in the survival of traditional art.‡

Further, much of the debate between Carroll and Beier is vitiated if it is recognized, as already suggested above, that in

* K. Carroll, *Yoruba Religious Carving* (1967), p. 53.

† U. Beier, *Art in Nigeria 1960* (1960), p. 14 f.

‡ W. Fagg and M. Plass, *African Sculpture* (1964), p. 7; and W. Fagg in Carroll's *Yoruba Religious Carving*, p. x.

African thought as in most cultures there is no division of sacred and profane. Some modern Western writers delight in describing the 'secularization of society' and the narrow world of the 'religious', though it could be objected that no societies are really secular. All cultures are motivated by beliefs; and even modern China is profoundly religious, however philosophically weak its faith. African carvers range delightedly across the whole field of human experience, depicting divine beings, priests and worshippers, in fully anthropomorphic fashion. Birds and beasts, fishes and reptiles, mingle in this panorama. A study of figures in an Ibo *mbari* cult-house reveals the entire spectrum of life. Administrators with sun-helmets, wrist-watches and motorcycles sit next to baboons or dancing girls. Tailors with sewing machines jostle fabulous elephants. Pornographic scenes appear side by side with nurses and stretcher patients. But the central figure is always Ala herself, the earth mother goddess, usually with a child on her knees like a Madonna. Facing her is often a male counterpart, Amadi-oha the storm god, and other figures are Ekunochie a water goddess and a boa-constrictor which is a regular symbol of Ala.*

Of course a great deal of African carving serves no immediate religious function, but even the most 'humanistic' or 'secular' carving expresses a love of the natural world which arises from the world-affirming character of African belief. For this reason African art gives a very good report of the everyday life of the people, as well as of leaders and special events. When depicting royal personages and ceremonials it is the best documentation available and old stone carvings, like those of Esié, are invaluable for the light they shed on the costumes and manners of past centuries.

While the gods may appear in sculptured form, notably Ala of the Ibo, it is noteworthy that many carvings represent worshippers rather than gods. The gods may manifest their presence through symbols: axes, metal snakes, pots or plants. The 'idols', against which some observers used to rage, were often simply carvings of worshippers or lay figures. Well known temples of Shango, the Yoruba storm god, or Tano the Ashanti river god, contain no

* U. Beier, *African Mud Sculpture* (1963), p. 26 f.

image of the deity but low altars bearing thunder stones or other symbols. There may be a screen of carved figures, but these may be ordinary men and women, warriors, and even Muslims with prayer beads. Certainly the Supreme Being, whether his name is Nyame, Olorun or Chukwu, never appears in sculptured form. Despite the proliferation of sculpture among the Yoruba and Ibo it has clearly been felt that the heavenly God can no more be depicted in visible form than he can be enclosed in a building for worship.

In modern times much wood carving and brass casting has degenerated into commercialism, and it expresses the low view of a money economy. But a good deal of the old work is done in villages, and artistic impulses turn to other forms. These may be styles that require more continued effort than the stone or brass figure which, once made, needs no renewal. Mud, or even cement, sculpture expresses the continuity of life and the renewal of creation. The luxuriant forest is always alive and must constantly be kept back; the fertile earth is ever yielding crops in lands where rainfall is heavy and heat continuous. In the same way human life persists and the dead are believed to return as creepers circle round a post on the veranda of a house. Art is a means of expressing a basic philosophy of life and power, and of all the powers that work together for good in a harmony that must be maintained.

2 Philosophy and Cosmology

To speak of the philosophy of cultures that had no literature may seem inappropriate, but there are parallels for this. The ancient Hindus compiled the hymns of the Vedas and the dialogues of the Upanishads, which are imbued with philosophy and are often claimed as the oldest 'scriptures' but these were not written down for many centuries, until well into the Christian era. The ancient teachings were passed down by the priests of the Brahmin caste, in feats of memorization which were unique. Ancient African ideas were not transmitted so rigidly but there are myths which go back to time immemorial, proverbs which enshrine ancient wisdom, songs and rituals, and modern attitudes that reflect traditions of the past as well as thought about the present.

To say that African peoples have no systems of thought, explicit or assumed, would be to deny their humanity. The great philosophical phrase, 'I think, therefore I am', applies to all men. Some students of African life watch rituals, photograph masquerades, or dissect social organization, and then declare that Africans have no doctrines and that their religion is 'not thought out but danced out'. That fatuous statement came in fact from an armchair theorist, but it suggests that human beings dance for no reason and with their minds literally blank. But why are dances performed and repeated? There are many reasons, and powerful ones are that they express the life force, continuity with the past, and unity in the present community, and these are reasonable ideas.

The description of African religion as 'fetishism' has been abandoned by serious writers, because this would virtually limit it to magical and idolatrous practices, and sever Africa from other parts of the world where such practices are just as common. The word 'animism' is more frequent now, suggesting a belief that there is a 'soul' (*anima*) in every being and object. But African religion is more than a personification of nature, and some of its most important beliefs are in a Supreme Being and in the departed ancestors, neither of which is a strictly animistic belief. More central is the concept of 'power' or potent life, what Tempels calls 'vital force' and Smith 'dynamism'.* It is the importance of power, its increase or diminution, which is a constant concern in prayers and invocations, in spells and magic. All beings have their own power, and the most fortunate are those who have the greatest amount, whereas misfortune, disease and witchcraft are held to diminish power.

Fundamental to the notion of power is the dynamic nature of the universe and human life. Beings are not fixed in an unchanging nature, or condemned in fatalist manner to stay always in a pre-destined lot. The great efforts that are made to 'get up', to increase power and prestige, in wealth and learning, are evidence of this dynamic attitude. Indian religions are said to be world-denying, but African religion is more akin to that of the Bible in which the world is given as the creation of God to be used for human benefit, and body and soul are hardly distinguished but are united in one personality.

African thought sees different powers in the world, not just a universal 'mana' or dynamism spread over the earth like jam. The powers differ among themselves, divine and human, animal and plant, good and evil. Powers act upon one another, for man is a social being and he also lives in a vital relationship with the natural world. African natural science is based upon observation of the world, its powers, possibilities and effects upon human life. Much inherited and acquired wisdom is possessed by specialists in such observation; blacksmiths, farmers, hunters, herbalists and weathermen.

As study of art has often concentrated on West Africa, so investigation of philosophy has been particularly fruitful in the Congo and Burundi, with writers like Tempels and Kagame. But this shows how incomplete our knowledge still is of vast areas of

* P Tempels, *Bantu Philosophy* (English translation 1959), p. 30 f.; E. W. Smith, *African Ideas of God* (1950), p. 16 f.

African life and thought and how much work remains to be done. Alexis Kagame, who is himself a Bantu, distinguishes four basic concepts from the root Ntu. Muntu is the human being (plural Bantu), Kintu the thing, Hantu stands for place and time, and Kuntu for modality. Ntu is the cosmic force itself, the power in which Being and other beings are joined together. Tempels calls God the 'great Muntu', the powerful person and force from which all other beings flow. Muntu is not merely a force, but it has intelligence and might be described as Mind or a neuter supreme consciousness like the Hindu Brahman.*

The powers are not only individual but are ranged in proper order, in a hierarchy. The greatest power is God, the creator or cause, described by Smith as the apex of a pyramid. The two sides of the pyramid are the ancestors and the nature gods, the base is composed of lower magical powers, and in the centre is man subject to influences from every side. The Supreme Being, by definition, has power in himself but he is related to other powers in giving them vitality and increasing or diminishing their strength. The first men, the founding fathers, derived their power from God and passed it on through their descendants. They may be ancestors or gods, who are either ancient heroes or more purely nature spirits, but all are powers related to men.

Lienhardt, writing of the Dinka of the eastern Sudan, prefers to use the word Divinity rather than God, for the notion of the power above man (*nhialic*). Sometimes it is a being, supreme, creator, personal and father; but also it is a kind of activity which 'sums up the activities of a multiplicity of beings'. Yet it is not just Nature, or supernature, but 'divine' power that is in all these. Divinity is one, yet there are personal beings that Lienhardt calls 'free-divinities' and others which are 'clan-divinities'. If we find it easier in writing of African religion in general to use the names God, gods and ancestors, it is with the recognition that these words are useful but in the African context they are not to be fully equated with the more static conceptions of European philosophy and theology.†

African philosophy of being is not too far distant from that

* A. Kagame, *La Philosophie bantu-rwandaise de l'Être* (1956), p. 328f., etc.
† G. Lienhardt, *Divinity and Experience* (1961), p. 28 ff.

philosophy of life, power and consciousness which appears in the writings of Teilhard de Chardin, notably in *The Phenomenon of Man*, and in modern physics. The older European notion of 'dead matter' has been replaced by a science that sees mind or life from the lowest level of creation to the highest. Scientists also share the vision of Wordsworth who felt 'a sentiment of being spread o'er all that moves and all that seemeth still'. This may be a kind of pantheism though, as Chardin insists, for Christian belief it must be a personal pantheism, and the same may be said for African belief.*

African psychology sees in man a living power, the greatest of all created beings. Though he is not the strongest man he is able by his intelligence, like the hare in popular African fables, to outwit those who are physically more powerful. His power is both physical and mental, and the coordination of the two makes him a full man. But man is dependent on God, and on powers greater than himself, and so religion is essential to his well-being because it shows him how to remain in fullest communion with the saints. The power of man may grow or diminish, and all kinds of magical and other aids are justified by their usefulness to it. Men belong to a community and they are related to other beings, both living and dead. The power of a dead man, if not his whole personality, may return in a kind of reincarnation to strengthen his name, his property and his clan.

African ethics receive sanction from a consideration whether actions help or harm human power. There is a profound conviction of the wickedness of witches, sorcerers, and any others who are thought to damage the life and health of beings, prevent childbirth or spoil the crops. A true man, who is unified and in harmony with God and the spirits, lives according to the principles of this philosophy, recognizing human worth and not exploiting others, continuing the traditions of the past and adding new power to them. A man who is puffed up with pride and ambition, seeking power simply for his own ends and crushing others, is bound to come to an evil end by the laws of the universe. Morality is bound up with religion and receives its sanction from

* P. Teilhard de Chardin, *The Phenomenon of Man* (English translation 1959), pp. 309 and 57 n.

the Creator who gives the order of the world. What is ethically good must be ontologically good also.

Mythology of Creation

Systematic philosophy worked out in written form in Africa is only now being developed, and it is a difficult and complicated task. But in picture language there is much traditional wisdom, and assumptions become apparent that reveal much of attitudes towards the world and life. All peoples have myths, stories which try to explain the origins of the world and men, the mysteries of birth and death, and the activities of celestial and mundane beings.

Collections of myths have been made from all over the continent, in detail for some people, sketchily for others, and for some not at all. The collections vary a good deal in value, but from them some general pictures can be drawn, which give light on philosophy and theology. There is need for more complete and careful collections, in the original languages as well as translation, before these tales are lost or change beyond recognition. They cannot be dated, but many of the myths are clearly old and can be placed before ancient migrations, since resemblances are found between the stories of widely separated peoples. The myths answer questions about the origins of the world, for it is not reasonable to suppose that life and thinking man came from nothing.

The primal myth of most cosmologies the world over is that of creation. Sometimes God is thought to have created from nothing, and at other times from an already existent primal matter. The Dogon of Mali and Upper Volta say that the first invention of God (Amma) was to create the sun and moon, the former white and surrounded by eight red copper rings, and the latter with rings of white copper. The earth was made from a lump of clay which was thrown into space, where it spread out flat like a body lying face upwards. In his loneliness Amma sought union with the earth, but had first to excise its clitoris which was like a termite hill. This myth is used to justify female excision and attempts at suppressing this practice are resisted. The trouble over the divine-earth union resulted first in the birth of a jackal who caused mischief later. Further union produced twins called Nummo, half-human and half-snake, green and red, and embodying the principle of movement and energy in water. Further beings were made which were bi-sexual, and it is believed that all men and women are bi-sexual before circumcision and excision.

Yoruba myth in Nigeria says that Ol-orun, 'owner of the sky', lived in heaven with other divinities. Below there was a waste marsh without solid ground, where divinities sometimes came down to play and hunt. God called a divine agent, Orishanla or Great God, and gave him a snail shell filled with soil, a pigeon and a hen, and sent them down below. When the soil was poured out on the marsh the birds scattered it about till earth was formed. The original place of the appearance of solid ground was called Ifé, which means 'wide', and this was the site of the town of Ilé-Ifé, 'the house of Ifé', the most sacred city of the Yoruba, whose foundation is linked to this myth of the first creation and makes it the centre of the world. God also shared the work of making men with Orishanla, leaving him to mould men out of clay but reserving the breathing of life into them to himself.

The Fon of Dahomey tell of the creation of gods and men from an original pair, called Mawu and Lisa. Lisa is the male, like the sun, fierce and strong. Mawu is female and mild like the moon. But the myths are not always consistent and Mawu often appears alone as a male or sexless creator. From the original twins seven other pairs of gods were born, and ruled over the different departments of nature, storm, earth, sea, and so on. Mawu travelled around with a great snake, forming mountains and tracing out the courses of rivers. The snake is the principle of life and motion, and on its coils the earth is supported so that it does not sink into the ocean that surrounds it. Another symbol is the calabash, the top half of which represents heaven and the bottom the earth, with the horizon where the two meet. Calabashes, decorated with abstract and pictorial designs, are placed in houses and temples and contain offerings or symbolical objects.

Luyia cosmology, in Kenya, says that God (Welé) created the world in several stages. He made heaven first, supporting it by pillars like a hut to stop it falling. God created it like lightning and it is always bright through his presence. Then he made the sun and moon, but they quarrelled and the moon was thrown into the mud, so that now the moon is darker than the sun and only shines at night for thieves and witches. Then God made the clouds and a red cockerel which crows whenever it thunders. He made rain and two rainbows, the male being narrow and the female wider. Welé made two assistants miraculously and gave them the earth as a place for their work, creating mountains and valleys and sending rain to form rivers and lakes. Then he made a man, a woman and animals.

Other cosmologies are similar, with local variations, but the symbolisms should be noted. The calabash with two halves is representative of heaven and earth, or the sea with the earth floating in it. A snake curled round in a circle, swallowing its own tail, is a widespread symbol of eternity, continuity and immortality. Twins, especially male and female pairs, may represent the first people or spirits. Twins are still often held to be sacred, though some people regard them as abnormal and animal-like and so dangerous to the community.

Many myths then go on to say that having created the world and having lived here in olden days, God retired to the heavens where he is now. The stories are not unlike the Biblical narrative of the Garden of Eden, since man is blamed for the separation of God from men. But in African myth it is God who withdraws, and not man who is expelled, and the parallel is closer to other myths of the Near East which told of a separation of heaven and earth by their children. It is noteworthy that there are similarities between these African stories in widely separated countries.

The Mende of Sierra Leone say that God was formerly nearer to men than he is now and he gave them whatever they needed. But they troubled him so often that he decided to make a dwelling place far away. He went off while men were asleep and when they woke up they saw him spread out in all directions in the sky. A commoner story, told in the Ivory Coast, Ghana, Togo, Dahomey and Nigeria, at least, says that God was formerly so near to men that they grew over-familiar with him. Children wiped their hands on the sky after eating and women tore pieces off it to put in the soup. Women knocked against the sky when they were pounding grain, and finally one woman hit it so hard with her pestle that the sky moved away in anger to its present distance.

There is virtual identification of God with the sky in these stories, though in other myths it is God himself who moves away. It is remarkable that almost identical myths are told in eastern Africa. The Nuba of the Sudan say that the sky once pressed down so low that women could not lift their spoons high enough to stir the porridge without getting their hands burnt on the pots. One day a woman forced her spoon right through the sky and it went off in anger. Another version says that people used to eat pieces of the clouds till they went away. The Dinka also say that the sky was low and was hit by a woman pounding extra grain in her mortar. But another Dinka story says that man was in heaven at that time, kept in by a wall, but when he ate part of it God pushed him down to the earth. Women are often blamed in these myths for the disruption of primeval bliss, perhaps because the stories were invented by men.

A common theme is that a rope, ladder or spider's web used to join earth and heaven. The Dinka say that men used to climb up it to God, but when the women had offended him God sent a blue bird to cut the rope. The Nuer say that men used to climb the rope after death and they became young again, but a hyena and a weaver bird cut the rope and since then men have not been rejuvenated.

Many people of central and southern Africa say that God (Mulungu) lived on earth at first, but men began to kill his servants and set fire to the bush, and so God retired to heaven on one of those giant spiders' webs that seem to hang from the sky in morning mists. In Burundi, however, it is said that having made good children God created a cripple, and its parents were so angry that they tried to kill God and he went away. The Lozi (Barotse) of Zambia say that when God lived on earth there was a man called Kamonu who was very clever. He imitated God in making iron and forged a spear with which he killed an antelope. God rebuked him for slaying his brother and drove him out. Kamonu pleaded to be allowed back, but later he killed a buffalo and other animals. Then God sent misfortune, so that Kamonu's own child died, and God himself retired. He went first with his family to an island in a river, but Kamonu followed them, and they went up a high mountain. Kamonu still came on and God asked his diviner, the wagtail, where to go next. He was told to ask the spider, which spun a thread so that God and his family went up to heaven, and the spider's eyes were put out so that it could not follow them. Kamonu piled up trees in a vain attempt to climb up to the sky, but they all fell down.

A Pygmy myth, perhaps under the influence of a Negro story, says that God (Mugasa) used to live on earth with his family, two boys and a girl. But they did not see him for he lived in a big house where he worked at a smithy. The girl brought firewood and water to God every day and left them outside the house, but at last she was curious to see God and hid herself to watch. She saw a big arm, covered with metal bracelets, come out and take the pot of water. But God saw the girl, and being angry at her disobedience he went off, but he left behind weapons and tools for his children. The girl married her brothers but her first child died, and so death came to the world.

These myths explain creation and the separation of man and God. They look back to a golden age when God lived among men and there was no pain or death. Some writers consider that they depict an original fall of man from a state of innocence, as in the Bible, but this seems to be forcing a theological explanation into stories that are more concerned to explain the distance of the sky and God from man, rather than the expulsion of man from paradise.

Origins of Man

Although many myths attribute the creation of the world to God, and some represent man as coming from heaven or created by the action of God, there are other stories that give to man a more natural origin. An Ashanti narrative says that one Monday night a worm made a hole up through the ground, and from it emerged seven men, some women, a leopard and a dog. The names of these people are still repeated sometimes, on Mondays and Tuesdays. The people were afraid at the sight of the earth but their leader,

Adu Ogyinae, laid his hands on them and calmed them on the Tuesday. But on Wednesday he was killed by a falling tree when they were building huts. Then the dog went out to look for fire and they cooked food. Finally they met the God of creation (Odomankoma) and he took one of these people as his helper. Annual ceremonies are still held to commemorate these first people.

The Zulu say that the first man and woman came out of a reed, and the Thonga of Mozambique say that a reed exploded and men emerged. The Herero of South-West Africa said that their ancestors came from a tree which is still in the veld. Their cattle also originated from this tree, but Bushmen, sheep and goats came out of a hole in the ground.

A Pygmy story introduces the chameleon, a reptile which often appears in myth and fable. The chameleon once heard a noise in a tree, like the sound of birds or water, though there was no water in the world at that time. It took an axe, cut the tree open, and a flood of water poured out which covered the earth. A man and a woman also emerged from the tree, more light-skinned than most pygmies, and they lived on earth as the first people.

The Shilluk of the Sudan say that the founder of their royal house, Nyikang, came from heaven and married a woman who had the attributes of a crocodile. Their neighbours, the Dinka, tell of the first man and woman, Garang and Abuk, who were made of clay and kept in a small pot, till it was opened and they became much bigger. It was Abuk who was greedy and pounded so much grain that she hit the sky till it went away.

The Gikuyu of Kenya say that God made the 'mountain of brightness', Kere Nyaga which Europeans call Mount Kenya, as a dwelling place where he could be invoked. His three sons were fathers of Gikuyu, Masai and Kamba peoples, and he showed them the world from the top of the mountain and told them to choose their tools. Masai took a spear and went to be a herdsman in the plains, Kamba selected a bow and was told to hunt in the forest, while Gikuyu took a digging stick and practised agriculture in the fertile land in the middle of the country where fig trees grow.

A Malagasy story says that God made two men and a woman,

34

who at first lived on earth separately. One man carved a woman from wood and talked to it. The second man came across the image and covered it with clothes and jewels. Then the woman saw the image and took it to bed with her, so that it came to life and became a beautiful girl. Then the two men arrived and quarrelled over the two women. God intervened and said that the first man was father of the girl and the woman its mother, so the second man should marry the girl. The first man and woman also married and the two couples are the parents of all mankind.

The complex mythology of the Dogon, as recorded by Griaule, says that after the Nummo spirits the first human beings were four sets of twins. They lived in heaven but the Nummo separated them to prevent quarrels. However men broke the Nummo orders and decided to leave heaven. The first ancestor stole fire from the Nummo smiths and slid down a rainbow with it to earth. He came so fast that his sinuous limbs were broken, and so all men now have joints in arms and legs. The first ancestor marked out land and distributed it among the other men and each took a special craft: smithery, leatherwork, minstrelsy, and so on. Men were organized into eight families, of which the eighth was superior since it gained the power of speech.

Sometimes it appears that the first men and women had no knowledge of the process of procreation. Another Ashanti story says that a man and woman came from heaven with a python. The latter asked them if they had any children and offered to show them how to make the woman conceive. He stood the couple facing each other and sprayed water on their bellies, saying 'kus, kus', a formula still used in clan rituals. Then he sent them home to lie together and children were born who took the spirit of the river where the python lived as their tutelary spirit. The python is taboo to them, it must not be killed, and must be buried in a white cloth if it is found dead. The phallic symbolism of the snake is clear, as in Genesis.

A Luyia myth says that the first man and woman tried to have union in several ways but did not know how, until the man watched his wife climbing into a granary and saw the way. She refused the union at first and suffered great pain, but eventually she bore a son and daughter. A Pygmy myth says that God made a pygmy, a Negro and a girl. The Negro complained that his sister was always bleeding and he did not know how to stop it. God had told the pygmy the meaning of this phenomenon and he offered to cure the wound. The girl bore him children, and later bore others to the Negro. Like some other myths this is incestuous, but it explains the mystery of birth.

The Coming of Death

There are many African stories that tell of the first appearance of death. All death is thought to be unnatural, it did not exist among men at the beginning, its coming was due to the fault of some creature, usually an animal, and it is still abnormal and is blamed on witches and sorcerers.

In Sierra Leone the Kono say that God told the first man and woman that they would not die for he would give them new skins. He sent these in a bundle carried by a dog. But the dog stopped on the way and foolishly told other animals what was in his bundle. The snake heard him and stole the bundle, sharing the skins with his relatives. So the snake changes its skin and does not die, but men die and try to kill snakes. Some of these myths are rather like the Greek story of Pandora's Box.

The Lamba of Zambia say that when the first man, who was a nomad, wanted to settle down he asked God (Leza) for some seeds. They were sent by messengers in small bundles, with strict instructions not to open one of them in particular. This aroused their curiosity and on the way the messengers opened this bundle and death came out into the world. The Ila of Zambia say that God offered the first man and woman two bags, one holding life and the other death. They chose the one which shone brightly, but death came out of it, and their child who was sick died.

The theme of the faulty messengers is very common. The Mende of Sierra Leone say that the dog and toad were sent to take messages from God to men. The dog was to say that men would not die, and the toad to say that they would. They left together but the dog stopped to eat, and the toad went on without delay and called out in the town of men that death had come. Although the dog then came crying that life had come, it was too late. A Zulu story blames the chameleon for coming too slowly with the message that men would not die, for it stopped to eat fruit on the way. God sent the lizard later with the message of death, but it arrived first and men accepted its word before the chameleon came along.

A Luyia story says that the son of their first ancestor refused to give food to the chameleon, who cursed him with a promise of death. The chameleon went and asked a snake for food, was given it, and promised immortality to the snake. But another Luyia myth says that formerly when people died they returned after four days. A boy who died was sent back by his mother, who declared that when he was dead, he should stay dead, so he cursed the people by saying that none of them would return from death.

The Nuba say that when at first men died God told them to put the bodies aside and next morning these had returned to life. But one day a hare told people to bury the corpse of their relative in the ground, and God was angry at this disobedience so that men have not returned since then. A Nuer tale says that God put a piece of gourd in water, as a sign that men would live because the gourd floated. But the woman who was sent to bring the message threw a piece of earthen pot into water instead of a gourd and it sank. Men have died since that time.

A Dinka story, like some Hindu speculations, said that men die because if they all lived there would be no room for them on earth. At first God promised that men would return fifteen days after death, but they objected that if they did there would be no room for agriculture or houses. In Burundi a story says that God was chasing death away with his hounds, but death ran into a woman and promised that if she hid him he would help all her family. The woman opened her mouth and death jumped inside, and when God came up she said she had not seen death. But God sees all and knew what had happened, and he said that in future death would destroy them all.

In Buganda the explanation of the arrival of death comes in the long stories of the first man, Kintu, and his wife Nambi whom he fetched from heaven. When the married couple were returning to earth the king of heaven, Gulu, warned them not to go back for anything. But Nambi forgot grain for her fowls and returned to get some. Her brother death followed her and lived with the couple on earth. He asked for one of their children as cook, and when they refused he killed it. Other children died and Kintu went up to heaven to complain. Gulu told him it was Nambi's fault but after some pleading he sent another brother, Kaizuki, to stop death killing the children. Kaizuki told everybody to stay at home while he hunted for death, but some children went out with their goats and death was warned and escaped. So Kaizuki returned to heaven and death has lived on earth since then, killing whom he can and hiding in the ground.

Many stories are told of the world beyond, either of a land of the dead underground, like the Greek Hades or Hebrew Sheol, or in heaven as in Christian story. Such myths, and the many tales that relate the coming of death, express a firm belief in life beyond the grave. There is the conviction, as in Genesis, that men were not meant to die. There is the further conviction that death is not the end. This is a universal belief, which is just as clear in Africa as anywhere else. It is not an unwillingness to face the fact of death, for that is recognized in the many funeral and memorial services, but it is a faith that the human spirit and the life force are indestructible. The details of the stories are of secondary importance, they are not meant to be taken literally or passed on as infallible truth, but behind them is one of the most deep-rooted of all the ideals of mankind.

Other myths are concerned with spiritual beings and forces; with nature gods in relationships with the Supreme Being and man, or with their own activities among themselves. These will be referred to later when the gods are discussed more fully. There are tales of witches or monsters, many of them fanciful and told for amusement, while others express the fear of unknown powers or uncanny places. Legends, which refer to heroes of the past, with factual or fanciful detail, differ with every tribe and give sanction to local customs and loyalties.

3 Unity, the Supreme Being

From the earlier view that African religion was crudely fetishistic, with an idea of God where it existed being an importation, informed opinion has now swung round to the conviction that most, if not all, African peoples have had a belief in a Supreme Being as an integral part of their world view and practised religion. The symposium *African Ideas of God* did much to establish this finally, but it has been supported by countless books and articles. Missionaries have found, often to their surprise, that they did not need to argue for the existence of God, or faith in a life after death, for both these fundamentals of world religion are deeply rooted in Africa.

Some writers refer to 'the High God', but this term sounds derogatory to educated African ears, suggesting that God is merely distant or transcendent. Here we shall speak of the Supreme Being, or God, as in normal English usage. It has been seen that African myths express many beliefs about God in graphic form. It is not necessary to accept the myths as true in detail; but they express a conviction in the spiritual direction of the universe. Modern science may express its theories in different ways, and in new symbols, but it is also making a religious search for truth and purpose in the universe. Myths speak about God in picture language, and other sources for an understanding of his character in African traditional religion are found in prayers, songs, proverbs, riddles, and some rituals.

The nature of God in African belief can be gathered from the qualities attributed to him. These correspond generally to many of the divine attributes postulated in other religions. That God is almighty is one of the most obvious assertions, since supremacy implies it. All-powerful is a common name for him and he receives many similar titles: creator, allotter, giver of rain and sunshine, the one who began the forest, the one 'who gives and rots', maker of souls, father of the placenta, the one who exists by himself. The omnipresence of God, less commonly expressed, is found in sayings such as 'the one who is met everywhere', and 'the great ocean whose head-dress is the horizon'. More clearly God is omniscient: the wise one, the all-seeing, the 'one who brings round the seasons'.*

These attributes imply the transcendence of God, and to some extent his immanence. God is always creator and ruler, the one beyond all thanks, the ancient of days who is from the first, the everlasting who has no limits, and he who alone is full of abundance. The Zulu particularly delighted in such titles: 'he who bends down even majesties', the irresistible, and 'he who roars so that all nations are struck with terror'. Then the nearness of God comes in such titles as 'the one you meet everywhere', 'the great pool contemporary of everything', and 'the one who fills everything'. In his immanence God may be conceived more physically or naturally. He may be found in big trees or thickets, on mountains or rocky places, and especially in rivers and streams. He may be spoken of as one but many, invisible at ordinary times but seen by a man about to die, and his voice may be heard when the bush is burnt or when a whirlwind blows.

It is clear that God exists by himself; he is not the creature of any other being but is the cause of everything else. His pre-eminence and his greatness go together. But since he is greater than any other spirit or man, God is mysterious and nobody can understand him, he creates and destroys, he gives and takes away. God is invisible, infinite and unchangeable. Although his wife or wives and children appear in myths, yet in himself God is one, and only rarely is the notion found of a twin deity. Heaven and earth, sun and moon, day and night, man and woman, are dual but God is the unity beyond all this. The duality is not discussed as it is in Hindu speculation, but the unity of God follows from his pre-eminence and sole creation. It has been said that God might have been banished from Greek thought without damaging its logical architecture, but this cannot be said of African thought, as God is both the creator and the principle of unity that holds

* See the Index of God-names in *African Ideas of God*, p. 305 f.

everything together. He is the source and essence of force, Ntu, which inspires the whole vital organism.

The character of God appears not just in abstract attributes, but in more humane and moral qualities. Although he is supremely great, mysterious and irresistible, yet he is also kindly disposed towards men and his providence is mentioned not infrequently. He is the God of destinies but also of comfort, the kindly-disposed and 'the providence which watches over all like the sun'; he can be angry but is also 'full of pity', the father of babies and the great friend. In the enigmatic Akan title he is 'the one on whom men lean and do not fall'.

The natural attributes of God come from his primary function as creator. Not only did he make the world, but he established the laws of society and the existence of justice depends upon obedience to him. Creation is not only in the past; the divine work is continued in sustaining the universe, and men turn to God if things go wrong today, complaining if they have been treated unjustly. God is the giver of destinies, and may appear harsh or inscrutable, but that does not make people fatalistic or console them if justice is perverted.

A well known Ila story tells of an old woman who came from a large family and had many troubles. God, Leza, 'the one who besets', smote all the family in turn. Her parents died and then other relatives. Although she married and had children, her husband died and then the children. Some had borne her grandchildren but these also passed away. The crone was left and hoped to die, but strangely she grew young again (some would have said that she had eaten the soul-stuff of her relatives), and she decided to use her new powers to find out God and get an explanation of her troubles. First she tried to make a ladder to heaven out of forest trees, but as this Tower of Babel neared the sky the whole structure collapsed. So the woman resolved to travel to every country till she found the place where heaven touches earth and provides the road to God. In every land that she visited people asked why she was travelling and she replied that she had suffered so much at the hands of God that she was seeking him out. But her hearers said this was not strange, for such troubles come to all people and nobody can ever get free of them.

Although the ways of God are beyond man and can never be fully known, yet numerous titles speak of his sustaining and cherishing work. He gives rain and sun, health and fertility. He is also the deliverer and Saviour, moulder and providence. Disease and poverty, drought and famine, locusts and death come to plague man, but they are part of the mystery of nature. Although life is viewed, inevitably, from the human standpoint, yet man is not the centre of the universe in African thought, any more than in Christian theology. It is God who is supreme and the central moving force, and man submits to him as the great chief.

How far God is regarded in anthropomorphic fashion, as a big man projected into the heavens, or a glorified ancestor, has been debated. Human titles have been given to him: ruler, father, mother, and even more grandfather, the originator of the people. J. B. Danquah asserted that for the Akan God is the Great Ancestor, but other writers disagree. It seems rare for God to be thought of as linked to man in a family relationship. Rather man is his creation and God is the inscrutable maker. Other gods are spoken of but it is not normal to find the same generic term for 'a god' applied to the Supreme Being, who is in a class apart. And it has been noted that there are few, if any, sculptures of the great God.

Occasionally God may be spoken about in terms of either sex. Mawu-Lisa of the Fon is the supreme female-male, and Dr Aggrey, the Ghanaian educationalist, spoke of 'Father-mother God'. The southern Nuba, who have a system of matrilineal descent, refer to God as 'the Great Mother' and when praying beside a dying person they say, 'Our God, who has brought us into this world, may she take you.'* This is very unusual, and though most African languages have no sex in the pronoun, God is generally clearly personified as a great male ruler. In mythology God may have a wife and children, servants and messengers, and other gods act as his partners or agents in creation. God may be described with a body, head, eyes, ears, mouth, arms and legs. But both the Bible and the Koran speak of the divine body in this way, though theologians take such language as symbolical or, in a common Muslim phrase, assert the paradox that God has two eyes 'but without asking how'. Men have to use language, with

* *African Ideas of God*, p. 215 f.

42

its solid imagery, even when speaking of the invisible and indescribable God, and anything more than negatives is bound to involve metaphor.

Similarly God is related to heavenly objects, and at times apparently identified with them. His virtual identification with the sky, in myths of divine withdrawal, has been noted. In other stories God is closely linked with the sun, though this is not common. Some peoples may seem almost to identify God with the sun, but this appears to be metaphorical and due to the similarity of words used about God and the sun. The sun is sometimes personified in myths, or is regarded as a manifestation of God, but there are few clear indications that the sun is God or God is the sun. There is little ritual in connexion with the sun, such as that which was performed in ancient Europe or Japan to make the sun return from its winter journey to the south. In the tropics the sun is always overhead, and needs no encouragement to shine. However, as it is supreme in the heavens the sun may be an apt symbol for God, and stories are told of men visiting the sky and reaching the sun or God.

The Bakuta of the Congo speak of two supreme Gods: Nzambi above and Nzambi below. Often regarded as twins they act heroic roles in many stories, and have villages and families in heaven and earth. But in myths of creation it is Nzambi above who is supreme and his twin disappears, so that the function of Nzambi is creation. His first children were twins, the sun and moon, and death is attributed to his faulty messenger, here the goat. As in other myths it is said that Nzambi retired from the earth after a human offence and he has no regular worship. But he still has a concern for men and death is under his control. His name occurs in proverbs and exclamations: 'God sees him' is said about a man who escapes punishment from earthly courts, 'we have the grace of Nzambi' is uttered when people are spared by flashes of lightning, and 'Nzambi is with me' is said by a woman after childbirth. Some writers have identified this celestial Nzambi with the sun, but men prayed to him also at night, looking up to the sky, and when a thunderbolt falls at night it is his axe.

Any of the celestial bodies may be connected with God. The Akan of Ghana also say that thunderbolts are God's axes, though some other peoples have storm gods, inferior to the Supreme Being, who control the thunder. The rainbow is God's bow, and lightning is his weapon against evildoers. Different reasons are given for eclipses; they are due to the quarrel of sun and moon, or to clouds or storms devouring the moon, but ultimately God is responsible. An eclipse is viewed with alarm, since all nature goes quiet at this time, and drums are beaten to ensure the victory of good, but wise men know that the darkness never lasts long.

Earthly objects, and especially high mountains like Mount Kenya, are apt symbols for the dwelling or place of manifestation of a transcendent God, as in the Bible. They provide places where prayers and sacrifices can be made in time of need. Groves of trees are sacred, and the Gikuyu on important occasions pray to the Supreme Being there in the open. There are spirits of the earth, but unusual phenomena like earthquakes or floods may be ascribed to the direct action of God, and desolate places may be thought of as his special abodes, and precious metals in the ground as his gift. The regularity of nature is also ascribed to him, the succession of day and night, heat and cold, dry and rainy seasons. Although nature gods and ancestors are both objects of prayers for good harvests and plentiful rain, yet ultimately they are the concern of the supreme God.

Worship of God

The relationship of men with God is complex. Man is always the creature of the Most High, as mythology shows. The first man and woman are often called children of God, even though some stories say that they came from the earth instead of from heaven. Traffic between heaven and earth was easy in the olden days, according to the stories, but the separation came about by human fault, usually that of a woman. One result of the misunderstanding between God and man is that death has come, though a further reason is often given for this, and generally an animal is blamed.

Human life should be conducted according to principles which God gave to the founding fathers of the clan. Every clan has traditional history, some of it fact, some legend, but always

CHESTER COLLEGE LIBRARY

important for revealing ideals and attitudes. The ancient heroes are often described as coming from God, or entrusted by him with ordering their lives and settling on their land. Morality is traditional, but it depends on the ultimate creation and the purpose of the world to maintain harmony and prosperity. Rewards and punishments for good or bad acts may be applied in this present life. Even notorious evildoers who manage to flourish like the green bay tree and avoid justice for a long time are believed, rather optimistically, to be due for punishment before death. Only rarely, it seems, is a judgement predicted for good and evil men after death. But the Yoruba say that all that is done on earth will be accounted for in heaven, and men will have to state their case kneeling before God. Then the final lot of the righteous will be a heaven of cool breezes, and for the wicked a heaven of potsherds, a sort of celestial rubbish-heap like the midden of every village where refuse and broken pots are thrown.

The above statements suggest that God is close to most African peoples and that he receives regular worship, as in Christianity or Islam. Therefore it is surprising to find that there is little ordered worship of God and few places where rituals are performed for him. That a Supreme Being is widely believed in, that he is the background of life, and is thought to be near to many people, is true, though there are exceptions. But regular worship is not usual.

The Dogon have group altars for Amma, at which the village chief usually officiates. Additional altars are made if some special object is found which is imbued with the divine presence, and there are special priests and priestesses who sacrifice here and at annual communal rites. Rattray provided invaluable photographs of temples of Nyame in Ashanti, with their priests, and of the small 'God's altars', forked sticks holding bowls for offerings which stood in front of houses. But the temples were relatively few even in the 1920s, and many of the forked altars have disappeared today, though the worship of God has increased through the Christian churches. The Gikuyu and Shona also worship God on occasion or at special and communal ceremonies, but few other African peoples have organized cults for him.

Generally there are no temples or priests for God, though there

45

may be many temples for the nature gods, and there are always sacrifices and prayers made to the ancestors. Yet occasional worship of God, by libation or simple invocation, is quite common. Prayer is worship, and it can be made by any layman or woman, at any place or time. When the gods and ancestors fail, or when appeal is needed to the highest authority, then despite his greatness God can be appealed to directly, without any special formula or intermediary priest.

The lesser spirits are also important in this connexion. Although they may appear to receive most attention in sacrifices, it is often said that they receive the externals of the offering but the essence of it is taken by them to God. The gods are subordinates and may pray to God for men, and in prayers to them the Supreme Being is often mentioned first, in a recital of the spiritual powers that are being invoked. Even when God is thought to be far away and fearsome, he can be called upon in time of distress because 'his ears are long'.

The study of the idea of God in Africa has been weakened by theorists, some of whom think that there has been an inevitable evolution from fetishism, to animism, to polytheism, and finally to monotheism. Others consider that there was an original monotheism from which all Africans fell, in a kind of Fall of Adam. Looking at things as they are today there is a picture of a mixed religion, which is not mere animism, nor a democratic polytheism, nor a pure monotheism. E. B. Idowu calls it 'diffused monotheism'.

Evans-Pritchard, in one of his thoughtful conclusions, says that 'a theistic religion need not be either monotheistic or polytheistic. It may be both. It is a question of the level, or situation, of thought rather than of exclusive types of thought. On one level Nuer religion may be regarded as monotheistic, at another level as polytheistic; and it can also be regarded at other levels as totemistic or fetishistic. These conceptions of spiritual activity are not incompatible. They are rather different ways of thinking of the numinous at different levels of experience. . . . At no level of thought and experience is Spirit thought of as something altogether different from God.'*

* *Nuer Religion* (1956), p. 316.

4 Plurality, Powers of the Universe

The many powers that are important in life can be described in different ways. Gods and ancestors may be spoken of as such, or described more generally as Divinity or Spiritual Activity. But all such terms carry a suggestion of separateness from man, or an opposition of spiritual and material, of sacred and secular, which is commonplace in the West but foreign to African and most other conceptions of the universe. It is said by the Dinka that 'Divinity is one', meaning not only that gods are dependent on the Supreme Being, but that all power, divine and human, is interrelated. Whether the complex of power is thought of as a hierarchy or a pyramid, it is still linked in all its parts, and there is only a difference of degree between man and the spirits by whom he is surrounded. This explains the apparently blasphemous way in which people blame their gods or ancestors, though never the Supreme Being, because prayers have not been answered.

Perhaps it is better to speak of spirits than of nature gods, but with the understanding that man himself is a spirit. It is natural that men in all ages have considered spiritual powers to be at work in all material phenomena, and while old-fashioned materialism rejected this, the modern scientific mind discovers life or mind in so-called inert matter and in rudimentary forms throughout the universe. Everything in nature is living, or at least pre-living, and there is no such thing as absolutely dead matter. This is the truth that lies behind belief in nature 'gods' or polytheism, a belief that seems crude and false but which is based upon an apprehension of life and purpose in the world. Science is now giving more evidence of what poets like Wordsworth, and myth-makers all over the world, have long felt to be true.

To the monotheist, Muslim or Christian, the error of polytheism seems to lie in the personalization of the powers of nature into 'gods', and he may congratulate himself that in holding to one God, high and lifted up, he is at a more exalted level of spiritual evolution to which the polytheist must one day raise himself. But it is by no means sure that a bare monotheism produces, or is produced by, a higher culture. India has produced some of the finest cultures of history, yet most of its people could be called polytheistic, worshipping both natural and local gods and goddesses. In fact thoughtful Hindus believe that all divinities are manifestations of the one Brahman. Moreover a bare monotheism leads easily to deism, in which God is useful in providing an explanation of the creation of the world, but he is then dismissed and no longer intervenes or is invoked. In contrast to this arid deism, the immanence of divinity and its intermingling with the life of man, is the important faith taught by what are roughly described as both pantheism and polytheism. The significance of this belief in manifold divinity upon the spiritual outlook can be illustrated from the effect of westernization on Africa. Western political systems, education, communications, trade, and Christian missions have exerted constant pressures upon Africa, but for most people the African world view has not changed very much. As Williamson and Dickson say, 'Christianity and Akan religion meet without common ground for conversation, except in one respect, the concept within Akan religion of a Supreme Being.'* But even here the conversation is superficial, for God tends to be isolated from other spiritual powers which traditionally men have believed were closely related to him.

Furthermore, although African gods are said to be personal, having names, temples, images, priests and cults, the personification need not be taken too literally, but rather as poetical expression through the use of abundant metaphor. Modern theologians warn us not to think of God as 'up there', an 'old man in the sky', and they talk as if their opinion were something new, a kind of abstract religion which they imagine will appeal to the man in the street. But respectable theologians have always known that these embodiments and locations of God are metaphorical. Origen in the third century and Luther in the sixteenth both said that to think of God as sitting on a throne or rainbow above the bright

* *Akan Religion and the Christian Faith* (1965), p. 167.

blue sky was a child's picture-book description. And not only theologians but ordinary people do not necessarily take all religious language literally; they also understand poetry. The uneducated Italian peasant may speak of the pearly gates of heaven and St Peter with the keys, but he will listen to a joke about St Peter without being shocked. Poetry, in metaphor, proverb, fable and myth, forms a large part of language for ordinary people, and it does not have to be logically consistent or literally true. The many African gods can be considered in this light.

Sky and Storm

The over-arching sky appears to be wider than the earth and powerful forces operate within it. The firmament itself may be personalized, but often it is vaguely associated with the Supreme Being, and it has been seen that in myths of the divine withdrawal the two are virtually identified.

The sun has been considered, when discussing its relationship with the Supreme Being. It may have a personal name and sometimes a temple, but there are few sun cults, and generally it is the warm power that makes trees and crops grow, and that is enough.

The moon shines more brightly at night in the tropics than in temperate regions, because it is higher up in the sky. It is beneficial in the cool nights, when people dance or tell stories in its genial brilliance. But there are few cults of the moon, and it is less important for people in the forests than for those of the burning deserts who need to travel by moonlight. The moon may be saluted when it appears as new, and libations of milk are poured on graves at this time. The Fon have 'moon-glorifiers' who sound horns to call mothers to lift up their newborn babies to the moon for blessing, to obtain prosperity and long life.

The Bushmen and Hottentots have myths about the moon, which seems more important to them than to their Negro neighbours. It is the moon who sends messengers to men to say that they will return from death to live again, just as the moon comes back to power with each new crescent. In one version the moon told a young hare not to cry when his mother died, since she would come back. But he refused to believe, and in anger the moon cursed him and struck his lip which has been cleft ever since. Pygmy stories tell of the moon creating the first man, and also telling the lightning about the mystery of procreation.

The stars are even less important in ritual, though it must be said that little research has yet been done into African knowledge of astral movements. There seems to be little astrology, and most systems of divination ignore the stars. But recent investigations in central Africa suggest that some people have more detailed knowledge of the stars and their variations than had been imagined. In the fields of African knowledge of both astronomy and botany there is urgent need for fuller study, for Dieterlen and Zahan have revealed an extensive and systematic classification of plant life among the Bambara which was hitherto unsuspected.

The most important cults concern the storms that are powerful and terrifying forces in African life. Storm and whirlwind, thunder and lightning, thunderbolt and rainbow, are the subject of myths and rituals. The storm may be closely associated with the Supreme Being, as when the Ashanti call thunderbolts 'God's axes' and place them in the forked posts which are 'God's trees'. Sometimes these thunderbolts are real pieces of meteorites, but often they are old stone axes which are found in the ground in the Sudan.

The rainbow is strange and is often believed to give magical powers. The Luyia say that God made two rainbows to stop rain out of season, the narrow male rainbow appears first and if it is followed by the broader female then the two together bring rain to an end. In Fon symbolism the rainbow is the cosmic snake, the red part being male and the blue female, or one is twined round the earth while the other appears in the sky. There is a widespread fantasy of finding treasure 'where the rainbow ends', a treasure which may be the brightly coloured Aggrey beads used in necklaces, or some great fortune in the mountains. But in southern Africa it is considered fatal to come to the end of the rainbow, and it is unlucky to point at it, though the Ila of Zambia point pestles at rainbows to send them away. The Zulu call a rainbow the Queen's Arch which frames the house of the queen of heaven, but the Gikuyu say that it eats men and animals.

Altogether the rainbow is regarded as uncanny and even dangerous, rather than decoratively beautiful.

The best known storm god is Shango of the Yoruba who has a
double function, so ensuring special attention. He was a historical
or legendary king, the fourth monarch of Oyo, ruling over an
extensive territory. Tyrannical like Solomon, he resembled him
also in possessing esoteric powers. Shango breathed fire from his
mouth to kill enemies, and he could call down fire from heaven,
like Elijah. Eventually his ministers rose against Shango and he
fled with his wives to the forest. Finally it is said that he hanged
himself at a place called Koso, though his followers still maintain
that he did 'not hang' (*ko-so*). Their version is that Shango
climbed up to heaven by a chain, and his power on high is shown
by the thunderbolts and fire which he sends down. His priests
still claim to have this power, with which offenders are punished,
but they can also protect the faithful followers of Shango. They
carry 'thunder axes', symbolical axes with finely decorated metal
blades. Shango is personified in songs, which praise his power,
justice and protection. He strikes the stupid to the ground, he
kills the liar and dances wildly before the impertinent, and casts
down the obstinate. But he wishes long life to warriors, makes the
old man marry again, and there is no danger for his follower.*

The Hottentots worshipped a great rain and hero god called
Tsui'goab. It is said that he warred with a chief, Gaunab, who
was sometimes identified with death. At first Gaunab was win-
ning, but each battle made the hero stronger and he finally
destroyed the enemy, but as Gaunab lay dying he smote Tsui'goab
on the knee and this gave the hero his name, meaning 'wounded
knee'. It is said that he made the first man and woman, or the
rocks from which they came. He died in the end but was then
believed to live in the clouds and send rain from there. He was
worshipped at dawn, called Father of our fathers, and in drought
implored to send thunderclouds and feed men and their flocks
and give them health. Men swore oaths in the name of Tsui'goab,
showing that he was a moral divinity, and some writers have
taken him to be the Supreme Being, but now it is more general to
consider him as a rain and hero god.

* P. Verger, *Notes sur le Culte des Orisa et Vodun* (1957), p. 308 f.

The storm may be one of the activities of other spirits. Deng of the Dinka is sometimes said to be son of heaven and earth and ancestor of the Dinka, but he is closely associated with the storm and his name is used for the rain. The lightning is called Deng's Club, and both rain and human birth are his manifestations.

Weather forecasters, rain-makers and rain-stoppers are students of the storm and other heavenly phenomena. Even some modern African writers claim that rain-makers can bring rain in the dry season and drive it away in the wet, and it is said that there is a science of rain-making which can be acquired on payment of fees to older teachers and giving respect to their taboos. But anyone who knows the tropics realizes that there is no time of the year when rain may not fall, and no completely wet or dry season. Rain-makers are men closely in touch with nature, often farmers or hunters, who have a fund of weather lore based upon years of observation. Like Elijah, they watch for the tiny clouds which indicate unusual storms, and they study the direction of the winds which may carry them away from their village. A writer on the Dinka describes the rain-maker straining his eyes to the hills, and after long silence declaring that there would be plentiful rain in one region and parching wind and drought in another. Of course with this there is a good deal of suggestive ritual, which may be practised to encourage the faith of clients. Rain-makers may abstain from washing for long periods, because by sympathetic magic that should make the rain stop falling. Fires are made with green wood to create large black clouds, which are supposed to encourage the formation of rain clouds in the sky. Rain-makers who abuse their powers can be deprived of office, and they usually sell their knowledge to other members of their families who are more willing to respect the taboos.

The most famous rain-making rites were performed by the Rain-queens Mujaji, of the Lovedu people of the Transvaal, who were made notorious in Rider Haggard's novel *She*, though he knew little more about them than their reputation. A succession of queens has ruled the Lovedu in recent centuries who are called 'transformers of clouds' and give rain to their people. Like many other sacred rulers, the queen must be kept in perfect health as this is important to the people, whose prosperity depends upon her powers and well-being. The queen does not work actively every time there is rain, but in a crisis or drought it is said that 'the people are crying', and the rituals are set to work. The queen has her own rain-doctor and helpers, who use divination to discover the reasons for drought and try to remove the obstacles to the working of the royal powers by the use of medicine. Specific medicines are kept in secret, and the rain-queen has to obtain the help of her ancestors to bring a storm. If there is no rain this is attributed to the anger of the ancestors at human neglect. Above the ancestors is God, from whom the queen has derived her powers. More popular and obvious medicines are also used, such as those which produce dark clouds to attract the storm.

The Earth

Heaven and earth provide the stage where the human drama is played out. Men lift up their eyes to the sky and naturally regard its spirit as transcendent and mighty. But they live on the earth, plant seeds in it, derive food from it, and in its depths the dead are buried. So Mother Earth is nearest to men and linked with them by many bonds.

For the Ibo the earth mother is Ala, the greatest deity after Chukwu, the heavenly creator. She is as near to them as the ancestors, for they are buried in her pocket or womb. Ala sends the dead back again in rebirth, and she is the spirit of fertility both for the family and for the land. Barren women, or mothers whose children have died, pray to Ala for children, and men ask her for success in trade and increase of their livestock. So Ala is a kindly spirit and she helps her children if they are troubled by other deities. But if people offend her and disregard repeated warnings, she will punish them and a hardened evildoer may receive the final humiliation, refusal of burial in the earth.

The land is generally sacred, for it belongs to the earth spirit, and to the ancestors as well as to the living community; attempts at selling land are unpopular and in olden days they were impossible. This was a major cause of the Mau Mau troubles in Kenya; when settlers to whom land had been leased thought they had

...ught it. The Ibo dislike selling land because of their reverence for Ala, and they appease her if it has to be done. Their ancestors founded the 'face of the earth'(*ihu ala*), which became sacred for the people and was the place where major decisions, such as warfare or ritual oaths were made and strictly respected.

There are temples for Ala all over Ibo country, but special Mbari houses are erected in the southern regions near Owerri. These are built when the priests say that the spirit has sent a sign, like a nest of bees, and men and women are set aside for weeks or months to make the building. After it is finished the house is left until it decays and is finally abandoned. In 1960 Beier found that four new Mbari houses had been built in the past five years, and some were already decaying. Mbari houses have a central room for the goddess and verandas on the four sides. The walls are painted with abstract and representational patterns, and the verandas are filled with up to fifty clay sculptures, life-size figures of all manner of beings, divine, human and animal. Ala is always in the middle, faced by other deities and flanked by many figures. There are policemen and tailors, hunters and women in childbirth, and sometimes figures of Jesus as a schoolboy or of the Virgin Mary.

In other places there are no special temples but the earth is still venerated. The Ashanti say that 'the earth is not a goddess, she does not divine'; yet work on the land is taboo on Thursday because it is sacred to Asase Yaa, Mother Earth, Yaa being the name given to women born on a Thursday. When a farmer hoes his field at the beginning of the rains he offers a fowl to the earth, and gives another with the first fruits at harvest. Similarly when a grave is dug in the ground a libation is made to the spirit, a custom that was taken to America by the slaves. Sometimes Ashanti drummers address the earth in words which Rattray recorded in the original and in translation:

> Earth, while I am yet alive,
> It is upon you that I put my trust ...
> We are addressing you,
> And you will understand.*

* *Ashanti* (1923), p. 278.

The earth is associated with other powers, and in Dahomey and Nigeria it is linked with the fearful disease of smallpox. Here Sapata or Shopona is called King of the Earth, King of Pearls or Lord of the Open. Smallpox was formerly such a scourge that it seems to have absorbed the earth cult. Shopona is a fierce king whose actions must be described in euphemisms; so of a man who had smallpox it was said that 'he has the king' or 'the king makes him suffer'. The fever of smallpox is like the hot ground which makes people uneasy, so Shopona is called 'hot earth'; of a small-pox victim it was said that 'hot earth has seized him' and if he died 'hot earth has taken him away'. The dislike for even mentioning the hard facts made people say 'the ground is cold' when they meant the opposite.

The cult of Shopona has been prohibited in Nigeria since 1917 because of fears that priests spread the disease, though some shrines remain. But in Dahomey Sapata has more priests and shrines than any other god. At the entrance to most villages is a low mound, with a block of ironstone for offerings of oil and blood, a pot of water, and a cactus plant. Sapata is in that outside place which connects fields and village, and he is also the dangerous power which may harm or protect those who pass by.

The powers of earth include the spirits of hills, and great mountains like Mount Cameroun and Kilimanjaro. Mount Kenya figures in the mythology of creation and also as a place where men still invoke God. Even small hills, like those of Ibadan, have rituals recording the foundation of the city there. Every year there is a holiday when work stops, and fires are extinguished till they are relit by the priest who is the 'worshipper of the hill'. Rocks and outstanding formations are likely to be regarded as centres where special power is manifested and available.

The Canaanites worshipped 'on every high hill and under every green tree', and most races of men have done the same. Most people still observe this nature worship under various guises, at natural shrines, in pilgrimages and on holiday. Great trees such as the African oak, mahogany, silk cotton, or baobab are obvious haunts of spiritual power. If a shoot springs up spontaneously that is a sign of good luck, and if a tree is cut down its power must be propitiated so that no harm comes to the woodcutter. Some trees are dangerous, or may be considered the abode of witches, especially if great bats cluster in their branches and emerge to flap across the sky in the evening dusk.

Metals are found in the earth and many peoples have tales of their first users, who are sometimes believed to have descended from heaven with metal weapons and tools to clear the forest. Blacksmithery is an expert profession, and many smiths are priests of the god of metal, or also of the storm. Other priests are hunters or herbalists in their spare time. The use of iron for tools and weapons meant that the presiding spirit had a large clientele. Tribal wars have declined in modern times, or were doing so until recently, but there are still plenty of uses for metals. Lorry drivers and cyclists pay their respects to the spirit of metals, using charms or offering sacrifices. Hunting guns may explode, since flintlocks are still used, and the god of metal is addressed in songs not only as protector and strong, but as one who kills or washes himself in blood. Like storm and smallpox, the spirit of metal has a power which may destroy as well as bless.

The Ashanti god of blacksmiths was Ta Yao, worshipped on a Thursday. Because of his connexion with war he was addressed on the talking drums as 'aggressor' and 'eager for war'. At the time of battle symbols of the gods were taken to the scene, but nowadays such objects are carried in annual processions. In Buganda the god of war, Kibuka, was also connected with the storm. During a battle it was believed that he hovered over the field and shot arrows at the enemy, but he was himself killed by treachery. A temple was built for him which was said to enclose his jawbone, as in shrines of Buganda kings, and his priests went with the armies to war and gave messages from Kibuka.

The Waters

All waters are places of power; wells and springs, rivers and streams. People who live in villages on river banks hold annual rites in which everyone joins, and since a principal purpose of the festival is to increase fertility this may be one of the few occasions of permitted licence. However not all villagers have the same ideas, and people on one side of the river may disregard the taboos of those on the other side and provoke communal strife.

Shrines of river spirits are usually on the banks, and here people swear oaths in ordeals to prove their innocence. If they swear falsely it is thought that they will drown in the river, or their limbs will swell up with water, and they will be refused burial in the ground. Those who drown by accident are thought to be taken away by the river spirit, and if the bodies are recovered they may be buried on the river bank.

The river Tano of Ghana is one of the chief spirits of that country, whose fame spread far away into Togo and the Ivory Coast. In mythology Tano struggled with a rival river, Bia, and also with death himself who had come to claim victims from a village of mortals. After a great fight the two contestants agreed on the compromise that whichever of them reached a sick man first would have him, and so sometimes death wins and sometimes Tano saves the sick. The priests of Tano dress in white and are renowned for the oracular messages which they give from the river god.

Even peoples who have accepted Islam for centuries may hold to some of the powerful pagan cults which remain from ancient times. The river Niger is regarded as a great source of potency by those who live on its banks and depend on its fish for life itself. So the Songhay, who have been Muslims for 500 years, observe the minimal daily prayers and go to the mosque on Fridays, but on Sundays they have popular drummings and dances where people are possessed by river spirits called Zin or Jinn. The great rivers of East and South Africa are also associated with spiritual beings, and sometimes with royal personages; in Buganda rivers are said to have sprung from the son and daughter of King Tembo. The importance of water for washing away uncleanness and receiving the power of the water is shown in the continued practice of full immersion in baptism in the independent Christian churches. On many Sundays in South Africa candidates are plunged into the rivers, rubbed free from impurities and tremble with the infusion of new life.

Great lakes are homes of many fishes and reptiles which swarm in the tepid waters, and no doubt of other powers as well. Lake

Bosomtwe in Ghana is a circular expanse about five miles across and, like the Dead Sea, it has no outlet. Streams flow into it, but as the lake is surrounded by hills with high cliffs, the water evaporates in the intense heat; and accumulations of decaying matter brought into the lake cause explosions from time to time. The lake is said to be the home of a spirit who long ago came out of the water and made love to an old woman who lived nearby. He promised that if she bore a child she would only have to knock on the water and fish would come to her, so she founded the clan of fishermen who still live there. Canoes, metal hooks and fishing nets are forbidden there, and the fishermen go on the lake on logs, paddling with their hands, and catching fish in reed baskets. It is said that the lake spirit, Bosom-twe, 'god Twe', used to come out of the lake to greet his worshippers on the Sunday that was devoted to him, and occasionally the lake 'explodes its gunpowder' as a sign of his power.

Of course the sea is the home of powerful spirits, their leader often represented as a great king who lives in an underwater palace with mermaids and mermen as his attendants. From time to time he tries to flood the earth, and in some stories there may be links with Asian tales of a primitive deluge. One of the most famous bronzes of Ifé is called after Ol-okun, 'owner of the sea', though it may represent an early king with crown and robes. In bronzes and mud sculptures of Benin the same deity appears full length, a king, but with two fishes in place of legs. The Owner of the Sea is very wealthy and a giver of riches and fertility. Proud of his wealth and fond of fine costume, he challenged the Supreme Being, Ol-orun, Owner of the Sky, to meet and compare with him in dress. But God sent his messenger, the chameleon, to fetch the sea god and the latter was astonished to see that even the messenger's dress was finer than his own. He changed robes seven times, but was always outdone by the messenger, so he gave up the contest, realizing that God must be greater than his servant.

Along with water spirits may be included the snakes which are revered in many places, though it seems to be particularly in the neighbourhood of waters that they are most honoured; by lagoons, sea, and river banks. While all snakes are respected, and the most dangerous ones are feared and killed when possible, it is the non-poisonous python that receives special attention. Many people refuse to kill pythons, and if they find a dead one it is buried in a white cloth like a human being. If a python attacks a man's fowls he will gently put it outside his garden, or call a priest of the snake temple to take charge of it. The very pious man of Dahomey or the Niger Delta kisses the ground in front of a python and calls it father. In Whydah, on the sea coast, there is a celebrated snake temple, a mud building at the foot of a sacred tree. Here pythons are kept and fed by priests who, though usually male, are called 'snake wives' (*dangbe-si*). Women mediums, here and elsewhere, go into trances and give messages from the spirits. They are true pythonesses, like the inspired women at Delphi and other places in the classical world, and the pythoness of Acts 16, 16. The Ijaw and Ibibio of the Niger Delta have many carved wooden figures of pythons, sometimes with heads like those of early Portuguese traders.

There are many other spirits to which attention is paid, when it is thought necessary. In West Africa there are regular cults, temples and priests to many gods, whereas in East and South Africa there may often be only a general feeling that spirits haunt notable places, but no regular cult, unless there is a special manifestation of power or a great need for help. Wild places, rocky hills or thick forest, seem to be haunted. The ghosts of people who have not been properly buried, demons and grotesque giants, and fairies who make pacts with hunters to give them secret knowledge may all be thought to lurk in the unknown bush. The books of Amos Tutuola, and especially *My Life in the Bush of Ghosts*, reveal such a world of imagination, in which surprises mingle with fear.

The Shona of Rhodesia look on the ruins of Zimbabwe as an uncanny and sacred place. It is said that if one tries to break a twig from a tree there it cries out 'do not break me'. No living creature may be killed there, and if an animal is pursued into the ruins it calls out 'do not kill me'. In the olden days great gatherings were held here every two or three years, at which sacrifices and prayers were offered to the Supreme Being.

Oracles

Many of the spirits are noted for the oracular powers of their priests, and giving advice is one of their chief functions. Priests go into trances themselves or employ mediums who do so regularly. Although these are apparently normal people in everyday life, yet they go into ecstasy spontaneously or by techniques perfected by long practice. This is a universal phenomenon, such as may still be seen among Muslim dervishes and Christian Pentecostalists who speak in tongues.

The oracles often function as final courts of appeal in disputed quarrels for individuals and communities, and in this way they make valuable links between such communities. There are many oracles and they compete for popularity, but successful ones attract trade, while those whose predictions are proved wrong become neglected. The oracles generally confirm ordinary judgements, but they add spiritual sanctions. They help to resolve dilemmas or debated points, though like the Delphic oracle they may give enigmatic or mysterious answers to problems. The diviner or priest is generally a man of wisdom and commonsense, with a thorough knowledge of village life, and often with agents who supply him with additional information.

This clearly happened with the 'long Juju' (*ibini okpabe*) of Aro Chukwu in Eastern Nigeria. The Aro people were enterprising traders who had contacts in many places, and so built up a network of intelligence services through Aros abroad. Clients came from long distances, and were passed from contact to contact till their origins and needs were known. The oracle was given from a cave up a river bank, and the client stood in the river and declared his needs. If the oracle declared against him he was said to be 'eaten', and disappeared into the cave to be sold into slavery. This trade was suppressed in 1900, though the oracle is still respected.

A similar oracle has been described by an Ibo diviner (*dibia*) who sought further help because he and his fellow diviners could not stop people dying prematurely. He set out for the oracle of Igwe and was passed from diviner to diviner, each taking a fee, for three weeks. When he finally arrived at the temple the whole place shook as the oracle appeared, and though he was a diviner he shivered too. The oracle knew the client's name and those of his parents, and of the six young people who had recently died in his family. It demanded a great fee, the equivalent of the dowries of ten women. Then it declared that the deaths had been due to the burial in the diviner's compound of the head of a premature baby. Another diviner was sent to remove this, and it is said that the deaths then ceased. The client was grateful and impressed, but the many fees 'paid out impoverished him for life'.* This illustrates the easy abuse that comes from the exercise of secret information, and though many diviners are honest and respected, yet temptations to abuse are considerable.

The most famous oracular system of West Africa, centred on the Yoruba but used by a number of other peoples, is the Ifa divination. Ifa is said to have been a superhuman being, sent by God from heaven to teach the use of medicine, give help in illness and guidance in secret affairs. He established himself at the ancestral home of his people, Ilé-Ifé, which is still the chief centre for consultation of the oracle and training of new diviners. Ifa is often virtually identified with an oracle deity, Orun-mila, 'heaven knows salvation'. This god is associated with creation in some myths, and came down from heaven on a rope. In Dahomey this oracle is said to be the writing which is created with every man and by which he discovers what god he should worship.

The Ifa oracular system uses sixteen palm nuts, which are thrown from one hand of the diviner to the other. According to whether one or two nuts remain from the throw, two or one marks are made on a divining board which is covered with powder or sand. At least eight throws are made for each consultation, producing a figure of eight single or double marks arranged in two columns. There are 256 possible combinations of single or double strokes in two columns and, depending on which combination appears, a traditional answer is given by the diviner from a proverbial saying or story connected with this pattern. A simpler method, producing the same result, is practised by using a cord in which are fixed eight concave and convex nuts, four at each end. These are cast on the ground, making two columns of

* V. C. Uchendu, *The Igbo of Southeast Nigeria* (1965), p. 101.

concave or convex surfaces, which are interpreted as in the longer system. Similar systems are found in the Sudan, where Muslim diviners interpret sixteen patterns from Arabic textbooks.*

Oracles are consulted for many purposes. At the birth of a child the parents ask about his god and destiny. A complete horoscope may be made then, or at adolescence, to show the proper Ifa pattern for the child, and this is kept for consultation at later periods when guidance is needed in a crisis, or to discover affinity in marriage. Oracles have been regularly consulted at the choice of chiefs, and even if the procedure of succession is regularly laid down the oracle provides a guarantee of divine blessing. In cases of chronic sickness, strange dreams, trouble from ancestors, barrenness, or sorcery, the oracle is asked to unveil the cause of trouble. Though much of this may seem like guesswork, yet diviners are usually concerned with the well-being of their clients and try to help them if possible.

Similar systems are found all across Africa, from Senegal to Malagasy. In Mozambique the diviners of the Thonga take six half-shells, three called male and three female. These are thrown on a mat and the manner of their fall gives the result, a convex side uppermost indicating blessing. The whole pattern is taken together to discover a complex meaning. Bones are also used for throwing, and the basket of divinatory bones represents all the elements of social life, indicating its institutions, so that when the bones fall they suggest a pattern of future social events.

The Sotho use four bones, two male and two female, which are decorated to allow for the interpretation of each in four ways. This allows of sixty-four primary combinations and further subsidiaries. The Venda of the Transvaal use four pieces of ivory, and others use wooden dice carved with animals and reptiles. The four dice are identified as old and young men, and old and young women, and are thrown into sixteen combinations.

Another oracular method is the divining bowl. It may be filled with water, in which shells, stones and beads are placed. By gazing intently into the water the diviner arrives at a solution by the order in which the objects appear. The Venda, and the Karanga of Rhodesia, use such bowls which have patterns round the sides,

* For details of the Ifa system see my *West African Religion* (2nd edn, 1961), p. 137 ff.

and in the middle a cowrie shell to represent maternal spirits. Such bowls are not common nowadays but similar objects, made of soapstone and ornamented with figures, were found at Zimbabwe.

The numerous oracles of the Azande of the Sudan have become well known through the writings of Evans-Pritchard. The most important is the poison oracle, whose decisions can have the force of law. The poison is administered to fowls, though in days gone by in other parts of Africa the poison was given to human beings, as in medieval Europe. The oracle is consulted in secret and each person brings fowls which are handed to the operator. Poison and water are mixed into paste and poured down the fowl's throat, and the oracle is then addressed inside the fowl and told to kill it if there is wrong and spare it if there is right. 'Is the illness due to anyone living here?' If the fowl survives, the answer is 'No'. There are other Azande oracles; a minor poison procedure, a rubbing board, or the use of termites. The rubbing board is carved from wood, with a flat surface and a lid. The lid is moistened in water and jerked backwards and forwards to give an answer. The rubbing board is the most commonly used, but it is of human manufacture and the termite oracle may be regarded as more impartial. A branch of a tree is inserted into a termite mound and questions are addressed to it. According to the way in which the branches are eaten, the answers are discovered.*

With the oracle spirits there are other divine messengers that are believed to help the free traffic between men and spiritual powers. Legba of Dahomey and Eshu of the Yoruba are both associated with the Ifa oracle. Legba-Eshu is a mischievous being, by earlier writers called 'the Devil', but nowadays regarded as a dangerous trickster. Like a fierce dog he is used to keep away intruders, but he will help the householder that feeds him. Images of Legba-Eshu are placed at the entrance to villages, in market-places, and at doors of houses. These are often small clay mounds, darkened with oil and blood, but often they are life-size mud sculptures, in human form and with glaring features. The phallic element is prominent, along with old or modern dress, such as sun-helmet and wrist-watch. The spirit is prayed to for fertility, and regularly for protection during the day.

* *Witchcraft, Oracles and Magic among the Azande* (1937), pp. 294 ff., 352 ff.

Legba-Eshu is messenger of Ifa, taking his oracles to men and returning with sacrifices to heaven. He opens the sixteen eyes (nuts) of Ifa, or the sixteen doors of the future. His many shrines are places from which he reports to God on the behaviour of men. But there are stories of him tricking God himself, and in one of these he inspired the woman who was responsible for the withdrawal of the sky from earth. This mischievous figure is both feared and cajoled but he is a very important character in daily life. In other places also there are intermediary and messenger spirits, who help men by rising up through the spiritual hierarchy to the source of all power.

Magic, Sorcery and Witchcraft

Magic is a further invocation of powers, and although it involves the manipulation of material apparatus, it is not merely mechanical. Most of the powers involved are impersonal, or only lightly personalized, and so there is not so clear dependence on a higher power. If the magical procedure is accomplished the result should follow, like putting down an electric switch. Hence it is said that 'magic demands, religion implores'. Magical acts are religious in that they are thought to involve spiritual powers, but these are impersonal and do not have a higher will like the gods.

Magic may be divided for convenience of discussion into personal and public, protective and offensive. All of these involve elements of sympathy or contagion between the individual or community and the magical object. Many magical charms are personal, worn on the body, hung over the house door or put in shops. Rings, bracelets, armlets, necklaces, girdles, anklets and many other decorations have magical as well as ornamental purpose. Nowadays texts from the Koran and Bible are also used as protective amulets.

Public magical objects are placed at the entrance to a village to ward off evil spirits and disease. A protective arch is a common sight on the main village road, or a magical fence all round the village during an epidemic. Bundles of leaves or feathers are put in sticks in fields or laid on piles of stone, as protection against blight and thieves.

Most magical medicine is protective, and since it is very common the magicians or medicine men are popular figures, who do a great trade with their concoctions. Many markets contain the ingredients which customers are asked to bring for a magical preparation: porcupine quills, red parrot feathers, dried bats, dried rats, snake skins, and all manner of leaves and roots. The expert prepares these to make them effective.

Harmful magic, or 'black magic', is anti-social and much feared. The 'sorcerer' works in secret and at night and prepares harmful medicines, for a price. These may be simply suggestive things, like black powder which is laid across a doorway to frighten the victim. Or they may be spells and curses uttered against him, clay images in which thorns are stuck to hurt him, or plain poison to be dropped in his soup. All of these have evil intentions, and where possible the sorcerer is punished and his power nullified.

Sorcery is often confused with witchcraft, but the latter term is best reserved for those people who are thought to have no magical apparatus, but work harm on others by devouring their souls. The witchcraft beliefs of Africa, which have many similarities with the ancient witch fears of Europe, include the belief that witches fly by night to orgies. They are said to be accompanied by familiar animals and birds, and they feast on human flesh. But this is imaginary, and Africans say that it is only 'the soul of the flesh' which is eaten. The victim may be ill, but even his toes are not nibbled when the witch has confessed to eating them. In fact witches are the scapegoats for the ills of society, its mysterious diseases, social tensions, quarrels of wives, jealousy of old women, high infant mortality, and barrenness. In reality there are no witches, but only accusations against people who are blamed for the troubles of others. There are witch-doctors, but they are not witches themselves, since they try to cure those who are ill.*

In modern times these magical and witchcraft beliefs ought to disappear with the growth of education. There may be some

* See my *Witchcraft, European and African* (1963).

decline in their power, but since new tensions arise in society, new fears and illnesses, so men resort to the old superstitions. Even when the higher levels of religion fade or are changed into a new faith, the lower levels tend to linger on for centuries. And there are new charlatans who sell worthless but expensive remedies for every human ill, from loss of potency to failure in examinations. Unlike the old medicine men these quacks have no care for their clients, but only try to extract as much money from them as possible. No doubt in time people will learn the true causes of their troubles; there will be better health, children will not die, education will enlighten minds, and a better faith will guide human actions.

5 Ritual Word and Action

Prayers to God

'Great Spirit, piling up the rocks like mountains, sewing the sky like cloth, calling forth the branching trees, you bring out the shoots so that they stand erect. You fill the earth with mankind, the dust rises on high. O Lord, wonderful one, you live in the midst of the sheltering rocks, you give rain to men. You are on high with the spirits of the great. You raise the grass-covered hills above the earth and you create the rivers. Gracious one.'*

This rain prayer of the Shona of Rhodesia reveals better than many explanations the nature of an African faith in God, his greatness, character and attitude towards men. It is not a solitary example, for from all over Africa there are being recorded prayers made on many occasions, which are enriching the literature on African traditional religion and providing the materials for something like a prayer book of African worship.

The attributes of God are expressed in 'praise names', which are repeated and savoured like salutations to a great chief, and they resemble epithets used in collects and prayers of other religions. Anyone who has listened to African prayers must have been impressed by the sonorous rehearsals of divine qualities. Olorun, Olodumare, Baba, Alaanu julo; God, Almighty, Father, Most merciful; so the Yorubas begin many prayers, and continue with rolling sentences in which praise and prayer are mingled.

The poetry of African prayer, delight in expressive words, and the subtleties of traditional aphorisms, are not allowed to detract from practical purpose. Faith in God implies his providence, his interest in men and his ability to help them in time of need. This is illustrated by a prayer made at sacrifices by the Gikuyu: 'You who make mountains tremble and rivers flood; we offer you this sacrifice so that you may bring us rain. People and children are

* A. T. and G. M. Culwick, *Ubena of the Rivers* (1935), p. 100.

crying; sheep, goats and cattle are crying. We beseech you to accept this sacrifice and bring us prosperity.'*

The need for rain is one of the great concerns of people in the drier parts of Sudanese and eastern Africa, and it is much less important in the damp forest regions. Another constant demand is for children and so people look to God as the creator of all life. In Burundi it is said that there is little prayer to God, Imana, though he is constantly in people's thoughts and speech, but a baby song has been recorded which expresses petition. 'Hush, child of my mother. . . . Imana who gave you to me, if only I could meet him I would fall on my knees and pray to him, I would pray for little babies. . . . You came when Imana lit the fire, you came when he was in a generous mood.' But in suffering or barrenness laments and reproaches may be addressed to God: 'Imana, why are you punishing me? Why have you not made me like other people? Could you not even give me one little child?'†

All family affairs can be matters of prayer, whether they are good or bad, and sometimes a prayer may be almost a curse, as in the Old Testament. A Mende, whose son had left home against his father's will, was prayed against in these words to God, Ngewo: 'O Ngewo, you know this is my son; I begat him and trained him and laboured for him, and now that he should do some work for me he refuses. In anything he does now in the world may he not prosper until he comes back and begs my pardon.' Such a breach with traditional custom and inherited crafts is common nowadays, with the attractions of big cities and easy money, but children often seek reconciliation with their parents, and if misfortune comes they may return home and ask forgiveness. The errant son finds his mother first, and they go with a gift of rice or money and sit or kneel at the father's feet. If he is moved with compassion the father prays again: 'O Ngewo, this is my son . . . he knows he cannot stand behind me; he has come now to beg me to pull the curse as I am doing now. Wherever he goes may he now prosper and have many children.' The assembled family responds by saying, 'God grant it'.‡

* J. Kenyatta, *Facing Mount Kenya* (1938), p. 247.
† R. Guillebaud in *African Ideas of God*, p. 197 ff.
‡ W. T. Harris in *African Ideas of God*, p. 283.

Ancestors

Not only children but ancestors are the constant concern of prayer. They are believed to show their power through the welfare or misfortunes of their family, in sending children and blessing the crops, or the reverse. They are often associated with God in prayer, and as a chief is approached through an intermediary so prayer may go to God through ancestral and other spirits. Or God may be asked to include all the forefathers in his blessing: 'O God, let it reach all our forefathers who are in your arms.' Prayers made directly to the ancestors may be longer than prayers to God, for they know all the intimate family concerns and will pass on to God the most pressing needs. They may be thought to answer prayers themselves, but only if God is willing.

Sometimes God and the ancestors are so closely associated that it is difficult to know which is being addressed. The Shilluk invoke their founder ancestor, Nyikang, and only rarely address God (Juok) directly, but their recorded prayers are ambiguous. 'There is no one above you, O God. You became the grandfather of Nyikang; it is you Nyikang who walk with God, you became the grandfather of man. If famine comes, is it not given by you ? . . . We praise you, you who are God. Protect us, we are in your hands, and protect us, save me. You and Nyikang, you are the ones who created. . . . The cow for sacrifice is here for you, and the blood will go to God and you.'*

These prayers are not fixed in form, and it is a widespread delusion that 'primitive' peoples always pray in exactly the same words, for fear of uttering a word out of place which would have harmful effects. Prayers are made in everyday language, to express general or particular needs, and they can be short and simple or long and complicated.

The ancestors are some of the most powerful spiritual forces in African belief, and in many places they take the place of the gods which are more prominent in West than in East or South Africa. The vexed question whether the ancestors are really worshipped, or simply revered like elders of the clan, finds a partial answer in the fact that prayers to ancestors differ little in tone and content

* G. Lienhardt in *African Worlds* (1954), p. 156 f.

from those directed to God and other spirits. Some of the best examples were recorded years ago by Rattray among the Ashanti, and his examples are models of care, given in the original language followed by English translation.

In Ashanti Adae ceremonies, performed every three weeks or so, water, mashed plantains, and sometimes meat, blood and alcohol are offered at the stools of the ancestors with words like these: 'My spirit grandfathers, today is the Wednesday Adae, come and receive this mashed plantain and eat; let this town prosper; and permit the bearers of children to bear children; and may all the people of this town get riches.' On another occasion when a chief offered a sheep these words were said: 'Ancient ones . . . who came from the Sky God, receive this sheep and eat, permit me to have a long reign, let this nation prosper, do not let it act foolishly.'*

Like God the ancestors are addressed not only in petitionary prayer, but in praise and epithet, and their characteristic virtues are recounted in funeral dirges. Particularly that benevolence is praised which is one of the most popular virtues of chiefs and is expected of the departed still: 'You are a mighty tree with big branches laden with fruit. When children come to you they find something to eat.' The dirges show both the loss to the community of the dead person and the continuing links with his family. 'Grandsire . . . with a slim but generous arm, fount of satisfaction . . . I depend on you for everything . . . . Although a man, you are a mother to children.' People are mentioned by their qualities and events that happened to them: 'Ataa the Priestess fell on a Friday, she was the one called by God.' And God himself is invoked in funeral dirges as the ruler of the departed: 'The Creator of the sun, receive this liquor and show me the way to the world of the dead.'†

Private prayers are often short, whether daily or in time of need or danger, but since much religious practice is formal there are priests or elders who lead prayers at public ceremonies, and as professional men they are proud of their fluency. At a sacrifice for a sick young man among the Dinka the leader seized a spear and

* *Ashanti*, pp. 96, 112.

† J. H. Nketia, *Funeral Dirges of the Akan People* (1955), pp. 35, 37, 156, 192.

addressed the ancestors, 'You of my father', and the spectators repeated the words in chorus. He continued, 'I call upon you because my child is ill', and the chorus repeated this, and so on throughout this prayer and others. 'The promise that you promised, you of my father, where is it? You, trees, hear my words, and you grass hear my words, and you Divinity hear my words, and you earth hear my words. O Divinity, because of sickness, you will help out my tongue.'*

Prayers are comprehensive and tend to include any spirit force that may give help. This may be shocking to a monotheist, but the purpose is to call all the varied powers to give health and well-being. This prayer was recorded at an annual Apo purification ceremony in Ashanti: 'Sky God, upon whom men lean and do not fall, Goddess of the Earth, Creature that rules the underworld, Leopard that possesses the forest, Tano River, by your kindness the edges of the year have met. . . . Stand behind us with a good standing. Let no bad thing whatever overtake us. We give our children. We give our wives. We give ourselves into your hand, let no evil come upon us.'†

Other prayers

The 'nature gods' are also objects of many petitions. They are praised in long chants which refer to past traditions, as well as to the present activities and characters of these powerful beings. These words are taken from songs (*oriki*) recorded of great divinities of the Yoruba. The Great God or King (Orishanla or Obatala) was the agent of creation under the Supreme Being: 'Obatala, powerful king, Obatala, owner of the sacred thing. . . . He gives to him who has and takes from him who has nothing; he remains calm and judges calmly; he looks from the corner of his eye without seeming to do so; with long hands he takes up the son who has fallen into a trap; he pours out quickly away from the hand of the evildoer; if he has something to eat he gives us to eat.' And to the great storm god, Shango, traditional songs are

* G. Lienhardt, *Divinity and Experience* (1961), p. 220 f.
† *Ashanti*, p. 165.

addressed: 'Shango can help us . . . hear if I speak, Shango, hear if I speak. . . . Come, O king, that we may all go and that the festival may be good.'*

Prayers usually assume that the divinity will help his suppliant by an intervention, either open or hidden, but powerful and effective. People know the regularity of nature, the revolution of the solar and agricultural year, and the proper times of rain and harvest. The Luyia ask God to 'let things take their normal course', and to 'let the sun rise and shine as usual'. When variations appear in the normal order of things these are not sent by God out of spite, but to punish people who have deviated from the natural order which he established. If children die it may be blamed on the mother's adultery, or it is witchcraft from a jealous co-wife or a withered grandmother. The argument may be mistaken, but it is based upon reasoning which looks for explanations.

Nevertheless the traditional conception of the world is not static but dynamic. God has not fixed an order that can never change or placed people in positions where they are doomed to stay for ever. The philosophy of forces pictures many different powers, under the supreme one, striving for improvement and progress. Great endeavours are made today by people and communities to 'get up', improve and modernize themselves and become successful, because of this dynamic idea. So prayer, petition and praise, all seek augmentation of force, by recognizing and invoking the powers of the spirits and the Supreme Being.

Sacrifices

Worship has been defined as the field of ritual action, and even the vaguest prayer is a kind of ritual, though it need not be fixed in form or ever repeated in precisely the same way. But beyond the utterance of words there is commonly in all religions the offering of a gift, a sacrifice, a 'thing made sacred'. The sacrifice may be a simple presentation of nuts, such as kola, placed in front of a small shrine or on an altar, or a libation of water or alcohol

* P. Verger, *Notes sur le culte des Orisa et Vodun*, pp. 391, 466.

poured out on the ground. It may be done daily, or at fixed intervals, or occasionally.

There have been many theories of the meaning of sacrifice. Some peoples have animal emblems which can be roughly compared with North American totems, but animals are never killed or eaten, and there is no communion feast on the flesh of the emblem. In Africa the principal purposes of sacrifice are gift and propitiation.

Daily sacrifices are usually simple gifts to keep a man in harmony with the spirits, and offer the essence of the food to the ancestors. Even in such simple offerings there are distinct steps of progression in sacrifice. First there is a formal presentation, briefly or elaborately made. This is followed by consecration, in words or actions, setting the gift apart for the deity. Then comes invocation, words addressed to the spirits. Finally there is the immolation of the animal or placing of nuts on the altar.

A gift may express simple thanksgiving, or it may be presented with the aim of ensuring a return blessing from the god. 'A gift expects a gift' is a common saying, and if this is so between men it also applies between men and God. In its crude sense this becomes a bargain, a gift made with the understanding that help is needed. Jacob expressed this in Genesis, 'If you bless me . . . then I will serve you.' It is not normally as blatant as this; a gift is presented in hope, but it is known that the deity is more powerful than the worshipper and 'thy will be done' is characteristic of all religions.

Sacrifices of propitiation try to remove sin, avert danger, or obtain a blessing. They are directed against misfortune, sickness, barrenness, quarrels, drought, and any disruption of normal life. The help of the god is requested as that supreme power that can set right the errors or shortcomings of mankind.

There is a communion sense in sacrifices, both in gift and propitiation. The latter may be a rite of consolidation, mending the breaches of order between men and the gods. It may be also a rite of incorporation, joining the family by ritual actions. A. I. Richards writes of a Bemba sacrifice: 'the ritual meal binds the living and the dead to fulfil their part in this complex scheme of family obligations. . . . Concrete demands are made of the spirits, to which the sacrifice pledges them to accede.'*

The elements of sacrifice are many, but three basic types can be singled out: vegetable, alcohol and animal. The power of alcohol shows that it is stronger than water and it is thought to be surpassed only by blood. Blood sacrifice has long been abandoned by most European and Asian peoples, but it was still practised in the temple at Jerusalem till its fall in A.D. 70, and it is found in some popular Indian cults today, such as that of Kali, the Great Mother. Some African gods are said to dislike blood and all have things which are 'hateful' to them, taboo. But offering chickens is very common, and also sheep, goats, dogs, and on great occasions bulls. Wild animals are rarely if ever sacrificed, only those animals which are part of human property. Usually it is the blood only, or entrails as well, which are given to the spirits; the rest of the flesh is cooked and eaten by the officiants and sometimes by the worshippers. Human sacrifices were rare, even in the olden days, and most human victims fell not at religious sacrifices but in ancestral rites which were meant to provide attendants and messengers for departed kings and great men.

Most sacrifice is communal, especially when large offerings were made involving the whole family or clan in expense and sharing of a meal. This has the purpose of strengthening family ties, particularly at family rites: naming, puberty, initiation, marriage and funerals. But small individual offerings are made in daily worship and in some agricultural rites.

Sacred People and Places

An individual sacrifice may be offered by any layman, and in time of sickness by the head of the family on behalf of his family group. But when sacrifice involves a whole lineage there will usually be a master of ceremonies, appointed for the task and trained in its performance. Some of these are properly called priests, men and women who are set apart and trained for the work, and who are often attached to a temple. They may work

* *Hunger and Work in a Savage Tribe* (1932), p. 187.

full-time at ritual functions, if they are popular and act on behalf of many people. Often they have a part-time priestly occupation, and work for the rest at jobs like smithery, hunting or agriculture. As in most religions, the priests are married, for celibacy is virtually unknown in traditional Africa. Priests are usually trained by older priests, alone or in the company of other neophytes, and they learn traditional wisdom, rituals and practices.

Priests may have prophetic functions but there are other people, sometimes called 'possessors of spirits', who claim to have spiritual powers lacking in others. Their developed psychic faculties may be thought to come from a familiar spirit, or by intuition from the divinity. Then there are seers, who claim to have second sight, but who often act through magical manipulations rather than by possession by a god, such as water-gazing or nowadays looking into a mirror.

There are many mediums who work under the control of priests or independently, going into trances and speaking on behalf of the spirits. This may be done regularly at festivals, or occasionally at the demand of inquirers. Mediums may be men or women, but women seem particularly adapted to the trance state. In Dahomey the training of mediums has been developed most elaborately; the candidates are chosen when they are possessed by spirits, taken into enclosed cult-houses and trained for months or years. The purpose of training is to produce a new personality, and at the end the medium emerges with a new name, a new language and an ability to be possessed on demand.*

Diviners are men who seek the will of the oracles, by methods of consultation which have been described above. Then there are medicine men, or doctors, who try to cure the sick in body and mind, by material and spiritual means. There are witch-doctors who have special powers by which they attempt to cure those who think themselves bewitched. There are herbalists who know the medicinal values of plants and apply them to the sick. There are many specialists in different departments of human life, but most of them have other occupations which provide economic support.

The organization of the priests and their assistants is usually local. In a town there may be half a dozen temples to the same god,

* See my *West African Religion*, Chapter 8.

whose servants have recognizable relationships with one another, the elders taking precedence in communal gatherings. In village or clan ceremonies there are leading priests or elders who perform rituals on behalf of the whole community, and in the old kingdoms there were officials who supervised all the cults and arranged annual and special ceremonies. But much African religious life has little organization and it is difficult to speak of it as a whole. There are no scriptures, but also no fixed creeds, and of course no missionary societies to spread the faith. This is not unusual. Other religions such as Hinduism and Judaism are national, almost tribal and local. Organization can be a heavy burden on religious energy, and the loose and simple arrangements of African priests and prophets are adequate for most needs.

There are no great stone temples in old Africa, and in the absence of soft building stone there are very few ancient constructions, apart from the three hundred or so stone ruins found at Zimbabwe and near-by places in Rhodesia. In the tropics, whether Africa or India, much religious ceremony has taken place in the open air on sites perhaps marked by small wooden or earthen shrines or altars. There are many small clay temples in West Africa; the Mbari houses of the Ibo have been mentioned and there are cult-houses in Dahomey for training priests and mediums. Such temples are often decorated with symbolical patterns in bright colours, and these may contain painted images of the gods and their assistants and worshippers. But many temples are so small that only a priest can enter, bowing low through the doorway to place a gift on the altar, while attendants wait in the courtyard outside.

Liturgies also are loosely arranged. The visitor to a traditional ceremony often receives an impression of casualness which almost seems irreverent. When prayers are uttered they may conform to a general pattern, but many prayers are virtually extempore, as in some other religions. The formal element in liturgy becomes apparent in the songs and dances that accompany or follow worship. Here there is room both for tradition and spontaneity, and the collections of traditional songs that have begun to be compiled, by Nketia, Verger and others, show the importance of ancient songs which are memorized easily with the music and passed down from generation to generation. Here is the nucleus of creed and religious history. The words, music and movement of the dance express the character and actions of the deity that is being praised, and the nature of human petitions to him. The dancers wear coloured and symbolical costumes, become possessed by the god, and reveal his nature in action. The importance of music in African religious life is that it gives expression to the deepest feelings, but it is not only feeling, for it points to belief in the life force that underlies religious thought. Dancing is symbolical and expressive in sound, gesture and costume, expressing the life of the family and society and the meaning of the world.

6 The Life Cycle

In reaction against the individualism of the West modern writers have stressed the corporate nature of African religion, and some extremists have excluded individual religion entirely. S. F. Nadel said that 'the self-abandonment of the mystic or visionary is utterly foreign to the Nupe. Never does the worshipper face his god in solitude, drawing only upon his inward experience or seeking private illumination.'*

If there were no mystical experience then African traditional religion would be seriously lacking in a major element of most religious life. By mysticism is meant nothing magical but, in the Oxford Dictionary definition, seeking 'by contemplation and self-surrender to obtain union with or absorption into the Deity'. There are plenty of examples of such self-surrender in the mediums who become absorbed in the divinity in African dances and rituals, to the extent of speaking with divine voices. In ordinary life these mediums seem to be normal people, not usually showing signs of neurosis in the general sense. But communion with the deity is not confined to the experiences of exceptional people, and mysticism in its exalted ranges is only different in degree from the experience of ordinary folk in their prayers and daily living in the consciousness of the presence of divine powers.

How can it be maintained that the individual never faces his god in solitude? By definition one cannot observe a man in solitude, and no one knows what he thinks in the privacy of his mind. Such denial of individual religion would imply a complete break in the new religions, for Christian prophets in Africa often retire into solitary meditation and there is no reason to suppose that older priests and seers have not done the same. Moreover

* S. F. Nadel, *Nupe Religion* (1954), p. 273.

there are traditional myths which tell of individuals, in the old and supposedly rigid tribal societies, who left home and travelled abroad to other villages and countries. The notion that ancient African society was such a tightly knit group that there was no individual freedom of thought, like a communist cell, seems to be a myth in itself.

Rites of Passage

BIRTH

However in rituals which are intended for individual blessings there is normally some communal participation. *Rites of Passage* is the name commonly given to those traditional rituals which mark stages in the life of an individual, passing from one stage to another through a sacred event. These are the rituals of birth, adolescence, marriage and death, and for some people ordination as well, corresponding to some of the sacraments of the church.

Rituals of birth concern the parents, especially the mother, as well as the baby. The physical facts of conception are known, but the blessing of the spirits is believed to be necessary to make it operative, with perhaps the reincarnation of the ancestors. There is a great desire to have children, no wife feels her marriage secure till she has borne a child, and no man feels that his family can be continued and his own funeral rites ensured till a son is born. Since African faith is world-affirming, marriage, sex and a family are the gifts of God. Barrenness is one of the commonest causes of divorce and the desire for more children is the usual reason for polygamy.

Expectant mothers may wear protective amulets and avoid taboo foods. At delivery prayers are made, and if it is difficult the woman is told to confess sins against purity. The cutting of the umbilical cord is done carefully, for a pointed navel is desirable for a child; then the cord may be buried at the foot of a tree which henceforth belongs to the child. Twins are usually regarded as unlucky and they used to be exposed or neglected in many places, though some people hold them sacred. Sickly children are loaded with charms to drive away evil, or called by scornful or disguised names so that disease will not think them worth taking away.

Name-giving ceremonies are popular and many names are bestowed on the infant at a family festival. Prayers are made and libations poured on the ground, even in Christian naming rites. The names depend on circumstances of birth, likeness to parents and ancestors, and choice of divinity through an oracle. This is followed by an outing ceremony for mother and child, though it has little religious content.

ADOLESCENCE

African children mix with adults from the beginning of their lives, sharing in ceremonies and feasts at home, in visits to fields and markets, and in watching tribunals and funerals. In modern times many children go to school, and this makes for a separation from the elders that was not so marked in the past. Children sleep with their parents, usually until they enter their teens or are married.

Traditionally many African societies were divided into age grades, and in adolescence the grade would pass through common ceremonies of initiation into adult life. Nowadays the rituals are often neglected, being interrupted by school, but grade divisions are still seen in dances and competitions, and in group pressures which guard the morality of the members.

Circumcision is practised widely but not everywhere. It may be done in childhood or left till adolescence in circumcision schools, as in Lesotho and Botswana. Female excision is also practised, even in modern Egypt, despite attempts to suppress it by reformers. The Ibo had 'fatting houses' where girls were prepared for marriage with the minimum of exercise, feeding on fats and having coils of metal and large solid ornaments fixed to their legs.

Some of the best known initiation societies are the Poro and Sandé of Sierra Leone and Guinea. They are examples of the so-called 'secret societies' which have the double function of initiating youths into adulthood and perpetuating the traditions of the ancestors. The Poro is for boys, controlled by a hierarchy of elders, different in each village, which meets in a sacred grove where the clan founder was buried. The purpose of initiation is the rebirth of the youths, who are said to be swallowed by the Poro spirit at the beginning and returned to their parents as reborn at the end of initiation. Not only is instruction given by elders in traditional rituals and social duties, but boys have to learn endurance by sleeping out of doors and fending for themselves.

The Sandé is a girls' society which has the same purpose of preparation for adult life and marriage, with sex instruction and beautification. In both these societies the leader dresses in a mask and robe whenever he appears in public, but during the initiation his identity is revealed. The public manifestations of the societies are notorious through the masked figures which appear to represent the dead. Their bodies are always completely covered and it is taboo to say that they are human beings. They are accompanied by attendants who keep away the crowds and sometimes women and children have to seclude themselves while the masqueraders are out. In many towns the masked processions are like the carnival figures of Europe. At night the maskers may sound 'bull roarers', flat pieces of wood tied on the end of cords so that uncanny irregular sounds are emitted. Such instruments, said to be the voices of spirits, are used in many parts of Africa, as well as in Australia and America.

MARRIAGE

Marriage is a social rather than a private affair, uniting two families as well as individuals. In the past this removed choice from the partners but it gave greater stability than marriage has today in some western countries. Although marriage is a rite of passage, going from one state to another, its religious side is not distinctive. It is regarded as the normal sequel to rites of adolescence, whose purpose was to prepare for this state.

There are laws of affinity which restrict the choice of partner, and taboos of certain forms of marriage, though these differ from place to place; whatever the form the regulations are fairly strictly observed, even where there is some relaxation in modern and town life. Betrothal takes a long time and includes arrangement of the marriage by both groups of parents and consultation of the ancestors. The girl's consent was often formally asked by her prospective bridegroom, and it is commoner now when many young people choose their own mate. The next step is payment of, or agreement upon, the dowry or bride-wealth. This is paid by the bridegroom to his wife's family to reimburse expenses they have made for her, even back to her education, and to act as a guarantee of fidelity. It is accompanied by many gifts in kind to parents and relatives. Modern marriage involves much more expense, in which church customs and clothes are added to traditional cost and often plunge the family into debt. But the basic contract is marked by a relatively small payment, or even a simple exchange of kola nuts and libation to ancestors.

FUNERALS AND ANCESTORS

There is much more ritual connected with death because these last rites of passage are intended to ensure that the dead person leaves this world with full ceremony and enters safely into the company of his fathers. In tropical heat a corpse cannot be preserved for more than a day or two and there is a speedy 'first burial'. The corpse is washed and dressed in its best, and traditionally interred in fine clothes, with nowadays usually as splendid a coffin as the family can afford. It used to be the custom, as in many other parts of the world, to bury the dead with tools or weapons used in life, and with fine robes and ornaments. But the latter are now generally removed before burial.

Death is thought to be like a river, as the Jordan, which must not be looked at before then but must be crossed safely. Money may be left in the corpse's hand to pay for the journey and provide gifts for the ancestors on arrival in the world beyond. When the body is placed in the grave prayers are said, and the spirit of the dead person may be asked for blessing and protection from harm. Burial, and not cremation, is the universal practice and only evil people or those with highly infectious diseases, such as leprosy and smallpox, are refused burial. Most graves are simple shafts, but some have a niche at the side into which the body is slid to prevent earth falling on it; this type of grave is found in both southern and western Africa.

A 'second burial' is fixed at a time to allow all the family and friends to gather and may vary from a few weeks to months after death. But if it is delayed too long it may be thought that the ghost of the dead person will appear in dreams to trouble his relatives. This final rite of passage is to 'make the grave firm' and separate off the dangerous powers of the dead finally from the living. In some places, such as south-east Dahomey, the head of the corpse is removed some time after burial and placed in a box or bag for annual commemoration ceremonies.

At these final rites the 'secret societies' appear again, with masked figures which sometimes impersonate the dead, visit their houses, speak in guttural voices, and bless their children. It is difficult to estimate how far adults still believe in such impersonation, but they are convinced of the continuity of the spirits of their loved ones. The many masks of the dead, which are made all over tropical Africa, testify to the importance of the departed to their relatives. Sometimes the masks are white and express coldness and impassivity in the dead, sometimes they are in animal form like totems, and sometimes they are abstract or nearly so and indicate the different powers and awesomeness of the deceased.

That life survives death is one of mankind's oldest convictions, found in all countries and at all periods. No doubt there is some wishful thinking in unwillingness to consider personal extermination, but there is a more rational basis to the conviction that the elements of the universe are not destroyed, and that although the form may change life continues in another manner. The new religions, Islam and Christianity, affirm survival of death as well, and add details about the afterlife, though they have not always sufficiently adjusted themselves yet to the full range of African traditional needs.

Some modern writers refer to ancestors as 'ghosts', which is unfortunate in English because the word means an apparition or spectre. Lienhardt says it would be wrong to suppose that when the Dinka offer food and drink to the 'ghosts' they imagine that these beings physically consume the offerings. That is true, and Africans generally, like people in other religions, would agree that only the essence of the sacrifice is received by the ancestor. But Lienhardt proceeds to say that 'ghosts' are not in any way materialized, and although they appear to their kinsmen in dreams

'I have never heard of an encounter with a ghost as occurring in the "external" "objective" physical world'.* Whether this is known among the Dinka or not, many other African peoples tell vivid stories of ghosts which appear to their relatives as apparently visible and tangible as in their lives on earth. Ghosts, says this writer, 'are to be understood as reflections of a kind of experience, not as a class of "beings"'. This may be a European explanation, but certainly elsewhere in Africa the ancestors are not just regarded as part of a man's experience only; they have life and power in themselves, they are dead persons who have survived as real and immortal beings. The profound conviction of the vitality and continuity of the dead as a 'great cloud of witnesses' cannot be explained, in African terms, as a simple experience of the survivors. Even if this were a scientific explanation it would not be what people believe.

REINCARNATION

The return of the dead, or some part of their life force, to their family is widely held in Africa, though there are many differences about the degree and manner in which this takes place. Although this belief where it is held in Africa resembles Indian belief in reincarnation, there are important differences. Indian ideas are based upon the conviction of the indestructibility of the soul which journeys from one body on earth to another. As with Plato, in the myth at the end of the *Republic*, Indian belief has a moral concomitant; the *karma* or entail of a man's 'deeds' brings him back to a higher or lower destiny in the next life. He may rise to the level of a priest or sink to that of an animal; the soul may be reborn as male or female and in any family. Even Buddhism, which tried to dispense with the soul, was unable to part with the belief in rebirth and tied it to behaviour in a previous life on earth.

African belief starts from different presuppositions and flows from its philosophy of power. It is not belief in a collection of individual souls coming back to higher or lower levels in this unreal world, and finally escaping altogether. That which is passed on from elders to children is the force which makes life possible and through which property is inherited. This is not based on

* *Divinity and Experience*, p. 153 f.

moral judgements, but anything which blocks the linking of power, like witchcraft which is thought to cause sterility or prevent babies from being born and surviving, is condemned as very evil. Rebirth is therefore into the same family, to strengthen it with sure links of continuity. And because the African world view, like the Biblical, is world-affirming there is none of the Indian notion of world-denial which sees punishment or loss in being born at all and holds out hope of escape into a featureless *nirvana*. For Africans return to this world of light and warmth is far preferable to the cold of the beyond.

Yet African belief is complex. Ancestors are reincarnated yet offerings are still made to them at their graves; they are in heaven, yet back on earth, and they may enter not only one body but perhaps several. That a dead person may be reborn in several descendants has suggested to some writers that Africans are not logical in their thinking, or are 'pre-logical', but in fact this agrees quite well with the philosophy of power, for one force can strengthen or weaken another or several, and wisdom and happiness are increased by the influence of the dead forebears. So it is not the single 'soul' of the ancestor that passes from one embodiment to another in an endless round or chain of existence. Rather it is the 'ontological influence', as Tempels calls it, which a forefather exerts on his grandson or grandsons, it is the immortal vitality that continues to reinforce and uplift.

The Ila of Zambia hold that all people are reborn, except evil ones who worked for sorcerers and have become wandering ghosts. After a child is born the parents go to a diviner who tells them the name of the ancestor who has come back. When the child is named he cries, till he is given the birth name of the proper forefather and then he stops. Some say that the ancestral spirit comes on him now, others that it came before birth at the moment of quickening. The Ila believe that a male spirit may return in a female child and also that the same spirit may descend upon two bodies. The parents accept the word of the diviner that this is so and say 'our father has returned to our home'. When there is a dispute over a chieftaincy, the candidate who can prove that he comes from a powerful ancestor has his case strengthened. E. W. Smith says, 'My old friend Mungalo now sitting smoking a pipe with me, or sitting yonder under the eaves of his hut and carving a wooden spoon, is the Mungalo who lived here a hundred years ago, and, furthermore, Mungalo is his *musedi*, his guardian spirit, shall we say, always accompanying him, guarding him, warning him of danger. There is here some metaphysical subtlety. The spirit that assumes a material body is not confined to that body; being spirit it cannot be imprisoned in the material. It is in the body and yet it is not of the body; it is there as a kind of aura, surrounding and protecting the body.'*

Among the Yoruba popular names are Babatunde and Yetunde, 'father returns' and 'mother returns'. Three months after birth the Ifa oracle is consulted to know which is the *ori*, the 'head' or 'life' of the child and he declares which ancestor has 'turned to be a child'. The same phrase is used at funerals, when mourners wish the relative the blessing that he may turn to be children for them, and that his turning may fill the house. This 'turning' may even be used of a living person, and seems to indicate that his power will be passed on without dying.†

There is widespread belief in 'born-to-die' children. These are babies who are so unhealthy that they keep dying, but each one is supposed to be identical with its predecessor and great efforts are made to break the chain of rebirth and redeath, by magic and medicine. Circumstantial stories are told of babies who had the same physical characteristics or deformations as their predecessors. Similar tales are told of a child and his returning ancestor; both had facial or other resemblances and so the diviner recognized which ancestor had been reborn. Differences of character and status are also explained by reference to the incarnating spirit, and part of the importance of the idea of reincarnation is that it provides an explanation of differences in the social hierarchy by the philosophy of power.

The Ibo believe that before birth the soul chooses between two bundles which the Creator offers to him, one of which contains high fortune and the other lower. If he makes a bad choice, however, he may still hope to change his lot in the next life by special

---

* E. W. Smith and A. M. Dale, *The Ila-speaking Peoples of Northern Rhodesia* (1920), ii, p. 152 f.; E. W. Smith, *Knowing the African*, p. 103 f.
† E. B. Idowu, *Olódùmarè, God in Yoruba Belief* (1962), p. 194 f.

efforts. Evil people are said to have an inauspicious reincarnation, so that a moral element enters in. A great curse on evildoers declares 'may you not be reincarnate in human form', and those who are born in an abnormal manner, with feet first or having teeth, are looked on with fear as bringing evil power to birth.*

There is little history of African religion because of the absence of reliable documents from the past, and in modern times so much is changing that it is difficult to know whether beliefs are the same as those of a century ago. But recent research into African communities that have survived from descendants of slaves in South America shed some light on beliefs which were imported over a hundred years ago and which have received no influence from Africa since then. No doubt there have been other influences, but they are different, and comparisons can be made between two kinds of African belief that are widely separated. Records of slaves in the eighteenth century show a high proportion of suicides, partly from despair but also it is said with the hope of being reborn in their native land. Because of this their owners cut off the heads of suicide slaves to suggest that they would be reborn mutilated. South American Africans today believe that dreams indicate which ancestor is being reborn in a child. A man can be reborn as a woman, but never as an animal, though animals can be reborn among themselves. An ancestor can be reborn in several people at once, and gifts may be presented to the newborn child under the ancestor's name, as well as to the ancestor himself at his grave. A reborn spirit is called 'the spirit which comes back to see the world'. Criminals become ghosts and are not usually believed to be reborn. There is normally thought to be a limit to the number of times rebirth takes place; some say three times, others up to twelve times, and after that the liberated soul becomes a soldier of the highest spirits.†

* V. C. Uchendu, *The Igbo of Southeast Nigeria*, p. 102.
† R. Bastide in *Réincarnation et vie mystique en Afrique Noire*, ed. D. Zahan (1965).

7 Society and Morals

Many modern writers on Africa have a special interest in social organization. They describe in great detail, though not always easy style, the agnates and cognates, affines and lineages, clans and tribes. All of this is important and its recording is a valuable element in building up the history of Africa. But a great deal is in process of change and the organization of hitherto untouched villages alters or even disappears in the multiplicity of great towns which have sprung up all over Africa. Further, in the sociological approach the place of religion, in past and present communities, may be interpreted in different ways. The social function of religion tends to be stressed at the expense both of its individual and ideological characters. Yet it is important to emphasize that a participant in public worship does not think that he is merely making a social cement. He has a personal faith, the light by which he lives, and in these days the power of ideology ought to be very clear.

Nevertheless religion has a social importance. A man and his family create and live in the midst of relationships, which extend both in space and time. Mythology seeks to explain and justify these relationships and link them with the wider field of the universe. Myths of creation make all clans descend from God, and he created the hero-ancestors from whom the present clans descend. Myth and actual genealogy overlap, as do the actions of God and ancestors.

Morality

The social relationships in which men live are links of authority, indicating the proper places of individuals and prescribing courses of conduct for them. Man lives in a moral community and his behaviour is prescribed by relationship. Morality is the *mores*, the manners and customs of society. Good morality is living in appropriate relationships with other people, high and low, old and young. The smaller the community the narrower is the scope of moral relationship. A foreigner is regarded with suspicion, because it is not known what relationships can be established with him, even if men do not throw bricks at him. This is modified to some extent by myths that include all men within the creation of the supreme God, though this belief may be vague and formal.

The sanctions of morality are the disapproval of the social group, expressed in reward and punishment. These vary greatly according to the status of the persons who have been favoured or offended; offence against a humble person is less dangerous than against an elder or priest. The ancestors also have their sanctions, but they are part of the social unit. They founded the clan, gave its laws and imposed taboos. Ultimately there is God, the final authority and court of appeal.

It has sometimes been doubted whether God is essential to morality, or whether religion is necessarily moral, since morality concerns society in its interrelationships, horizontally rather than vertically. But God is not to be separated off into some non-secular or supernatural world; he is both the Creator of all and the pinnacle of the hierarchy of beings. While he is high and lifted up, and his power may be delegated to lesser beings, yet he can no more be abstracted from the world view than the veiled chiefs could have disappeared without shaking society to its foundations. God is not only responsible for the abnormal, such as sudden deaths of the wicked; he is near to men in strange and lonely places, and also in the ordinary affairs of everyday life. That rewards and punishments are believed to come from God in reaction to human behaviour, shows that God is thought to be closely concerned with morality.

The relationships of authority in the past were static, and although there were deviations and individual aberrations these did not change the essential pattern. Rituals and sacrifices were made to renew the social order but not to change it. But in modern times the many changes that occur bring uncertainty as to the new powers that are operating and the proper ritual obligations that exist. It is commonly said that there is more witchcraft nowadays, and while there is no evidence at all for an increase in the belief because the incidence of it in past centuries is quite unknown, yet the assertion is evidence of modern uneasiness expressed in a conviction that there is more evil present now. An offence against society in the past was a breach of a well known custom or law, in a pattern of relationships that was relatively understood and unchanging. While this still holds in some areas of life, there are many new situations in which people are not sure what is the best course of conduct. Traditional religion suffers here, because although it had a vague and general world view, its obligations were largely local and tribal. The concepts of universal brotherhood and charity to a neighbour whatever his race have only made their appearance with Christianity.

It is easy to idealize the past and sigh for an imaginary Golden Age away from the disturbing present with its rapacious commerce, oppressive politics and bitter warfare. The facts are that even in the past there were unpleasant customs, tyrannical rulers, sudden deaths and human sacrifices. Although oracles and magic worked in favour of some people, they could work against others who had paid less. The bribing of diviners and ministers of ordeals is no new phenomenon. The new religions bring a disturbance of society and its values, but they also bring new values of their own which in time will create a new stability.

Old and New Authority

The divinity that hedges a king has been much written about. Whether the king is a god or not his office is regarded as sacred or awesome, and the sacrosanct nature of the office surrounds the ruler as well. Many African societies have been ruled by monarchs, paramount chiefs or kings, though their authority was rarely absolute or despotic. But many other societies are more loosely organized and may have no tribal ruler at all or only a figure of convenience; and most sacredness attaches to clan elders who perform ritual functions on behalf of the community.

Many of the Bantu of South Africa have had a chief who was not merely a convenient ruler but the embodiment of the unity of the people, administrator of traditional laws, leader in war, source of wealth, priest and rain-maker. Some of them rose to great power, like Shaka of the Zulu, born of an illegal union in 1787, but by his own efforts and genius building a great army and in fifteen years conquering an area larger than Europe. People fell before him in adoration and flattered Shaka with praise names, till he became harsh and cruel, though he himself considered some European practices were inhuman. Shaka was becoming receptive to more advanced European ideas when jealous brothers assassinated him and his empire was destroyed.

More traditional and peaceful were the kings of the neighbouring Swazi. They have retained their great annual ceremony, the Incwala, in which the king is the chief performer and recapitulates the history of his people. It is controlled by priests who wash the king in sea water to give him strength. A black ox is slaughtered and the king acts to break off from the old year and inaugurate the new. There is a long and elaborate ritual, which has been described by H. Kuper in *An African Aristocracy*. The king and his mother are the leaders of the kingdom, she is called 'mother of the people' and he is 'child of the people'; after enthronement the king is called Lion and his mother Lady Elephant. The mother has charge of national sacred objects, but if they are to be efficacious her son must manipulate them with her. The royal pair are called twins and any disagreement between them is believed to cause national disaster, such as drought and famine. A national anthem sung during the ceremony expresses some of the people's feelings towards the king.

> 'Here is the Inexplicable,
> Our Bull! Lion! Descend.
> Descend, Being of heaven,
> Unconquerable.
> Play like tides of the sea,
> You Inexplicable, Great Mountain.'*

The Rain-queen of the Lovedu has been mentioned in con-

* *An African Aristocracy* (1947), p. 205.

nexion with rituals of the storm (page 52 above). Among many other African peoples there are traditional rulers who are revered for the supernatural powers with which they are invested. However, in our day there are clashes with new powers of political life. In 1966 Sir Edward Mutesa (King Freddie), Kabaka of Buganda, fled his country after the army had seized the palace. The President announced the end of the Kabaka's government and the division of Buganda into four districts administered by the central government. Traditionally the Kabaka had been regarded as the source of the health of the nation and his absence would be disastrous. All the land was called his possession, and while he delegated the administration of justice and much of the ritual of sacrifice to officials, he was the final source of their power and authority. At his installation he was dressed in a barkcloth and skin, like those worn by the first ancestors when they took charge of Buganda, and very old drums were beaten.

Most monarchs of West Africa have experienced more gentle decline in influence, most of them still holding tenuous authority but overshadowed by politicians and soldiers. The Alafin of Oyo was once ruler of an empire that stretched from the Niger Delta to Togoland, but he was exiled a few years ago, and though he returned it was to much diminished influence. Traditionally the Alafin was direct descendant of Oranyan, a semi-divine founder of the nation who is still represented by a twenty foot stone pillar at Ifé which is called his staff. When the Alafin was enthroned he 'ate the king', making a token meal of his predecessor's heart in order to gain his power. Other rulers were surrounded with customs to emphasize their sanctity. They wore bead veils to hide their faces from the common gaze, and spoke only quietly or through spokesmen, the so-called 'linguists' of the courts. Men prostrated in the dust before them, and some do so still. Shoes are removed in their presence and the shoulders bared of robes, as at a shrine of divine spirits. The chiefs ate alone or behind curtains, since they were supposed not to need food. It was once an offence to have more riches than a chief, a bigger house or robes like his, but many rich men, soldiers and politicians now have more luxurious mansions and cars.

Traditional monarchs were great powers, surrounded by holiness and taboos. E. Meyerowitz, in *The Sacred State of the Akan*, claims that the king of Ashanti was fully divine, the child of the sun whose golden colour was sacred to him, and his body was dusted with gold in ceremonies. The queen mother was daughter of the moon, with silver as her emblem. This interpretation is disputed, but the king of Ashanti was undoubtedly invested with sacred powers and related to the Golden Stool. This is a national emblem, made by a priest Anotchi in the eighteenth century, and said to have come down from heaven in a black cloud. Stools are personal possessions and at death are used as shrines for ancestral cults. Anotchi said that the Golden Stool contained the soul of all the people of the Ashanti nation, and he made powder from the nails and hair of the king, queen and chiefs, which was put on the stool. Possession of the stool was believed to give the Ashanti victory in war and gold chains and masks of conquered kings were fixed to it. It was never sat on, but at his installation the king was lifted three times over it. After disappearing during wars with the British, who had demanded to sit on it, the Golden Stool was discovered and restored to the capital town of Kumasi again in 1921. But the power of the Omanhene, the king of Ashanti, has been much curtailed under colonial and later independent rule. President Nkrumah thought himself a much greater authority, and his followers declared that he would never die, but he took care not to visit Kumasi even at the height of his power.

Despite their power in the past most African rulers were not despots, with some exceptions like Shaka, and totalitarian rule is not a traditional phenomenon. Although the king was often monarch by right of descent, he could be deposed or could abdicate. He ruled with councils of elders, and if he abused his powers they were broken by making him perform some action that cut him off from the ancestral forces. An Ashanti king was de-stooled by whipping off his shoes so that he came into forbidden contact with the sacred power of the earth, or he was made to sit on the ground, or his body was mutilated. A Yoruba king was presented with parrot's eggs to eat, which was a traditional sign that he must abdicate or take poison.

As has been said, many other African societies were more loosely organized, though sometimes chiefs were foisted on them in modern times for convenience of imperial rule. Lugbara society in Uganda and the Congo is composed of some sixty clans, descended from founder heroes, which are dispersed among territorial tribes. But the tribes have no single head and the chief central authority is a rain-maker whose power is only exercised occasionally. Effective authority is expressed through heads of family clusters, and these elders differ in power according both to their position and personal qualities. The elder is in charge of shrines of the recent dead and also the special shrines of founding ancestors. He has various tokens of office, the most important being a special stool which is inherited and on which he alone may sit. He is called the one who sits on the stool, the one who stays with the shrines and puts meat in them, and the one who eats the elder's portion of meat, which includes special parts of the victim reserved to him at sacrifices. He consults oracles and has ritual authority, as well as secular power, for example in the allocation of land.*

Similarly loose and decentralized authority is found among the Ibo of Nigeria. There are some kings, as at Onitsha, but they are based on foreign patterns and even so are elected, not hereditary. In the villages government is fairly democratic, and all adult males share in the direction of communal affairs. The village rules its own concerns and since the houses are scattered about, a central government such as that practised among their neighbours in big towns is difficult. Beyond the village there is representative government in which all share equally, 'sharing kola nuts', and uniting for matters of common interest. The head of a family, or oldest member, has a ritual staff (*ofo*) as symbol of authority, and is respected as intermediary between the family and its ancestors. Priests and medicine men have similar wands of office. The family head sacrifices to Ala, the earth spirit, on behalf of all members of his lineage. Politically he is a president over committees which consider disputes, and he gives advice on custom and tradition, indicating where a proposed action agrees with or violates them. His effective powers are limited to cursing offenders on his ritual staff, which is rarely done. When decisions have been agreed upon by the whole group, the elder strikes his

* J. Middleton, *Lugbara Religion* (1960), p. 7 ff.

staff on the ground four times, declaring that it will kill those who disobey the law and all the assembly responds in support.*

This democratic system has survived the vagaries of modern rule. Under colonial administration it was assumed that the Ibos lived in 'ordered anarchy' without any chiefs, and so a direct centralized administration was imposed. 'Warrant chiefs', picked by district commissioners, were appointed to represent village groups. This led to various revolts, with women's riots in 1928, and so reforms were made in which new courts were instituted, 'customary courts' to regulate inter-village affairs, though the villages themselves are administered much as in the past.

Modern Change

The different kinds of social organization have been affected in modern times not only by politics but by religion. Of course politicians themselves claim supernormal powers, and religious attitudes cannot be divorced from political or any other departments of life. Similarly Islamic and Christian influences inevitably accompanied the political forces of the Berbers or the Europeans. These two religions are missionary forces but they have political effects. K. A. Busia, in one of the best studies of such culture-contact, says that 'Christianity came into immediate conflict with the chiefs in Ashanti'. The first converts were encouraged by their leaders to cut themselves off completely from 'heathen' customs, and in some cases separate villages were formed which removed Christians entirely from the traditional authority of the chiefs. Even where such segregation was not practised Christians were liable to reject the jurisdiction of the chief. They refused to work on Sunday but laboured on the land on Thursday which was taboo to the earth spirit; they rejected forced labour or Sunday courts; if called to a court they would not remove their shoes before the chief or swear oaths on symbols of the ancestors; they objected to libations and annual ceremonies to gods and ancestors. Busia says that the cleavage centred round the two vital questions of ancestral authority and the liberty of the Christian. These are

* V. C. Uchendu, *The Igbo of Southeast Nigeria*, p. 39 ff.

both political and religious. From the point of view of the chief, Christians were rejecting all traditional customs and the power of the ancestors which was incarnated in him. In 1941 the Confederacy Council of Chiefs decreed that those who farmed on Thursday committed an offence. Christians saw this as an attack both on religious belief and on their economic position, and appealed to the central government. The problem was insoluble and in the characteristic manner of compromise a decision was left in abeyance, in the hope that time would solve it.*

The new religions present many problems for traditional faith and customs. When they are still new intruders, with little power, they can be ignored or allowed as exceptions, but when their followers become numerous the dilemmas grow. With modern ease of communications and international links, these world-wide religions have many advantages over the old local cults. Christianity, with its stress on liberty, has tended to aim at personal salvation and responsibility. Islam, broadly speaking, has aimed more at the conversion of chiefs in the hope that the people will follow later. But chiefs still have many traditional customs to perform, which involve some recognition of spiritual powers that both the new religions declare to be non-existent. What happens, both with Muslim and Christian chiefs, is that traditional rites are performed, but often by a substitute who acts on behalf of the chief and allows him to attend church or mosque. A short note on characteristics of modern African religion as a whole will be found at the end of this book.

* K. A. Busia, *The Position of the Chief in the Modern Political System of Ashanti* (1951), p. 133 ff.

Statistics of African Religions

There are no figures available of the numbers of adherents of Traditional Religions in Africa. The population of the whole continent is estimated at about 330 million. Calculations of the numbers of Muslims and Christians will be found at the end of their respective sections, but there are, approximately, 125 million Muslims and 95 million Christians. This means that about 110 million may be reckoned as still holding to the old religion, though the growth and appeal of both Islam and Christianity are very strong and many people come within their scope of activity and are potential Muslims and Christians.*

* See T. A. Beetham, *Christianity and the New Africa* (1967), pp. 22, 164, and Europa publications, *The Middle East and North Africa* (1975) and *Africa South of the Sahara* (1975).

Part Two : Christianity

8 North Africa and Ethiopia

Christianity has the longest history of the great living religions of Africa. It is not necessary to discuss Christian doctrine here, or the organization of different churches, since these are the same as in other continents and can be studied in countless books. Rather than discuss Christian doctrine, in the way in which we have been considering the beliefs and customs of African traditional religion, we shall now consider the history of Christianity and its extension in modern times.

Christianity entered Africa in the first century of our era and it has had a continuous history in Egypt and Ethiopia, so that it is truly a traditional religion of Africa. There is a vast literature on the ancient Egyptian, Ethiopian and North African churches, and though the latter disappeared the influence of the writings of their leaders remained important. Here only a few sketches can be given of the early history and some account of the modern churches of Egypt and Ethiopia.

Egypt

The ancient civilization of Egypt is one of the two oldest in the world, the other being in Mesopotamia. Both were centred round rivers and the annual flooding of the narrow Nile valley enabled Egyptian agriculture and civilization to flourish. City-kingdoms arose here in prehistoric times, gradually joining into two major groups of Upper (south) and Lower (north) Egypt. At first these cultures were isolated in Africa but about 3000 B.C. links were formed with Mesopotamia, and also at this period the kingdoms of Upper and Lower Egypt were united under King Menes. This was followed by the age of building pyramids, immense royal tombs, many of which remain as some of the wonders of the world in their size and yet geometrically precise construction. Texts abound from the pyramids and later inscriptions which reveal ideas of religion and morality among the ancient Egyptians. There were local gods, often represented in animal form, and cosmic gods which appear as human. Re was a typical sun god, and Osiris a king and vegetation deity. There was great concern with life after death; the dead were embalmed as mummies, and the journeys of the soul are described in the Book of the Dead.

Some attempts have been made to link the religion of ancient Egypt with beliefs and practices of various parts of modern Africa, but few scholars see more than some vague resemblances in this. J. O. Lucas considered much of Yoruba religion as a degenerate form of Egyptian religion. He thought that the Yoruba 'must have' settled for many years in ancient Egypt, but there is no solid evidence for this. He said that 'not less than half' the words in modern Yoruba contain Egyptian roots. But the Egyptian language was related to Hamitic and not Negro-Bantu languages, and although it was written in picture form the signs indicate consonants and there is no certain knowledge of the vowels of most ancient Egyptian words. As an example of his method, Lucas dissected a Yoruba name for the Supreme Being, Olorun. Ol was dropped as a prefix, and n as a nasal; there remained Oru which Lucas said came from the Egyptian Horus, a sky god. But this method was as forced as the attempt of another writer to find a respectable ancestry for a central African name for God, Leza. Drop za as a suffix, reverse Le into El, and you have El or Elohim, a Hebrew name for God and so Africans have Jewish religion, Q.E.D. But E. B. Idowu says reasonably that the attraction of Egypt is a trap for students of Yoruba religion and he criticizes Lucas's etymologies as 'far-fetched'.*

In fact the ancient Egyptians do not seem to have exported their religious ideas even to near-by peoples, let alone into the tropics. Some of the Hebrews were in captivity in Egypt about 1300 B.C. and were always close neighbours, but they show few signs of that great preoccupation with life after death which characterized the

* J. O. Lucas, *The Religion of the Yorubas* (1948), and E. B. Idowu, *Olódùmarè*, p. 32 n.

Egyptians. Tropical African religions were much farther away, and they have very different conceptions of the universe as a dynamic field for the interplay of spiritual powers.

After leading the world in culture for thousands of years Egypt gradually declined, submitting to the Persians in 525 B.C., to Alexander the Great in 332 and to the Romans in 30 B.C. Egypt became fully incorporated into the Mediterranean world; some of its religious cults spread to Greece and Rome, but in Egypt itself they slowly declined under the growing pressures of Greek culture, Judaism, Christianity, and finally Islam. Even the Egyptian language eventually disappeared, to be replaced by Arabic, and the only remains of the old tongue are in the liturgy of the Coptic Church.

Alexandria, named after the emperor, came to be the most cultured city of the Roman empire, with a large Jewish population. Its academies and schools drew scholars from all over the Mediterranean world to study Greek philosophy and rhetoric. The Roman empire provided peace, organization and roads for easy communication between countries. The Greek language was spoken by most educated people and became the great medium for the circulation of ideas. It was only natural for the first Christian writers, who were nearly all Jews, to compose the New Testament in Greek. In the first century A.D. Christians spread from the Holy Land to Asia Minor, Greece, Rome, and no doubt into Egypt, though the early history of the church of Alexandria is obscure.

That Jesus himself went to Egypt is asserted by St Matthew in recounting the story of the flight of Joseph, Mary and the child from the wrath of Herod. Nothing more is known certainly about this journey and sojourn, but apocryphal writers in later centuries delighted to tell of the places where the family stopped in Egypt, the trees that bent down to give them fruit, and the water that sprang out of the ground for their needs. There are four sites of the Flight still venerated by both Christians and Muslims in Egypt, which are said to make Egypt a land of peace. Other tales about Jesus learning the religion or magic of the Egyptians are pure fantasy, for the Gospel says that he was taken back to Nazareth while still a child.

Simon of Cyrene, who carried the cross of Jesus, was probably a Jewish settler from part of what is now Libya. Other Jews from Cyrene who became Christians are mentioned in the Acts of the Apostles, and they preached to Greeks as well as to Jews. A notable Christian was Apollos, who is called a Jew but 'an Alexandrian by race, a learned man' (Acts 18, 24), but it is not known where he became a Christian and he first appears in activity at Ephesus.

The Coptic Christians claim that the Egyptian church was founded by St Mark, the writer of the second Gospel, cousin of Barnabas, companion of Paul and interpreter of Peter. The first written evidence for this is in A.D. 311 in the church history of Eusebius, who says 'they say that' Mark founded the church of Alexandria, but it is curious that when Dionysius of Alexandria discussed the career of Mark he did not mention his connexion with Alexandria. In a Syrian writing, the Clementine Homilies, it is said that Barnabas first preached in the streets of Alexandria. However, the Egyptian church holds to Mark, and for centuries the patriarchs of Alexandria were elected beside a tomb which was believed to hold his body.

Christianity spread in Egypt no doubt first among the Jews, who numbered about a million in the whole country. In Alexandria and the towns of the Nile delta it made headway among intellectuals. In the country the native Egyptians, later called Copts (meaning Egyptians), were devoted to the cult of Osiris. This taught the murder of the god by his brother Set, the search for Osiris by his wife Isis, and the posthumous birth of his son Horus. Osiris was brought back to life and given the kingdom of the dead. Although there are only vague resemblances between this myth and the Christian history of the Crucifixion, there was a clear appeal in the preaching of the Saviour who had conquered death, that constant preoccupation of Egyptians. The church took a strong hold on the people and later there were many ascetics and martyrs.

For the first two centuries Christian progress in Egypt was relatively peaceful, and it seems that there was no widespread persecution until that of Septimius Severus (193–211). The first house-churches were soon replaced by special buildings for worship with a kind of freehold land. But church organization and discipline was not rigid, perhaps because of the high standing of the congregations; bishops were not yet clearly distinguished from presbyters. The Alexandrian church was more tolerant than some towards Greek philosophy, and other books as well as those of the Bible were used, including a Gospel according to the Egyptians which seems, from the few references made to it, to have been a secondary work with some ideas which have little basis in the canonical Gospels.

In such an atmosphere it was not surprising that there was latitude towards speculations of Gnostics who taught theories of gnosis, 'knowledge', which divided most churches in the second century. From pagan roots this movement spread throughout the church, but split into sects by the end of the second century. One of the leading Gnostics was Valentinus, who is said to have been a native of Egypt, but who lived at Rome from 136 to 165, seceded from the church and went to Cyprus. He distinguished between the supreme and unknowable God and a creator god or Demiurge. Christ was regarded as a divine emanation who came bringing gnosis, but he was not properly human and did not die, either being a spirit who lived in the human Jesus for a while or a merely phantom human appearance. Such ideas were later to influence the Coptic Church and Islam. The recently discovered Jung Codex and other manuscripts from Nag Hammadi near Luxor are fourth-century Gnostic texts which show the spread of the doctrines in Egypt.

Orthodox Christians could not accept teachings which denied the humanity of Jesus and the reality of his death, but attempts to bridge the gulf between Jewish and Greek thought were made more significantly by a succession of great Alexandrian teachers, with whom knowledge of the church and its doctrines really begins. A famous Catechetical School was founded which was unrivalled in the world. Clement of Alexandria came from Athens, where he had studied philosophy, and became head of the Alexandrian school for twelve years, till in 202 he was forced to flee during the persecution of Septimius Severus. Clement agreed with the Gnostics in seeking for 'knowledge', but he said that this was found in the church. He held that both Greek philosophy and

Hebrew theology came from God and that Christ, the Word, was the source of all human reason.

Even more famous was Clement's successor, Origen, who was born at Alexandria of Christian parents in 185. He saw his father die a martyr in 202, and Origen himself was tortured at length in the Decian persecution at Tyre in 250 and died soon after. Origen gave allegorical explanations of the Bible, trying to bring out the mystical sense of true knowledge in the union of the soul with the wisdom of the Word. He speculated on the salvation of all creatures, even the devil, and some of his theories were condemned by later authorities.

The persecutions of this time revealed the deep hold that Christianity had gained, especially in Egypt and North Africa where they were fiercest. The historian Eusebius speaks of these 'athletes of God' who suffered many tortures and varieties of death, especially in Alexandria, but also in all Thebais, the territory of Thebes five hundred miles up the Nile, which shows how far Christianity had expanded. He gives lists of church leaders who suffered, and himself saw large crowds in the Thebais confessing their faith and rushing to death. But the church continued to expand despite persecutions, and in 320 there were 100 bishops in Egypt, Thebais and Libya.

The Greek language was used in the Egyptian cities and in theological writings, but evidence of the penetration of Christianity among the people is found in translations of the Bible into other languages. There was a Sahidic version used in Upper Egypt in the third or fourth centuries, and a Bohairic one in the Nile delta later which became the official version of the Coptic Church. Some of the monks knew no Greek and were urged to study the scriptures in their own language. The church took deeper root by this use of the vernaculars, and its numbers in Egypt at the beginning of the fourth century have been estimated at over a million.

Persecutions and the wickedness of the world drove some Christians into the desert and began the great movements of hermits and monasteries which have remained to this day in Egypt and Ethiopia. Antony of Egypt is usually regarded as the founder of the hermit life. In 269 he gave away all his belongings and retired to the desert, where he is said to have fought with demons. Other hermits followed his example, including some negroes from the south. Pachomius, a Copt like Antony, founded a monastery in the Thebais and instituted rules for communal life in 320. At his death there were nine monasteries for men under his rule and two for women. These provided the pattern for the later European monastic organizations of Basil and Benedict.

Alexandrian teachers played a leading part in theological controversies that shook the whole church. Arius, the great heretic, was a Libyan in charge of an Alexandrian church who taught that Christ was a creature, subordinate to God. He was opposed by Athanasius, bishop of Alexandria, who triumphed over the Arians at the councils of Nicaea in 325 and Alexandria in 362. Athanasius taught both the full divinity and the full manhood of Christ, and also introduced knowledge of monastic movements to the West.

Debates on the nature of Christ continued so long and were so divisive that they left a permanent mark on the Coptic churches. Most eastern and western Christians held that there were two natures in Christ, divine and human, and this was affirmed at the Council of Chalcedon in 451. But Mono-physites taught 'one nature', which was divine, and they were especially strong in Egypt, Syria and Armenia. The battle cry of 'one nature' was taken up by African monks and the Coptic churches separated from most of the rest of the Orthodox on this issue, a separation that has remained. Only a few Orthodox were left in Egypt, called Melkites or Imperial Christians.

Nubia and North Africa

The first record of an African converted to Christianity is the Ethiopian eunuch (Acts 8, 26f.). Scholars consider that he probably came from the ancient kingdom of Meroé, between Aswan and Khartoum. He is called the treasurer of Candace, but this was a title like Pharaoh and the proper name of this queen is unknown. The eunuch was a literate man, reading the book of Isaiah no doubt in the Septuagint Greek version. He was baptized by

Philip and 'went on his way rejoicing', but nothing more certain is known about him. Later writers claimed, not unreasonably, that he became a missionary to his own people.

Christianity was taken to the Sudan or Nubia by missionaries from Egypt. But it seems that despite trade with Egypt, in which no doubt Christians took part, Christianity had not been accepted in the Sudan before a presbyter, Julian, went in 543 with royal approval. There were mass conversions by him and his successors, many churches were built and Christians reduced the Nubian language to writing. This was the first establishment of the church among the Negro races, and long after Egypt had become Muslim the Arab advances were resisted in Nubia. But from 1275 Arab expeditions entered the northern Sudan and there was Arab immigration which slowly spread Islam. Finally the fall of the Christian kingdom of 'Alwa in 1504 led to the disappearance of Christianity in the Sudan, till missions in modern times brought it again to tribes in the south.

Apart from the mention of Christians from Cyrene in the Acts of the Apostles little is known of the spread of the church along North Africa till the end of the second century. The first documentary evidence is in the Acts of the Scillitan martyrs, which describes how a dozen men and women were executed in 180 at Scillium in Numidia for refusing to recant their faith despite the persuasions of the authorities. In 203 a girl Perpetua and others were executed in the arena at Carthage after having been baptized as Christians.

Roman 'Africa' comprised roughly the countries which are now known as Libya, Tunisia, Algeria and Morocco. Here Latin was spoken and while even in Rome itself Greek was still used in the church, African Christians were writing in Latin and using Latin Bibles and liturgy. The chief centres were the Romanized towns on the African coast opposite Italy, but before long Christians were found as far west as Mauretania. In a synod at Carthage in A.D. 220 there were 71 African bishops, and some 250 by the following century.

There were many famous African Christian writers and leaders. Tertullian of Carthage (160–220) was the first Latin writer among Christian theologians, and the first to use the word

'Trinity'. He wrote to the prefects of the Roman provinces maintaining that Christians were good citizens, and said that 'the blood of the martyrs is the seed of the church'. But his puritanism led Tertullian away from public life and to support the Montanists who expected a speedy end to the world. He was followed by Cyprian, bishop of Carthage, a pagan rhetorician who was converted to Christianity and martyred in 258. In the fierce persecution by Diocletian in 303 many other African Christians suffered. Others denied their faith under threats, and these lapses caused divisions in the church. The Donatists refused to accept a bishop of Carthage whose consecrator had previously denied his faith, and they separated into their own churches led by Donatus. The rival churches were involved in quarrels and later were repressed by the state, but they remained till the Arab invasion.

The most renowned of all the African church fathers was Augustine, bishop of Hippo, who was born at Tagaste in 354. His Latin writings on the church and doctrine have been influential down the ages, and he opposed the Donatists in maintaining the unity of the church. At a council at Carthage in 411 there were 286 Catholic bishops and 279 Donatist bishops, but Augustine secured the condemnation of the Donatists. The evident large following of the Donatists is attributed not only to their rigorism but to their claim to be Africans as against the Romans, and they were successful in converting many Berbers to Christianity.

Other divisive forces were at work. The Vandals sacked Rome in 410 and as Augustine lay dying in 430 they besieged his city of Hippo. A Vandal kingdom was established in Africa for nearly a century, teaching Arian Christianity and persecuting the orthodox. Then the position was reversed when the Byzantines took Africa in 533, and Arians and Donatists suffered disabilities. Then Islam came on the scene.

Islam and Christianity

The Prophet Muhammad had friendly relationships with Christian Egypt and Ethiopia. Some of his followers fled to Axum in

Ethiopia from persecution in Mecca, and they held discussions on religious beliefs with the Christian authorities who protected them. When the Negus, the emperor of Ethiopia, died it is said that Muhammad prayed for him and asked God to forgive his sins. From the ruler of Egypt the Prophet received a Christian concubine called Mariyah. In the Koran it is said that Christians are 'nearest in love' to Muslims, and their monks are praised for piety and kindness.

After the death of the Prophet in 632 the Arab armies burst out of Arabia looking for worlds to conquer, and soon Syria, Palestine and Mesopotamia fell to them. In 640 the Arabs were in Egypt, knocking at the gates of Alexandria. The city had a garrison of 50,000 men, and a Byzantine navy was in the harbour, while the Arabs had no ships or siege machines. But the Copts were oppressed by Byzantine rule and the imperial Melkite church had tried to forbid Coptic worship. Yet now the Melkite patriarch, Cyrus, offered no resistance, and in 642 he surrendered the keys of the city to the Arabs. Tribute was paid to the Arabs, but religious toleration was guaranteed and the Coptic patriarch was restored to office. It was in the Arab interest to leave the government of the country in Egyptian hands, for the Arabs were soldiers and bent on further conquests. At first there was little pressure on Christians, for as 'People of the book' both Christians and Jews were respected by the best Muslims and only pagan idolaters were forced to accept Islam.

Little by little restrictions were introduced. New churches were not to be built, it was decreed later, or crosses displayed in public, and special dress was prescribed from time to time for Christians and Jews. The poll tax could be oppressive when collected by private revenue men, and when exemption was offered to converts to Islam thousands of Christians changed religion. There were revolts which were put down, followed by mob attacks on churches and monasteries in later centuries. But Christians could often travel freely to many places in the Islamic empire and beyond to visit other Christian lands.

The Arabs continued into the whole of North Africa, as will be described later under Islam, and here their triumph was more complete. It has been said that in the early centuries Christian

North Africa could look across the Mediterranean at largely pagan Europe, but from the eighth century Christian Europe looked across at Muslim Africa. This statement contains exaggerations, yet there is enough truth in it to raise the question why Christianity in the end disappeared from North Africa. The most serious defeat that Christianity has ever suffered was in the loss of Africa. Why did this happen?

Firstly, the loss was not complete. A strong minority church has remained all down the ages in Egypt, just because it was most deeply rooted there. Christianity remained in the Sudan till the sixteenth century, and it is the state religion of Ethiopia to this day, but that land was distant and difficult of access. Then the Arab conquest was by force of arms, an obvious statement but often neglected. Muslim rule was imposed on North Africa and has remained for thirteen hundred years. While there was toleration, there was also strong social pressure which increased with the centuries. Christian churches did not disappear at once, and there is growing evidence from archaeology of African churches and monasteries outside Egypt which long remained. But the North African churches were weakened both by divisions, such as Donatism, and also by the failure of their roots to go deep enough. The leaders were Roman or Byzantine, and Latin was the official church language. The Punic language of Carthage was used in preaching, though Augustine found it hard to get priests to use it. The Berber language was even less used, and it seems that the Bible was not translated into either Punic or Berber. When the Vandals came they used their vernacular in worship, and apparently most of their Arian clergy were Germans. Some of the Berbers were Christian, mostly Donatists, yet they formed the mass of the population and when Romans and Byzantines left the church was in their care. So dissension and anti-Roman feeling prepared the way for Islam.

Islam did not make exacting demands, beyond outward conformity from pagans, but it established itself slowly by peaceful penetration as well as by conquest. Using the methods of Christian hermits, Muslim holy men settled in lonely places to practise their religion, and gradually attracted serious people among their neighbours. So Islam took root and the last remnants of Christianity disappeared from North Africa outside Egypt.

Egyptian Churches

The oldest Christian churches in Africa are those of Egypt and Ethiopia. The supreme head of both Coptic churches is the Patriarch of Alexandria, who is also called Pope and successor of St Mark the Evangelist.

Mention has been made of the Melkites, a nickname meaning 'Emperor's men', by which the Coptic Monophysites mocked those Egyptian Christians who adhered to Byzantine imperial orthodoxy. The name was first used about 470, and by the time of the Arab invasion the Copts outnumbered the Melkite Orthodox by about thirty to one, nearly six million being Monophysites. The numbers of Melkites or Greek Orthodox in Egypt have continued tiny, though they have their own Patriarch, separate from the Coptic Patriarch. The Orthodox Patriarch of Alexandria is one of the five leading Patriarchs of the Orthodox churches, second only to Istanbul. But his following is mainly composed of Greeks living in Egypt and other parts of Africa, numbering about 120,000.

There are Greek Uniates, 'united' with Rome, in Egypt and Syria who are also called Melkites. They have a Patriarch of Antioch who is called Patriarch of Alexandria as well, and who lives alternately in Damascus and Cairo. This church uses Arabic in its liturgy, with fragments of Greek, and is a wealthy community. There is also a small Coptic Uniate church, with about 20,000 members, which uses the Coptic liturgy and has a Patriarch of Alexandria. A few Ethiopians and Eritreans are Uniates, governed by a Vicar-apostolic, and they use a Latin liturgy translated into their own language.

The Coptic church is the dominant church of Egypt. Its early history has been sketched above, and when Arab rule began it was promised 'protection and security' by the Arab general 'Amr. The church of St Mark had been burnt during the siege of Alexandria and it was rebuilt, together with other churches and monasteries, and their congregations were strengthened. Towards the end of the seventh century, however, the Patriarch was tortured till he produced money demanded by the governor. The Fatimid caliphs, who ruled for two hundred years from the tenth century, were tolerant at first. But there was harsh persecution under the 'mad caliph' Hakim, from 996. The Coptic Patriarch was spared but three thousand churches were destroyed and many Christians were forced to renounce their faith. But in all these centuries only one bishop apostasized. The Crusades led to the overthrow of the Fatimids but brought the Copts into conflict with Roman Christians. Saladin, in the thirteenth century, was harsh towards Christians, forbidding them to hold public office, have public processions, or display bells and crosses outside churches. There was tyranny also under some of the Mamluk rulers. Finally the Copts obtained full freedom under the British occupation of Egypt in 1882, though they shared in later nationalist movements for independence. Since the eleventh century the Coptic Patriarch had lived in Cairo, and in 1965 the government of President Nasser made a large gift towards building a new Coptic cathedral in Cairo.

Estimates of the numbers of Coptic Christians in Egypt today vary from about a million to six million, but members and adherents may be about three and a half million out of a total population of some thirty million. Most of the Copts are peasants, but among the educated many are merchants and professional men and they have taken a leading part in national affairs. A reforming party demands higher education for the clergy and more lay control of finance.

All the Copts speak Arabic, which is used in church sermons and Bible readings. But most of the liturgy, called that of St Mark, is in Coptic, the ancient Egyptian language, with a few Greek phrases. Service books have parallel Coptic and Arabic texts. In Old Cairo the most ancient Church is Abu Sarga, or St Sergius, largely underground, and said to contain a well where Jesus and Mary rested. On its walls are old paintings of the Last Supper, showing vegetables as well as loaves and wine on the table, a detail that also occurs in Islamic stories of the Gospel Table. Coptic churches are like other Orthodox churches, with a screen before the altar. Men and women sit separately and are divided by a partition at the chief liturgy. Coptic women, like most women in the towns of northern Egypt, are not veiled, unlike the Muslim women in the Sudan. Laymen read the Bible lessons in Arabic, and there are Arabic inscriptions under pictures and inlaid in screens.

The Coptic hierarchy is led by the Patriarch, who is elected by twelve bishops. As in other Orthodox churches the bishops are celibate, and they are taken from monasteries since most parish priests are married. There are numerous monasteries, from St Mercurius in Old Cairo to St Antony near the Red Sea.

From the nineteenth century Roman Catholic and Protestant missions founded churches in Egypt, Ethiopia and North Africa. The Church Missionary Society from 1825 did not try to proselytize but helped the Coptic church by education and translations of the Bible. J. R. T. Lieder spent forty years in Cairo, was supported by the Patriarch, and one of his pupils was later head of the Ethiopian church. After Lieder's death in 1865 there was an interval of twenty years before Anglican missions were resumed on a wider scale. Other Protestants like the American Presbyterians sought to 'occupy Cairo' and found their own churches, from 1854. Roman Catholics established a vicariate of Egypt in 1839, to work partly through Uniates, who were Orthodox but accepted 'unity' with Rome, and partly through the establishment of their own churches. Throughout North Africa they built up considerable congregations and centres, particularly during the French occupation which lasted over a century in Algeria. But perhaps the most influential Roman Catholic work has been in education and social service; their schools, institutes, hospitals, and orphanages have done much for African life. Together with some of the leading Protestants, Roman Catholic scholars have helped towards the study of Islam and the establishment of inter-religious dialogue after centuries of misunderstanding.

An important modern development has been the growth of the African Greek Orthodox Church of Uganda, under the rule of the Melkite Orthodox Patriarch of Alexandria. Reuben Spartas of Uganda left the Anglican Church there and, impressed by the writings of Marcus Garvey, the Jamaican-born American Negro leader, and by the foundation of an African Orthodox Church, mainly in the southern parts of the United States, was largely instrumental in establishing an Orthodox Church in Uganda. Ordination was given by an Archbishop Alexander from South Africa, who in turn had been ordained from America. The Orthodox Patriarch of Alexandria had ordained priests for Greek communities in South Africa and they were invited to visit the new African Orthodox in Uganda. The result was that the Ugandans severed relationships with the American branch and gained the authority of Alexandria. Spartas was blessed by the Orthodox Patriarch and in 1959 he accepted the rule of the newly appointed Greek Metropolitan for East Africa. Spartas translated the Orthodox liturgy into Luganda, a fine piece of work, and he did not hesitate to incorporate old pagan words for priest and king into the Christian service.*

Ethiopia

Ethiopia was called Cush in the Bible, and this is the word used in the popular verse, 'Ethiopia shall haste to stretch out her hands unto God' (Psalm 68, 31). Candace, who is called 'queen of the Ethiopians' in the Acts of the Apostles, is identified by Ethiopians with the Queen of Sheba and the royal line is said to spring from her union with Solomon. Less romantically it appears that Christianity reached Ethiopia through Frumentius of Tyre, who was enslaved and taken there. He became chancellor of the king and on his release he promised to return to the country. He went to Athanasius in Alexandria who consecrated Frumentius bishop and sent him back about 350. This story is confirmed in a letter preserved by Athanasius. Nothing is known of the work of Frumentius on his return, but Christianity was probably first confined to the coastal cities and Axum, the capital. Then about the year 500 there arrived 'Nine Roman Saints', meaning Byzantine monks, who established monasteries in northern Ethiopia and translated the New Testament into the Ge'ez language. Soon the court had become Christian and a cathedral was built at Axum. The Ethiopian church was dependent on

* F. B. Welbourn, *East African Rebels* (1961), p. 77 ff.

Egypt, followed its Monophysite teaching, and received its bishop (Abuna, our father) from there.

The next centuries in Ethiopia are obscure. There was persecution under a Jewish queen in the tenth century. After the foundation of the Solomonid dynasty in 1270 Christianity dominated the highlands of Ethiopia proper. The pressures of Islam, which was slowly spreading down the Nile, were repelled and confined to the plains. Some of the Roman Popes tried to bring the country under their obedience, but a Dominican mission in the thirteenth century was opposed by the emperor and destroyed.

In 1490 Portuguese missions arrived looking for Prester John, the Priest John who was thought in Europe to be a Christian king ruling all India, and thanks to this belief Portuguese traders had boldly ventured into the largely Muslim-controlled Indian Ocean. The Christian emperor of Ethiopia was the nearest the Portuguese found to a Priest-king, since he is head of church and state. Jesuit missionaries then came in numbers and had some success, their great triumph being the conversion of Emperor Susenyos to Roman Catholicism, which was declared the state religion in 1626. But the country was against him, led by Abuna and the monks, and the emperor abdicated. The Jesuits were expelled and some of them martyred. Roman Catholic missions returned in the nineteenth century and were especially favoured under the Italian rule from 1936 to 1941, but the Coptic church remains the dominant state religion.

Although closely attached to Egypt, by history and against Rome, there has been more independence in Ethiopian church life in recent years. Traditionally Abuna was appointed by the Coptic Patriarch of Alexandria and had to be an Egyptian monk, who normally knew no Ge'ez, the liturgical language. In an agreement signed with the Egyptian church in 1948 Abuna would be chosen from Ethiopian monks or bishops, though with the approval of the Alexandrian Patriarch, and the first to be consecrated was Anba Basilios in 1959. He is metropolitan of Ethiopia, with several suffragan bishops. The emperor held the fairly recent titles of Conquering Lion of the Tribe of Judah, Elect of God.

The Ethiopian church has long had a monastery in Jerusalem, which has provided a link for relationships with other churches. Pilgrimage to Jerusalem is almost as important for Ethiopian Christians as pilgrimage to Mecca is to Muslims. Ethiopia has been called 'an island of Christians in a sea of Muslims', though about a third of the nine or ten million people of the country are Muslims. Christianity is dominant in the central and northern areas, and modern missions have spread it to Eritrea, while Islam dominates in regions adjacent to the Somalis. There are pagan majorities in the extreme south and west. In its isolation Christianity united Ethiopia proper, though the isolation led to stagnation.

Down the centuries education has been in the hands of the church, and almost every village has its church with adjoining school. Instruction has been largely oral since books are scarce. Prayers and Biblical texts are learnt in the ancient liturgical tongue, which nobody speaks now, and there is also reading and writing in the current language of Amharic. Further education has been given in the monasteries. In modern times European forms of education have been promoted, by foreign missions and by the state, culminating in the university of Addis Ababa. There are over a dozen Protestant missions, from Britain, Scandinavia and America, and several Roman Catholic orders. English is widely taught as the second language.

The official canon of scriptures includes the Bible and some apocryphal works. It is in Ge‘ez but there is an authorized Amharic translation, and the two languages are also printed side by side in new liturgy books. Liturgical order is much the same as in Egypt.

Churches are round or rectangular, and there are famous churches carved out of rock. Round churches have four doorways facing the principal points of the compass. Churches are regarded as holy places, and the ordinary Ethiopian gets off his mule or bicycle to pass a church and kisses the gate or ground in front of it. There are three concentric parts of the church and only a priest can enter the holy of holies. In the sanctuary stands the altar and the Tabot, the Ark. This is a small wooden box which represents the Biblical Ark of the Covenant, and is an object of great veneration without which no church service can be held. This is circumambulated, keeping it on the left as in the circumambulation of the Ka'ba in Mecca.

There are two kinds of clergy, priests who administer sacraments but are not much educated, and more learned lay clerks (dabtaras) who chant church offices and teach in schools. The importance of lay orders is one of the striking features of Ethiopian church organization. Each church of any size has a lay leader (Alaka) who not only rules over the cantors and stewards, but also over priests and deacons.

There are many monasteries, and some monks practise extreme forms of asceticism which seem as natural to this country as to ancient Christian Egypt or India. The monks work on the land as well as pray in chapel, and have special times of prayer on Sundays and feasts of saints. In some monasteries there are no private possessions, but others do not insist on this.

There are special practices of the Ethiopian church, some of which have been attributed to Jewish influence, but it may be just as likely that they are due to general Semitic practice. Circumcision is performed on all Ethiopian Christians, and the uncircumcised person is regarded as not a Christian. But Muslims and many pagan African peoples also have this practice. Saturday is a holy day as well as Sunday, and since this was observed also in the early church it may have formed part of the Christian tradition when it reached Ethiopia. Male children are baptized forty days after birth, and girls after eighty days. At Epiphany, 6 January, there is a ceremony loosely called baptism, when the Tabot arks are taken to rivers for ritual washing. Jesuits who observed this were shocked to think that it was re-baptism of believers. The Tabot may be an imitation of Jewish practice, though in Jewish synagogues the ark is a cupboard containing the scrolls of the Law. There are many holy days, which are strictly observed, and fasting is thought by Ethiopians to be essential to religion; the Lenten fast is indispensable. Monogamous marriage is the rule of the church, but it is often left till late in life and there are many temporary unions. At funerals there are no candles but plenty of incense, and there are prayers for the dead and remembrance days.

The Ethiopian church was isolated for many centuries, practically its only link with the rest of Christendom being with Egypt. It had to face increasing pressures from Islam on every side. It has often been called degenerate and careless of the evangelization of the rest of Africa, but in southern Ethiopia and Eritrea considerable missionary efforts have been made in modern times, and it is claimed that over a hundred thousand pagans have been baptized. The national church has a great prestige, it forms a unique link between Europe and Africa, and between western Christianity and southern Orthodoxy, and it shows that Christianity can take deep and lasting root in the heart of Africa.

9 Early Modern Missions

First Attempts

The Christian mission in Africa, apart from Nubia and Ethiopia, was cut off by Islam from the seventh century and was hardly renewed for eight hundred years. Scattered Christian communities remained for long in North Africa, and groups of European traders and soldiers were allowed to have churches in Islamic countries but were usually forbidden to evangelize. There were a few visits by Franciscan, Dominican and Jesuit missionaries, the most notable being those of Ramon Lull to Tunis from 1292 till his martyrdom in 1314. But large scale proselytization had to await the explorations of the Portuguese.

The missions of the fifteenth century and after followed the blazing of trade routes round Africa to India and China. The Islamic grip on North Africa and the eastern Mediterranean was to be outflanked, and contact made with supposedly Christian kings in Africa and Asia, such as Prester John. These voyages were chiefly for trade, but evangelization was included and a papal indulgence was granted for this. It is now some five hundred years since West Africa was first visited by the Portuguese explorers. In 1470 La Mina, in what is now Ghana, had been reached, and in 1472 Benin was visited. A fortress of Portuguese stone was built at Elmina (La Mina), an altar erected, and prayers were offered for the conversion of the people. In 1484 stone pillars bearing crosses were erected on the banks of the river Congo.

The Canary and Madeira islands had been evangelized in the fifteenth century, and missionaries visited Senegambia. The Wolof chief Behemoi went to Portugal with twenty-five companions and was baptized in 1489, but after his return the missionaries were expelled. Jesuits began work in Sierra Leone in the late sixteenth century, but progress was slow for the first hundred years till the king and many of his people were baptized.

Alfonso d'Aveiro made considerable progress in Benin in the early sixteenth century, building churches and baptizing thousands of people. The king's son became a Christian, succeeding as King Oba Orhogbua in 1550. But the climate of 'the white man's grave' so decimated the number of missionaries that from the middle of the sixteenth century most of them were recalled, leaving Benin priests in charge who were visited occasionally till 1688. Finally the Benin church disappeared till modern times, leaving only three shrines called 'altars of God' which were taken into the traditional religion. In Dahomey the kingdom of Allada was visited by Capuchins for a short time in the seventeenth century, but all that remains is a copy of their catechism in a Spanish library.

The Portuguese went farther south, to the Congo and Angola. Missionaries arrived from 1490, taking with them skilled workmen for building stone churches and houses. The Congo kingdom was one of the largest tropical African states and the king, the Manikongo, lived at Mbanzakongo, which is the modern San Salvador in Angola. The Manikongo and some of his chiefs were converted to Christianity, much building was done, and many young men were sent to Europe for education. Nzinga Mbemba, who succeeded to the throne in 1507 with the baptismal name of Alfonso, ruled as an ardent Christian till his death in 1543, trying to fashion his kingdom on European lines; his son Henry was consecrated bishop of Utica in 1518. But the Portuguese changed their policy, and from early missionary aid turned their attention to the slave trade. To supply this traffic armed bands made raids on towns and villages, and before long attacked the Congo kingdom. Throughout the sixteenth and seventeenth centuries the Manikongos, who were all Christians in name, appealed to their missionaries and the Pope for help. Several Popes sent stern letters to Portugal but the government said it could not control its subjects in Angola. In 1660 the Congo people took to war and were defeated by the Portuguese and their allies. The kingdom broke up, missionary contacts were finally broken, and by the end of the eighteenth century Christianity in the Congo had withered away.

Similarly in Angola after a hopeful start missionary work slowly declined. A cathedral was built in San Paulo de Loanda, which became a bishopric in 1596. Yet all the churches came to be neglected or disappeared. When Livingstone visited Loanda in 1854 he saw one of the cathedrals used as a workshop and cattle feeding in another.

In South and East Africa the Portuguese built a stone church at Mossel Bay in 1501, and services were held when forts were built at Kilwa and Mombasa. There was no Portuguese settlement at the Cape, but missionaries landed in south-east Africa from 1560 and went inland, baptizing Thonga chiefs and proceeding to Shona country. Gonzalo da Silveira landed at Sofala, baptized Thonga rulers and four hundred subjects, and went up the Zambezi to the country of Monomotapa, in what is now Rhodesia. He baptized the king and his mother, but their Muslim advisers having suggested that the missionary was a spy for the viceroy of India, he was strangled and became the first Christian martyr in southern Africa. This Jesuit mission failed and was succeeded by Dominicans from Mozambique and Sofala, whence Dos Santos gave valuable descriptions of journeys on the coast and up the Zambezi to Monomotapa country. After religious and political struggles another king was baptized and in 1667 there were nine Dominican and six Jesuit places of worship on the lower Zambezi. But at the end of the century warfare drove the Monomotapas and their Portuguese overlords off the plateau, and all the missions finally disappeared. Other missionaries went to Mombasa and the north, but despite some baptisms the converts generally relapsed to Islam.

These first Christian missions in tropical and southern Africa were all Roman Catholic, shared between different orders. They struggled for up to two centuries, but all vanished eventually and there is no continuity with modern times. The field was wide open to them, for African rulers in general welcomed the strangers, whose educational work was appreciated. Sometimes there were mass baptisms, but this meant superficial conversions, and on the other hand rulers were usually too involved with ancestral rituals to break with the past. There seems to have been little of the liberal attitude towards ancestral cults which gave the Jesuits considerable success for a long time in China. Some vernacular work was done, but the liturgy remained in Latin and the Bible was not translated. Some missionaries were heroic, but others were time-serving clergy attached too closely to the traders and colonial rulers. African society was broken up in the interests of the slave trade in the west and in a scramble for gold in the east. The fall of Portuguese power, due to troubles in Europe as well as to the climate and warfare in Africa, took with it the missions, which in few places had taken much root.

There were not many Protestants in Africa before the nineteenth century. Trading forts were built at English and Dutch centres on the west coast, and there were also Danish, French and German trading posts. These stations had chaplains, but they were usually only concerned with the traders and their servants. Settlements were made at the Cape, by English and Dutch, and their founders piously hoped that the Hottentots also might become servants of God. From 1648 some Dutch settlers tried to educate the Hottentots in the Christian religion, and slaves who had been imported from Angola and Guinea were given some education. The first Hottentot convert, Eva, was baptized in 1662 and married a Danish surgeon. But before long there was opposition to the conversion of slaves, as then they could no longer be sold or bought.

Although most Protestant churches were still establishing themselves in Europe, the evangelical Moravians were moved by missionary impulses. George Schmidt was a Moravian sent by the Reformed Church in Holland to the Cape in 1737 to work among the Hottentots. But when he had baptized several his ordination was challenged by Dutch clergy and his baptisms were regarded as a breach of their prerogative. After seven years Schmidt was obliged to return home and the mission to Hottentots was not resumed for half a century. Also in 1737 two other Moravians, Huckoff and a mulatto, Protten, arrived in Elmina. Huckoff soon died and Protten returned to Europe, but he went back to Christiansborg later and translated portions of the Bible into Fanti. Nine other missionaries followed, but all died and the mission was closed.

The English Society for the Propagation of the Gospel had work in America, where John Wesley had met Moravians, and in

1751 it sent Thomas Thompson to Cape Coast, both as chaplain to traders and evangelist to the Fantis. He only stayed four years, but took three young Fantis to England. Two of them died, but Philip Quaqué was ordained an Anglican minister, the first non-European ordained in this church. He was sent home as chaplain and missionary in 1766 and served there till his death. Quaqué travelled about in Fanti country and engaged in trade, there were few baptisms but the example of Europeans was bad and public worship was sometimes suspended. After Quaqué's death decades elapsed before another missionary was sent by his society.

Early Nineteenth Century

Various influences can be traced in the growth of church missionary movements in modern times. Growing imperialist policies of Europe, expansion of trade, and increase in medical knowledge were all contributory factors. In reaction against an earlier stress on religious revival, it has become fashionable to emphasize social and political factors behind the missions. But these also can be exaggerated out of proportion, and the role of ideology is always significant in human affairs.

The Evangelical movement in Britain and America in the eighteenth century was linked with the continent of Europe and was potent in both state and free churches. It was hardly an accident that within twenty years of the death of the Methodist leader John Wesley, some of the most important Protestant missions were founded. The first was the Baptist in 1792, followed by the London in 1795, the Church in 1799 and the British and Foreign Bible Society in 1804. Other notable societies were founded about this time in Scotland, the Netherlands and America, and a little later in France, Germany, Switzerland and Scandinavia.

Sierra Leone was one of the first centres of attention. Chaplains had ministered to the traders but made little contact with Africans. Zachary Macaulay, father of the historian, was governor of the colony from 1794 to 1799 and took twenty-five Sierra Leonean children to England for education, where they were baptized.

From 1792 over a thousand Negro settlers had been brought to Sierra Leone from Nova Scotia, and as most of them belonged to the evangelical churches they directed their own religious life independently of a rather suspicious government. Two Baptist missionaries arrived in 1795 but did not stay long, and a party brought by Macaulay to work among the Muslim Fulani was also short-lived. Others came from Glasgow and London, but some died and others returned home.

Sierra Leone had been opened as a home for freed slaves, first from England, then Nova Scotia, and in 1800 there came Maroons from Jamaica, ex-slaves of the Spaniards. After the Act of Abolition of Slavery it became a crown colony and a centre for suppressing the slave trade. The first Church Missionary Society workers, who were German Lutheran pastors, arrived in 1804. Reinforcements came later, and despite the usual health troubles the colony was organized into parishes and education was established. Fourah Bay College was founded in 1827 and played a great role in West African education, being later affiliated to Durham University; its first student was the freed Yoruba, Samuel Ajayi Crowther. An African ministry began to be trained, but it was not till 1852 that the diocese of Sierra Leone was established, with an English bishop, so that clergy no longer had to travel to England to be ordained. In 1811 the Methodists sent a minister and three schoolmasters to Sierra Leone and began continuous work. Roman Catholic Sisters of St Joseph established themselves there in 1823. The Sisters of Cluny were settled in Gorée in Senegal from 1819.

Wesleyan Methodists went to the Gambia in 1821, trying without success to convert Muslims, but slowly building up a community among freed slaves and their descendants. Liberia was colonized by freed slaves from the United States, the first going to Sierra Leone but moving down to Monrovia which they founded. They had their own churches, but difficult relationships with the indigenous Africans. Five American missionary societies saw Liberia as a field of activity and an entry into the Muslim hinterland. Jesuits also came to 'Maryland in Africa' which had been established at Cape Palmas. In 1851 Anglicans from the West Indies started a mission in Rio Pongas, always a struggling cause and extending earlier work in Africa from American descendants of Africans.

There was little Christian impact on the Ivory Coast till the twentieth century, except in coastal towns like Grand Bassam which were linked with what was called the Gold Coast, later Ghana. The Basel Mission sent four missionaries to Christiansborg in 1828 but all were dead in two years. Others followed and were more successful in the interior, Kumasi being visited in 1839. Then William de Graft, a Fanti who had been educated at Cape Coast, formed a Society for Promoting Christian Knowledge and was imprisoned for subversion. De Graft later settled at Dixcove, and Methodist missionaries came to help him spread knowledge of the Bible. One of their leaders was Thomas Freeman, a mulatto who for twenty years was one of the most active Christian workers. He visited Kumasi, Abomey, Badagry and Abeokuta, becoming civil commandant of Accra and Christiansborg after resigning from his mission over a disagreement on expansion policy.

The German Bremen mission began work among the Ewe of Ghana and Togo in 1847 and suffered disabilities in the Ashanti wars, but persevered till in the twentieth century it became one of the first self-governing churches. Freeman had stationed an agent in Dahomey, at Whydah and later in Porto Novo, and the Methodist church there still remains and is now independent. The Roman Catholic African Mission of Lyons began at Whydah in 1861, among Portuguese mulattos and returned slaves from Brazil, and soon spread to Lagos and Abeokuta, but was less successful in Abomey and the hinterland.

Before the end of slavery many freed slaves from Freetown began to return to their homes along the coast, or to trade in the growing commercial centres. Christian Sierra Leoneans, as they were called, formed communities in most of the coastal towns of West Africa and some way into the interior, and missionaries and teachers followed them. The largest numbers went back to the Yoruba areas of what is now Nigeria, to Lagos, and especially to Abeokuta whence many had been captured by Dahomean armies. Methodist and Anglican churches were established there from 1846, and when Lagos was closed as a slave market they entered there immediately. Organization of churches and schools was arranged as in Sierra Leone, with African ministers for self-supporting churches, and missionaries finally concentrating on education and work in the interior.

Farther east, Presbyterian missions were established in the Calabar and Cross river regions by enterprises from Jamaica. Hope Waddell from the Scottish society arrived there in 1846, with colleagues from the West Indies, Chisholm and Miller. Meantime Jamaican Baptists had been responsible for beginning work in Fernando Po and the Cameroons. When Fernando Po changed from British to Spanish hands priests arrived and the Baptists had to leave, though Protestant churches revived later and still remain.

In South Africa the Moravian work among Hottentots was suspended for fifty years after the departure of Schmidt, but three more missionaries arrived in 1792. They found one of Schmidt's converts, with a Bible he had given her, and in the next twenty years seven hundred Hottentots were baptized. There had been no attempt yet made to evangelize any of the Bantu, whom Europeans generally called Kaffirs, a name curiously adopted from the Arabic and meaning 'unbelievers'. The pioneers were the London Missionary Society, led by the Dutch Dr Van der Kemp and three others who arrived at the Cape in 1799. Although they tried to work among the Xhosa they could gain no facilities and settled among the Hottentots near the present Port Elizabeth. Van der Kemp and some of his friends married coloured women, lived a simple life, and championed the rights of Hottentots as free men. Dr John Philip, who arrived in 1819, also championed the rights of Hottentots and joined his efforts to those made earlier by Van der Kemp, who had died in 1811, to free Hottentot workmen from oppression, cruel masters, and even murder. The two missionaries were reviled by white farmers, but when the Cape came under Britain from 1795 disabilities on the Hottentots were removed by 1828, thanks largely to Philip's advocacy there and in England. Philip also fought for the rights of the Bushmen, and warned of coming trouble with the Bantu, before the war of 1835 and the death of chief Hintza of the Xhosa.

Robert Moffat in 1816 went north to the Tswana and settled

among them for life. He gave up the Cape Dutch language, which others had used in evangelization, mastered Tswana and with the help of others translated the Bible into it. He became a friend of King Mzilikazi (Moselekatse) of the Ndebele (Matabele) and described his reception by the ruler, before an immense assembly, taking him by the arm and saying, 'the land is before you; you are come to your son'. Moffat was a patriarchal figure, whose fervent evangelicalism led him to underestimate African traditional religion; he thought that the Tswana had no word for God, which later research proved untrue.

In the same period French Protestants began work among the Sotho and made notable studies of their customs. Édouard Casalis was protected by king Moshesh and described this ruler and the peace of Lesotho before and after the devastation wrought, directly or indirectly, by the Zulu under Shaka and the Ndebele. Casalis described Moshesh as 'noble and assured', with 'a smile of great good will'. He became the confidential counsellor of Moshesh and was followed by Coillard who advised the Sotho till they became a protectorate under the British in 1884. By that time there were more than two thousand baptized and many more Christian adherents in the country. After twenty years among the Sotho, Coillard went to open a mission among the Rozi (Barotse), where the king Lewanika gave permission for church work, but more difficulties were encountered.

German and British Methodists were at work in Natal among the Zulus, and in 1853 an Anglican diocese was established with J. W. Colenso as first bishop. He was a man of independent views who got into trouble not only by his Biblical teaching, which today would be considered mild, that Moses was not the author of the first five books of the Old Testament, but also because Colenso considered that polygamists converted to Christianity should be baptized. Most missionaries, though not all, have refused to baptize polygamists, and insistence on European forms of morality before Biblical faith has caused many troubles. Colenso was sentenced to deposition and excommunication, and a rival bishop was appointed, but he refused to budge and stayed with his house and cathedral till his death in 1883, and the Natal schism was not healed till 1910.

Roman Catholics had been banned from the Cape under the Dutch, but established themselves under British rule, and appointed their first Vicar Apostolic in 1818 with headquarters in Mauritius. There were too many conflicting churches in South Africa, a portent of the sectarianism to come, and overlapping of mission stations might have been avoided if there had been a common policy. In 1840 a Quaker traveller, Backhouse, who had visited the stations of all the missions in South Africa, reported that there were 45 in Cape Colony, 18 in Kaffraria (mostly Xhosa), 6 among the Sotho, 7 among the Tswana, and 9 among the Namaqua and Griqua Hottentots.

In Malagasy (Madagascar) French Carmelites and Lazarists began missionary work in 1642, but this declined, was restarted, and finally collapsed when the colonists were massacred or withdrew in 1674. The Lazarists made two further attempts in the eighteenth century but these also failed. The London Missionary Society began a new mission in 1818, and David Jones gained the protection of King Radama, on condition that artisans were sent to improve Malagasy living standards. Twenty-eight converts were baptized in 1831, but in 1835 the new Queen Ranavalona started a violent persecution in which at least two hundred Christians were killed and others fled to the forests, while missionaries were expelled. Not till the death of the queen was freedom restored and then the outcasts returned from the forests, some marked by wounds and starvation. Despite persecution the numbers of Christians had multiplied fourfold, an increase which is attributed to the possession of the New Testament in Malagasy. After the peace other societies arrived as well, particularly Norwegian and French Protestants, while Roman Catholics began afresh. Today the Christian population of Malagasy is estimated at about forty per cent.

Later Nineteenth Century

African churches in the tropics and south were still weak and badly organized in the middle of the last century, and it was not till the seventies that some of them began to be impressive in numbers and distribution. Yet though they were small their influence was important and grew continually. Christians were great factors in the mutual understanding of Africa and Europe, representing white culture to Africans and making African needs known to Europe. They were foremost among the explorers. The Church Missionary Society employed a number of Germans, and Krapf and Rebmann in 1848 were the first Europeans to see Kilimanjaro and Mount Kenya. In South Africa it was the missionaries who lived farthest north. The most famous was David Livingstone who crossed the continent from east to west and back, virtually unarmed, and as a missionary he pleaded with Victorian England for Africa to be opened to 'commerce and Christianity'. He was chiefly a lonely explorer, though a great opponent of slavery, and it was through the Royal Geographical Society that he became a consul, travelled up the Zambezi to Lake Nyasa and spent his last years in the upper reaches of the Congo.

Following the travels of the journalist-explorer H. M. Stanley, missions sought to reach the heart of Africa. English Baptists went a thousand miles up the Congo, to be followed by American Presbyterians and many others. After experimenting with the segregation of their converts from pagan influences, the policy was adopted of sending out African Christians as village evangelists and this practice was gradually developed almost everywhere, forming one of the most effective means of naturalizing the church in a new environment. The Americans tried this first among the Luba of Kasai and by 1904 they had forty out-stations with three thousand church members. Almost alone in the Congo, it was at Katanga that missionaries succeeded in gaining the protection of the rulers, and they were criticized for undue dependence and treating Msidi as a great king.

It is strange that the interior of South and East Africa, where the climate was much easier, was little explored before that of West Africa. As climatic difficulties were being overcome in the west, and the hinterland explored, so it was in the south and east. The penetration of central Africa from the Zambezi was a project of Livingstone's, and the Universities Mission to Central Africa was formed with this objective. A party set off in 1862, but it failed to get far up the Zambezi and withdrew to Zanzibar for another twenty years. Stanley had appealed for missionaries for Uganda and the Church Missionary Society sent a party which arrived at Kampala in 1877 and was received by King Mutesa. The first baptisms took place five years later, but then Mutesa died. His son Mwanga began to persecute Baganda Christians and Bishop Hannington, perhaps through a misunderstanding, was speared to death. Hundreds of Christians were killed, and in one day in June 1886 thirty-two young men were burnt to death. Then Mwanga was banished, the church revived and in a few years there were seven thousand baptized members and many inquirers. But meanwhile rivalries with French Roman Catholic missionaries led to a civil war, in which Lugard supplied arms to the Anglicans so that they defeated the numerically stronger Roman Catholics. From then on chieftainships and control of land has been strictly divided between Anglican, Roman and small Muslim parties, with Anglicans dominant in administration and education.

Baganda Christians, whose countrymen had often fought neighbouring tribes, were now foremost in their evangelization. Apolo Kivebulaya ministered to the Toro, and made further contact with pygmies, translating the Bible into their language. Bishop Tucker planned a Native Anglican Church in 1897, which was opposed by his colleagues but remained an ideal for the future.

German-speaking missionaries and explorers were foremost in many parts of Africa and when Tanganyika came under German rule the Lutheran missions began to go ahead. They were particularly successful among the Chagga of the Kilimanjaro region and most of them became Christians. Kenya was evangelized rather later, from Uganda and the coast, and the first baptism was held in 1908. Many missionary societies followed and there are now large churches. The Universities Mission finally succeeded in reaching Lake Nyasa and work in Malawi was divided between it and the Scots, and there developed some of the best educational and industrial enterprises.

One of the most notable rulers converted to Christianity was Khama Boikano of the Bamangwato in Botswana. The first missionaries were Lutherans and Khama was baptized in 1862 while still a prince. Three years later his father drove him out for refusing to take part in tribal initiations but Khama held fast to his faith, succeeded to the throne and ruled for fifty years till 1923. As a traditional rain-maker he held church services when rains failed, and he campaigned untiringly against all forms of alcohol. When Rhodes tried to annex his country to South Africa, Khama appealed for and received British protection, and he succeeded in playing off the interests of foreigners against each other to strengthen the position of his people.

In West Africa new attempts were made to overcome the climatic troubles and consequent shortage of missionaries. The policy in Lagos and Freetown had been to gather small congregations round a missionary, send out catechists as work developed, and finally ordain clergy who would in time be independent, so that the mission would fade away before the church. This was the policy formulated by Henry Venn, secretary of the Church Missionary Society from 1841 to 1872, aiming at self-governing churches which would absorb the mission. A Native Pastorate had been established in Sierra Leone in 1860 and a bishop consecrated, but there was a succession of European bishops and no African. In Nigeria, however, the outlook was both difficult and challenging. A Niger Expedition in 1841 supported by Prince Albert and Gladstone, reached Lokoja, ridiculed by Dickens in *Bleak House* as Borrioboola-gha, and attempted settlement. The scheme failed completely, and of the 145 Europeans 130 had fever and 40 died. But 158 Africans had joined the expedition at Sierra Leone and of these eleven had fever and none died. Among them was a catechist, Samuel Ajayi Crowther.

Crowther was a Yoruba who had been saved from a slave ship and taken to Freetown. Baptized in 1825, he became the hope of the African mission and church. He returned to Abeokuta, found his mother and sister, and translated the baptismal service into Yoruba for them. Venn persuaded the archbishop to consecrate Crowther in Canterbury cathedral in 1864, the first Anglican African bishop. He was bishop 'on the Niger', a curious term that indicated the vagueness of his diocese, which might cover any part of Nigeria except Lagos, then under the bishop of Sierra Leone. Crowther had to face many difficulties. He and his Yoruba and Freetown clergy had to use interpreters to speak to the Ibos

and others among whom they worked, while to the north were
Muslims who were opposed to Christianity. Crowther had little
local support and depended on the missionary society in London,
for he was a missionary bishop. After the death of Venn the over-
seas support was uncertain, and in 1890 there was violent criticism
from young missionaries which led to a purge of the mission.
Crowther died the following year and his diocese was absorbed
into a new one based on Lagos, and there was no other independent African bishop for many years.

The church was still very weak on the upper Niger, but it was
strong in the Delta, with a cathedral at Bonny. Despite the difficulties, Crowther's work had gone farther inland than any other
West African mission; he had made contact with Islam, gained
the confidence of chiefs whom he always treated respectfully, and
secured their financial support for many schools. Part of his
diocese became a Niger Delta Native Pastorate Church, virtually
independent though not seceding from the mother church, and
finally reunited with a new diocese 'on the Niger' in 1921. Meanwhile other secessions had come, partly as a result of the reversal
of earlier mission policy of self-government, and independent
African churches were formed.

The Presbyterian church at Calabar was centred on the Cross
river and the chief pioneer into the interior was Mary Slessor
who was appointed vice-consul in 1892 and, after the breakup of
Aro power and the destruction of their oracle, settled among them
for nearly thirty years. The Basel mission went into the highlands
of Cameroun and by 1914 had ninety stations on the grasslands.
The same mission was also active in Ghana, and after the defeat of
King Prempeh in 1896, it went to Kumasi and farther north.
Other missions consolidated their position from this time on,
particularly in Togo, Ghana, Liberia and Sierra Leone.

Roman Catholic Revival

Roman Catholic missions, which had begun with the first explorations of Africa and for long held the field, had slipped well
behind in the early nineteenth century. In 1622 the Sacred

Congregation of the Propaganda was created, but Spanish and Portuguese colonies were not included in its jurisdiction and Africa was neglected. Then suddenly Roman Catholics became aware of the many Protestant missionary societies and saw that the world might become Protestant. The renewal of African missions is attributed to the foundation of the Congregation of the Sisters of St Joseph of Cluny which sent missionary sisters to Reunion in 1817 and to Senegal two years later. There was an abortive attempt in Liberia, where eight out of ten priests died in 1843 from the climate, and in 1841 Pius IX created the vicariates of 'the two Guineas' and Mauritius.

Most of the great Orders and Societies were founded about or after the middle of the nineteenth century. In 1868 Cardinal Lavigerie founded the Society of Our Lady in Africa, better known as the White Fathers, who from Algeria went to West and East Africa, and from the Great Lakes to Rhodesia. Lavigerie was Apostolic Delegate for the western Sahara and saw in Algeria the 'open port' to the continent of Africa. The first parties that tried to cross the Sahara were murdered by Tuaregs, though later settlements were made in desert places but with little immediate effect on the Muslim population. Charles de Foucauld lived alone at Tamanrasset from 1905 till his death in 1916, without making a convert.

Lavigerie gathered round him eighteen hundred children who had been orphaned after epidemics of cholera and typhus in Algeria and settled them in Christian villages. This method was followed by others, with freed slaves and orphans, and separated Christian villages were established in many parts of Africa. These were 'chapel-farms' in which farming and handicrafts were taught to make them self-supporting, but there was the danger of a ghetto existence and a prevalent paternalism hindered the development of an African church which would be independent and integrated into tribal life.

Many Roman Catholic missions went to Africa in the latter part of the nineteenth century. The older orders, such as Benedictines, Dominicans, Franciscans and Jesuits, all sent workers. There were new African foundations, like the Mill Hill Society of St Joseph and the Society of the Divine Word. The more favourable sea routes to West and East Africa replaced the dangerous desert crossings. The attraction of the kingdom of Buganda induced Lavigerie to send a mission there, despite appeals not to rival the Anglicans, and other Orders came later.

The White Fathers also turned south to Tanzania and had difficulty in getting a foothold through opposition from Arab slave traders. Only after the extension of colonial power, and the decline of slavery, did the mission begin to flourish. The White Fathers entered Nyasa in 1889 and the Fathers of the Holy Spirit went to Kenya in 1891, but some parts of the latter country still have few missions.

South Africa did not welcome Roman Catholics, but they went on to Lesotho, where King Moshesh received them in the land where French and Swiss Protestants had been at work for thirty years. Roman Catholics concentrated on Lesotho, pouring in men and money, and came to dominate education and much of public life.

In Angola and Mozambique the Portuguese always gave a privileged position to the Roman Catholic church, though there have been some large Protestant missions, notably the United Church of Canada in Angola. But until 1908 all education was under the control of the official church, and priests were virtually government officers. The old Portuguese missions had practically disappeared and in 1873 the priests of the Holy Spirit began new work, so successfully that within twenty years it was claimed that one eighth of the population of Angola was Christian. But methods of colonization, seeking to assimilate relatively few to Portuguese citizenship, have kept illiteracy high among the masses, and Protestant missions, especially American, have been viewed as politically dangerous.

The most spectacular Roman Catholic missions were in the Congo, where the White Fathers entered first from the Great Lakes in the east. These were French, but Belgians were also sent to please Leopold of Belgium, and other societies followed. Protestant missionaries had been in the Congo first in modern times, but were finally outnumbered by Roman Catholics and the government favoured the latter and for a long time only gave money for education to them. But despite hundreds of missionary priests and nuns conversions were slow at first, and by 1910 there were only fifty thousand Christians in the vast Congo area. It was not until after the First World War that the landslide occurred which brought more than a quarter of the population into the church.

Cameroun was also a successful area of mission eventually. Progress was slow, so that by the twentieth century only some two or three thousand were Catholics, but after that they poured in men and money and are now said to outnumber Protestants by four to one and to dominate entirely some parts of the country.

Roman Catholic work was also slow to begin in West Africa, after some first weak efforts in Senegal and failure in Liberia. The founder of the Lyons Society went to Sierra Leone with four companions in 1858, but all died of yellow fever in a few weeks. The work was taken up in Dahomey and Lagos in the sixties. Borghero, an Italian, celebrated Mass in the disused Portuguese fort at Whydah and went up to Dahomey, with a grandiose scheme for reaching to the desert far north. Though well received the mission struggled against many difficulties, of climate and indifference, and came to include Porto Novo, Abeokuta and Benin. Later the missionaries crossed the Niger and became most influential among the Ibo people.

Once they had got under way Roman Catholic missions in Africa were pursued with great determination, and countless lives and fortunes were expended. Their inherent nature made it difficult to establish independent churches and the celibacy demanded of the clergy, which was as foreign to African traditions as to other religions of the world, made the establishment of an indigenous clergy doubly difficult. As late as 1923 there were only sixty-six African Roman Catholic priests in all tropical and southern Africa, including Malagasy.

There were some areas of Africa which were closed to all Christian missions, as much by the European overlords as by African rulers. Thus they were banned from the northern Sudan, after the trouble over the Mahdi, but allowed to enter the pagan regions of the southern Sudan. Missions were prohibited in British Somaliland, but not in French and Italian Somalia. And in

Nigeria Lugard ruled that Christians could only enter the Hausa states 'if the ruling chief concurs'. Eventually they did manage to reach the still pagan tribes, though the northern Nigerian cities remained barred to Christians who had to build churches outside.

10 The Twentieth Century

The many efforts, starts and checks, and continuing spread of the churches throughout tropical and southern Africa in the nineteenth century, began to bear fruit in the twentieth, with the mission becoming the church. The old picture, in which only Egypt and Ethiopia had large Christian populations, was replaced by a new one in which nearly every state in Africa had at least a minority of Christians, and sometimes a majority. In the movements for political independence most of the African leaders in the tropics had had a Christian education, and often they did not hesitate to acknowledge the role that the church played in the development of their land.

Moves towards self-governing churches came from various sources. The First World War brought conflict between the German colonies in Africa and the British and French. One by one the German colonies fell and were never returned; the German missionaries were interned or deported, and their churches were cut off from the financial help that they had received from Germany. British and French societies tried to fill the gaps, and it was easier for Roman Catholic societies than for Protestants, for the latter were usually divided into national societies, and had different organizations and sometimes different doctrinal emphases from their German counterparts. But African leaders now saw their chance; Martin Nganischo of the Berlin mission in East Africa and R. D. Baëta of the Bremen field in Togo gave outstanding examples of holding and strengthening the church. The Ewe Presbyterian church of Togo became independent, though later it received help from British and French missions.

Powerful assertions of African independency came in the many prophetic movements that have marked this century, but these are so important and numerous that they must be discussed later on their own. Less obviously relevant, but eventually giving powerful impetus to independence, were the great educational works of the churches. As Professor Oliver has said, the churches sowed the dragon's teeth of education, and from them arose insistent demands for religious and spiritual independence. Some fundamentalist missions resisted education, considering that their task was evangelization and that the larger missions had betrayed themselves to the education departments; but few have been able in the end to oppose African demands for what Europe enjoys, and belief in the brotherhood of man implied equality of opportunity.

As demands for education increased governments were obliged to cooperate with missions, for they alone could furnish teachers at reasonably low pay, and only government had enough money for the growing numbers needed. In 1916 in Nigeria and Uganda government and missions considered educational policy jointly, and also in 1916 at Fort Hare in South Africa was opened the Native College, which became affiliated to Rhodes University and in which the churches ran halls of residence. Although its facilities never equalled those of the white universities, Fort Hare brought together Africans, Indians and Coloured, till after forty years it was segregated off into a merely tribal college.

Two education commissions under the American Phelps-Stokes fund surveyed the situation of African education; West and South Africa in 1920 and East and South Africa in 1924; and these and other commissions received evidence from the churches and included members from them. The result was to set up centres of higher education, such as Achimota in Ghana in 1924, where J. K. Aggrey was vice-principal, and training schools like Kabeté in Kenya and neighbouring countries. Though these were largely of Protestant impulse, Roman Catholics were soon urging their own representatives to cooperate fully in all governmental schemes for higher education.

In British-ruled territories the usual dominance of Protestants allowed government to subsidize educational work, and support Roman Catholics equally, without fear that any church would have a monopoly. Also British use of vernacular languages in elementary education made it more easy to teach and paid respect to African culture. Under Portuguese and Spanish rule Roman

Catholics were heavily favoured, and stress on assimilation led to forbidding African languages in schools; since priests were Portuguese and Spanish they had natural advantages. In the Belgian Congo Roman Catholics and Protestants virtually monopolized education, though at a relatively low level. The French government was in theory responsible for all education, which was given in French in its colonies, with the aim of assimilation to France; official education gave a greater chance to fewer numbers and African languages were neglected. Perhaps because of this it is the French-speaking African writers who have been the most insistent on a return to *négritude*. Missions in French territories ran schools under great difficulties and received little or no help from government until after the Second World War. Then aid flowed comparably to the British scale, and corresponded to a recognition of African independence on the British model in place of assimilation.

After the Second World War there came advances to university standard. Fourah Bay had long been affiliated to Durham and by 1950 some three hundred of its students had received Durham degrees; now it has become an independent university. University colleges were established at Achimota, Ibadan, Makereré and Salisbury; like Gordon College, Khartoum, they were first linked with London University but eventually became independent. Colleges of arts and technology were founded, which after independence became more universities. The French founded Dakar University and the Belgians Lovanium. The latter was of Roman Catholic origin, as was Roma in Lesotho, but most of the modern universities are fully governmental institutions. In South Africa, apart from Fort Hare, the universities are now all white, though the English-speaking Witwatersrand, Capetown and Durban had coloured students until forcibly segregated by government. Yet the churches had laid the foundations for the highest forms of education, and many university lecturers came to serve from a Christian inspiration.

The churches were also foremost in literature. Tropical African languages, apart from those of a few Sudanese Muslim peoples, were not written down till modern times. Missionaries learned the languages and were often the only Europeans who could speak to Africans in their own tongues. With their African converts they reduced the languages to writing, produced grammars and dictionaries, reading books, and especially the Bible. The Bible in their own language is the first and great classic for many African people, even more significant than the Authorized Version was for the English-speaking world. Part of the answer to the question whether Africa will remain Christian may be seen in the way in which many people, of all churches, have made the Bible their own. Many other books and periodicals flowed in a growing stream from bookshops and centres of Christian literature.

Roland Oliver has said that Christianity defied the law of the survival of the fittest, in saving the destitute, healing the sick, and caring for orphans. From early days the churches were engaged in medical work, though the scale of sickness was always too vast for them to tackle thoroughly. No doubt the best known doctor was Albert Schweitzer, who lived at Lambaréné in the Gabon from 1913 with intervals abroad till 1965. He was widely honoured, yet his dry old-fashioned paternalism can be illustrated by his complete lack of interest in African traditional religion, despite a notable work on Indian philosophy. Leper hospitals and settlements were organized by many churches, and even in the Muslim Sudan the government erected a leper home at Omdurman and placed it under the Church Missionary Society. By 1938 it was estimated that half a million lepers had been discovered in Africa, and most of the treatment given was in church homes. The growth of medical science and conquest of leprosy enabled these centres to turn to other urgent health problems, such as tuberculosis. The churches could never afford the great training and specialist hospitals which only government could build, like the five hundred bed hospital at Ibadan, which costs hundreds of thousands a year to run. But cottage hospitals, village dispensaries and church settlements had a widespread influence and in some ways they were better fitted for ordinary cases of sickness than great impersonal institutions. The association of physical and spiritual sickness is very close in African traditional belief; the churches took this into account, whereas governments ignored it and so gained less public confidence.

One of the most important tasks for the churches was to train leaders, teachers for schools, and particularly clergy for the congregations. This had been done since Crowther's day, often by sending the brighter candidates to seminaries in Europe, or to Fourah Bay. Rising standards of general education demanded higher levels for the ministry, and churches began to feel that by sharing training work they would increase efficiency and diminish the divisions of the churches. Anglicans, Presbyterians and Methodists were the chief collaborators, at Limuru in Kenya, Umuahia in Nigeria and Kumasi in Ghana. Much later similar sharing began at Alice in South Africa, Yaoundé in Cameroun, and in association with the new universities, as at Immanuel in Ibadan.

After the setback following the death of Crowther, leadership of the churches long remained only in European hands. Africans became suffragan bishops, but not till 1951 were they made independent diocesan bishops, at Lagos and Ibadan. A little earlier Methodists appointed an African Chairman, on an elective basis. Roman Catholics, it has been seen, were also slow in training clergy, insisting on celibacy and a long period of training which meant numerous failures. But once the formation of the clergy had got under way there was a great increase, from 66 in all Africa in 1923, to 1,248 in 1951. The increase was most striking in central Africa, and in Rwanda where the mission began in 1900 there were over ninety priests fifty years later. The first African Vicar Apostolic was Bishop Kiwanuka of Uganda appointed in 1939, and the first Cardinal Mgr Rugambwa of Tanzania in 1960.

The twentieth century saw a proliferation of missions to Africa. The continent was easily accessible under imperial rule and later independence. The climate had been virtually conquered, though some foolish 'faith' missionaries died young, of yellow fever, malaria or dysentery. There was general peace and, apart from the Congo, foreigners have been respected during wars and revolutions. Most Protestants went first to British-ruled territories, where language and government were most favourable, but increasingly after the First World War they also entered French, Belgian and Portuguese territories. Between the two world wars the number of Protestant missionaries in the Congo doubled;

they came from all over Europe and North America. Their diversity, and sometimes mutual opposition, brought confusion to African life, and no doubt this was one cause for the growth of many African independent churches. Some of the older missions were alarmed at mission rivalry, and attempts were made at delimiting territory and agreeing on spheres of influence. Congresses and federations of churches were also held, to give advice and discuss joint action on matters of common interest, generally social rather than religious.

The twentieth century is the great age of conferences. Never has so much talking been done, almost as a substitute for action, and some modern studies of the churches consist largely of accounts of continual conferences between much the same people. A World Missionary Conference at Edinburgh in 1910 is generally recognized as the first or most significant, which stimulated regional conferences in Africa and other continents. To begin with these were missionary conferences, but with the growth of African self-rule they gave way to Christian Councils, as in Zambia where the first missionary conference was held in 1914 but became in 1944 a Christian Council. Similar councils were formed in Ghana in 1929 and Kenya in 1942.

These local councils were useful in bringing together members of different churches, though some of the extreme fundamentalist groups refused to cooperate, unless they were hard pressed, as in French or Portuguese territory. But there was still no overall strategy, or even study of the problems of the whole continent, except by individuals. In 1948 the World Council of Churches was founded and it absorbed an earlier international missionary council. In 1959 the first All-Africa Conference of Churches was held at Ibadan, and it considered matters of education, youth, literature, family, urbanization and independency. A further conference was held at Kampala in 1963 to consider politics, refugees, universities and traditional religions.

At present there are some twenty Christian Councils of African countries, with eight publications in English and French, and many Bible societies cooperate for translation and distribution. There is an All-Africa Church Music Association, a Society for African Church History, and widespread branches of the World

Student Christian Federation working in universities and colleges. In 1967 appeared the first number of a Journal of Religion in Africa, in English and French, to consider all forms of religion in Africa. The Christian Councils have not hitherto included Roman Catholics, though since Pope John XXIII barriers are breaking down. There is no general African office of the Roman Catholic Church, though there are Apostolic Delegates, and consultations of orders are held at high levels.*

The countless church buildings which are found in most African countries have added greatly to the architecture of the continent, though it cannot be said that their builders have shown much imagination. Far too often they have tried to copy Gothic or Norman fortress type European churches in concrete in Africa. Some of the most pleasing are village thatched churches, and in Cameroun American Baptists have used African carving and drums in church decoration. But thatch will not do in towns and only rarely is there creative use of the best modern techniques, as in George Pace's Chapel of the Resurrection at Ibadan University. Church worship also has followed European patterns. Liturgies have been transliterated into African languages, but far too often the tunes used have been those of Victorian hymnody. Since most African languages are tonal, the combination of African tones with the jumpy tunes of Moody and Sankey has produced clashes and even gibberish. Only a few individuals until recently have produced African hymns, written to indigenous tunes, but now broadcasting companies are doing much to stimulate creative musical work of this kind. Yet a great deal needs to be done to make church worship intelligible and an expression of African culture.

Church organization in Africa has been imposed from European patterns. Bishops, Chairmen and Moderators abound, but titles are not objectionable to African life and it is at the lower levels that the organizations creak most noticeably. Class tickets are useful methods of ensuring a steady income, but they should not be used as authorizations to communion or passports to heaven, buried in the hands of corpses. The whole system of paid clergy and catechists, and whether it can survive the financial crises of

* See appendices in T. A. Beetham, *Christianity and the New Africa*.

the present day, needs rigorous examination. Comparison needs to be made with the system of ordained laymen of South India or the worker priests of France. Closer comparison still can be made with the priesthood of African traditional religions, which is often a part-time occupation and dependent on occasional gifts from consultants.

The relationships of Christianity and Islam in Africa have been fragmentary and little studied. The Dominicans have set aside men for the study of Islam, and in 1952 and 1961 J. S. Trimingham began travels under Protestant mission sponsorship in West and East Africa, which not only resulted in monumental studies of Islam but also produced penetrating criticisms of the Christian approach to Islam. These were followed by the establishment of an Islam in Africa project to help the church understand Muslims, for Trimingham had said that 'the attitude of Christians towards Islam largely determines the attitudes of Muslims towards Christianity'. Christian scholars have been stationed in various parts of Africa, some of whom are competent Arabists, with the task of understanding Islam historically and in its African setting. The aim is dialogue before proselytization.

Similar studies of the relationships of Christianity to secularism and Communism have been undertaken, but at a less systematic and scholarly level, and generally at some of the many conferences held in different African countries.

The second half of the twentieth century has seen increasing independence and African leadership in the churches. The churches were often ahead of government; an independent Anglican Province of West Africa was established before any West African country attained political independence. Elsewhere political changes hastened church independence, first of all in the old German colonies after the First World War, and much later in the Congo and Angola where missionaries had to leave their followers to stand by themselves. Christian Councils gave more prominence to Africans, though they still tended to have foreign officials. Also while the councils could include missions of most diverse doctrine, they rarely admitted independent churches of undoubted doctrinal orthodoxy whose sole difference from the parent church might be that of self-rule or the permission of polygamy. But the tendency is towards self-rule for African churches and larger unions can be expected.

Reaction

When Britain seized the Cape there were 21,000 whites there most of whom were connected with the Dutch Reformed Church, with ten ministers paid by the Dutch East India Company and under the Classis of Amsterdam. Britain at first continued to pay the salaries of the clergy but before long issued a church ordinance which gave autonomy to the church but ended state aid. In 1836 some of the Dutch went on the Great Trek to the Transvaal to be free of the British. Ministers had come to them from Holland, but also from Scotland, especially the Murrays, of whom John became one of the first professors of the theological seminary at Stellenbosch in 1859, and Andrew who was an evangelistic reformer and became first minister at Bloemfontein. Divisions arose over the supposedly Methodistic revivalism; the majority of the Dutch held to the Nederduits Gereformeerde Kerk but two smaller bodies split away.

It has been seen that some of the early Dutch made efforts to teach the Hottentots, and George Schmidt had to leave for baptizing some; but then the work declined for lack of teachers. In 1799 Dr Van der Kemp initiated an inter-denominational South African Missionary Society and a little later the Dutch Reformed Church ordained a missionary to work among the indigenous people. In the second half of the nineteenth century local churches undertook missions, under the inspiration of the younger Andrew Murray and a training school for missionaries was established. Bantu converts were at first attached to white churches, which regarded them paternally, but before long separate congregations were formed with autonomous synods. The Dutch Reformed Churches have had important missions outside South Africa, in Malawi, Zambia, Rhodesia, the Sudan and Nigeria. Their missions were often foremost in producing vernacular literature, for they disliked teaching and writing in English. But it is not surprising that the most numerous independent church movements have developed in the apartheid atmosphere of South Africa.

The traditional policies of racial segregation were more ruthlessly imposed under the title of apartheid or 'separateness' after the General Election of 1948, won by a small majority of seats (without getting a majority of white votes) by the party of Afrikaner nationalism. This theory of the ultimate total separation of white, black, coloured and Indian, was rejected by most of the churches, Anglican, Methodist, Roman Catholic and others. In 1960 a conference of the World Council of Churches in Johannesburg rejected apartheid by eighty per cent of the votes. But because of this the three Dutch Reformed Churches withdrew from the Council the following year; they had a majority among the Afrikaners, but Anglicans were dominant among Christians of British descent, and the Methodists were the most numerous among the Africans. In 1964 the Methodists elected their first African President of the annual Conference, the Rev. Seth Mokhitimi, and in 1966 the Anglicans elected A. H. Zulu their first African bishop, but the government refused him permission to attend a council in Geneva. After the Sharpeville shooting in 1960 Bishop Reeves was deported, and in 1967 Bishop Crowther of Kimberley was expelled.

Within the Dutch Reformed Churches there was some protest against racialism. In 1956 Professor Basil Keet of Stellenbosch attacked apartheid in *Whither - South Africa?* and in 1962 Professor A. S. Geyser of Pretoria was deposed from the ministry, though later reinstated and given an independent chair at Witwatersrand. The Dutch Reformed Churches had a patriarchal mentality and considered the separation of apartheid to be justified by the Biblical curse on the descendants of Ham, but their Professor Ben Marais of Pretoria denounced this as 'Nazi theology'. They gave full support to the Bantu Education Act of 1953, whereby all education remaining in the hands of the churches was reduced to tight government control and directed by racial principles. Other churches were faced with the alternatives of closing schools or running them without government help as private institutions. Adams College, the oldest in Natal, run by the American Board of Missions, was closed in 1956 and the

Johannesburg diocese closed all its schools. Roman Catholics launched a great campaign to keep schools under their own control, but most churches decided to lease their five thousand schools to the government, since to close them would be to deprive African children of any education at all.

Rhodesia had an interracial Christian Council, though its meetings became more difficult after the declaration of independence. Some missionaries were then expelled, mostly Americans of the United Church of Christ who had attacked segregation, and several African ministers were imprisoned.

Christian leaders were liable to restriction or expulsion in South Africa and Rhodesia, but in Angola, the Congo and the Sudan they might lose their lives. From time to time news came of suffering in Angola, and in 1961 the American Methodist Board said that 17 pastors were dead, 30 in prison, 90 unaccounted for, and many churches and schools had been destroyed. Restrictions on the return of missionaries to their field reduced their numbers from 256 to 140. From 1964 numerous missionaries and Congolese Christians were mutilated or killed in the Congo civil wars. In the same year the Sudanese government deported all 300 missionaries working in the southern Sudan, 272 of them Roman Catholics. In 1965 a theological college at Mundri in the Sudan was burnt down by troops and Bishop Ngalamu escaped only after lying naked under leaves. At Rumbek the Roman Catholic Vicar-general, Archangel Ali, was killed, and at Juba hundreds of people were massacred in the Anglican cathedral and thousands more fled into Uganda and the Congo.

11 Independency

Before the twentieth century moves had begun for African church self-government, and it is remarkable that from the beginning they were linked not only with freedom from foreign control but aimed at the evangelization of Africa by modern methods. It used to be said that African Christians were not concerned about the propagation of their faith, but recent studies have shown that the independent churches have often been the most effective means of spreading the faith. In fact in both mission and independent churches it was the ordinary Christians who were the principal agents of Christian expansion. There is a great deal of literature from the independent churches, most of it unknown outside their ranks, which reveals a constant preoccupation with evangelization.

The first independent movements began in West and South Africa in the nineteenth century, and they were followed by similar schisms in Central and East Africa before the end of the century. Today there are over 500 separate church bodies of independents in West Africa and 500 in Central Africa, about 300 in East Africa and around 3,000 in South Africa. Although new movements are constantly appearing, and some die out, yet it is remarkable that about ninety per cent of these churches have survived since their foundation.

The first West African movements were inspired by Edward Blyden, who was born in the Dutch West Indies, ordained in 1858 into the Presbyterian Church, travelled in Europe and Africa and became a politician. Blyden rejected the notion favoured by some anthropologists of the time that Negroes were inferior, but he thought it would be more African to pass through Islam before rising to Christianity. His writings were known in West Africa and in 1891 Blyden lectured in Lagos on the 'Return of the Exiles and the West African Church', maintaining that the evangelization of Africa would never be accomplished as long as it lay in foreign hands and was imposed in alien forms. This was the year of the death of Crowther, after a purge of his Niger Mission by fanatical young missionaries, and there were rumours of separation. But the first move was a modest United Native African Church in Lagos, founded not as an alternative to the missions but as a more effective means of evangelization. There had already been a Baptist schism in Lagos in 1888, after a pastor had been dismissed, but the loose Baptist organization was not greatly upset and the breach was healed in 1915. One of the Baptist leaders, Mojola Agbebi, founded many Baptist churches in the Niger Delta. But in 1901 Anglican dissatisfaction erupted and a major secession formed the African Church Organization, which aimed at providing alternative churches in every town and village. There were other separations, that from the Nigerian Methodists in 1917 being one of the few which specifically seceded over the issue of allowing polygamy to members.

These independent churches were formed not because of differences over doctrine, for there have been few formal African heresies. They were expressions of the need for independence, sometimes against dictatorial missionaries, sometimes against the formalism of foreign ways which led to 'quenching the spirit'. There was a general feeling that African customs, laws, dancing, family, marriage, language, clothing, court etiquette, sayings and philosophy, were decaying where they were not crushed. The new churches kept to the Bible, prayer books and hymn books of the parent missions, but they added colour in costume and music, using drums and calabashes instead of the dreary harmonium. Although polygamy was not a major cause of division, most of them came to permit it to members though not usually to the clergy, since this restriction is the only one that appears in the New Testament (1 Timothy 3, 2 and 12). Schools were started, though the missions always had the advantage here of trained men and more funds. Today there are hopes of closer cooperation, since the mother churches are no longer missions and they can work together through Christian Councils.

Another kind of independency movement, though not entirely different, appeared with the prophetic figures so prominent in twentieth-century African Christianity. One of the first and most famous was William Wadé Harris of Liberia who made his name in the Ivory Coast. A Grebo (Kru) of Cape Palmas he was for ten years a teacher in the Protestant Episcopal church and was imprisoned several times for political disturbances. After a prophetic call Harris went in 1913 along the coast eastwards to French and British ruled territory, quite independently of any foreign mission. He was an impressive figure, carrying a cross and Bible, and wearing a white gown and turban, perhaps in imitation of the Hausas he had seen on journeys to Lagos. Although Harris had to preach through interpreters (one of whom, named after the god Tano, helped the present writer in 1935), he was far more successful in converting the Ivory Coast people than the Roman Catholic missionaries who were already there. With a simple message against idolatry and a call to repentance and baptism, Harris attracted thousands of the coastal Ivory and Gold Coast people. But the French rulers were suspicious of this English-speaking orator and in 1915 he was expelled to Liberia and forbidden to return. Up to a hundred thousand people remained faithful to the baptism of Harris, built churches, bought English and then French Bibles, and waited for more teachers. Fanti preachers from Ghana encouraged them by visits, till British Methodist missionaries arrived in 1924, and the tiny French-speaking Methodist church of Dahomey sent African ministers and catechists to help in the Ivory Coast for a number of years. Many of the converts joined the Methodists, though some remained in independent Harrist churches. Harris himself lived on peacefully at Cape Palmas till his death in 1929. As a result of his work the lower Ivory Coast is largely Christian and a great stimulus was given to the churches in Ghana.

The influence of Harris led to the formation of other churches as well as strengthening the missions. The Church of the Twelve Apostles in western Ghana takes its name from the practice of Harris in appointing twelve apostles to each congregation gathered among his followers. Another prophet, Appiah or Jehu, founded in 1919 the Army of the Cross of Christ Church, which is the largest of the Ghanaian independents. In 1920 Samson Opong was a powerful prophet in Ashanti, much like Harris, and working mainly within the older churches which became more deeply rooted and widespread in Ashanti through his work. Other Ghanaian groups began with later prophets, or under influences from Nigeria. Professor C. G. Baëta, in his study of them, notes their Old Testament tendencies, taboos and ritualism. Their separate communities, villages or 'gardens', resemble the unity of old tribal life round religious and family leaders, but tend towards the separation from the rest of the community which was a criticism levelled against mission segregated farms and hospitals.*

In the Niger Delta Pastorage Church in 1909 Garrick Braid found that he possessed healing powers, but these were exercised within the Anglican church for some years, till a popular movement spread from him into a number of centres. Bishop James Johnson was impressed at first by the spiritual revival and mass baptisms, for Braid's followers destroyed idols and renounced alcohol; but soon they regarded Braid as above the church, his words superseding the scriptures and ordinary medicines were denounced in favour of his holy water. The bishop disciplined some of the extremists and they separated into the Christ Army church. Braid died in 1918 and 43,000 Christians in the Delta were members of his church, which still exists in many forms.

A little later similar movements began in the Yoruba country of Nigeria, which developed into widespread churches of the 'praying people' (Al-adura). They were influenced by literature from the Faith Tabernacle of America, though no missionaries visited them. The Faith Tabernacle stressed healing through faith, and consequently both traditional African and modern European medicines were rejected. They also condemned infant baptism, and their followers in Nigeria rapidly adopted mass adult baptisms by immersion in rivers and the sea, and this fitted African patterns of cleansing by water. In 1928 a mechanic at Ilesha, Joseph Babalola, started a great revival movement that affected all churches and greatly strengthened the prayer societies. Other groups had been formed before this, such as the Cherubim and Seraphim, which laid stress on dreams and visions, and it was said that angel helpers such as cherubim appeared to heal the

* C. G. Baëta, *Prophetism in Ghana* (1962), p. 132 f.

sick and aid the perplexed. These new churches spread into neighbouring countries and branches of them are found in Ghana, Liberia and Sierra Leone. These latter countries also have prophets and prophetesses, far too numerous to mention, and there are more in the Ivory Coast, Togo and Dahomey.

The prayer and faith churches had different origins from the separatists of the African Church Organization, but they shared the same desire to evangelize Africa by their own methods. They went far beyond the moderate adaptations made by the 'Africans' in liturgy and discipline, since they were spiritual revivals of a Pentecostal type, insisting on baptism of adults by full immersion, and on healing the sick by faith and laying on hands. Prayers, dreams, visions and divine guidance are their daily fare. But H. W. Turner, who has made the first full scale and objective study of their faith, life and worship, says that these independents cannot be denied the name of Christian churches. They are strongly Biblical, make no conscious deviations from orthodox doctrine, and are zealous in evangelism. A study of their preaching revealed that it was not in fact weighted too much towards the Old Testament, as some critics have suggested, though two of the most popular Bible books are Proverbs and James, with their resemblance to African proverbial lore. Their preaching does not lay great emphasis upon the life of Christ and the Kingdom of God, but while such stress is typical of modern Western Christianity it was not so in medieval times, which made much of angelic visions and the power of the living Spirit and also stressed the Crucifixion and Resurrection.*

Although all these churches are African, seeking to put their own interpretation upon Christianity, they are not generally anti-European and they have taken little or no part in political agitation past or present. In fact the leaders of national independence movements generally came from the mission churches. A political National Church of Nigeria had little success and nothing like the great following that the prayer churches attract with their strictly religious emphasis. One or two small groups in West Africa are called 'Ethiopian' churches, and they have tried to mix Christianity, Islam and traditional religions, but with

* H. W. Turner, *African Independent Church* (1967), 2, p. 368 f.

little appeal. Much is made of the verse of Psalm 68, 'Ethiopia shall soon stretch out her hands to God', but this is applied to Negro Africa and has no connexion with Abyssinia. The Watch Tower Movement, or Jehovah's Witnesses, has made some impression and publishes literature in several African languages, but it is a foreign mission with only a superficial resemblance to the indigenous prayer movements.

In 1921 a prophetic movement began in the lower Congo, which like some others of the time has been related to the influenza epidemic, which it sought to cure or halt. Simon Kimbangu was a Baptist who found he had the power of healing, which he resisted at first but his fame spread so far that hospitals were deserted and even the dead were brought to him to be raised. Opponents claimed that pagan practices were used but they could not deny that charms and images were burnt, that polygamists put away their extra wives, and that church services were crowded. Then other prophets arose and both Roman Catholic and Protestant church leaders were disturbed. The Belgian government took fright at civil disturbances, they arrested Kimbangu and sentenced him to death. On the appeal of missionaries he was reprieved, but others were deported to penal servitude, though no evidence of political subversion was given at their trials. Kimbangu was imprisoned for thirty years, often in chains. He died in 1951, a true martyr. His Church of Christ on Earth through the Prophet Simon Kimbangu was persecuted but non-violent, not recognized officially till 1959, but today it claims three million followers in the Congo.

In Uganda Chief J. K. Mugema had renounced medicine through Christian conviction from 1885, but this belief did not lead to a schism till 1914 when he founded a movement known as the Society of the One Almighty God. It was supported by a church teacher called Malaki, after whom its followers were named Bamalaki. A popular movement began, with mass baptisms, building churches, and drawing members from both the missions and from traditional religion. Malaki obtained the permission of the Kabaka of Buganda to preach widely, but later the government intervened, Mugema was dismissed from his chiefdom and Malaki imprisoned for a time. After the Bamalaki had resisted vaccination, their leaders were deported in 1929. Malaki died in a hunger strike, and Mugema was allowed to return home to die in 1942.

A larger movement against mission paternalism in Uganda was led by Reuben Spartas with the foundation of the African Greek Orthodox Church, mentioned earlier. But clearly it was not against doctrine or even traditional authority, as the acceptance of Greek rule shows. This church posed a problem for the Anglican Church, which accepts the ordination of Greek Orthodoxy, but normally rejects that of African sects. Another Uganda movement, the Mengo Gospel Church, was founded by an English missionary, Mabel Ensor, but it broke away from the older churches and introduced adult baptism by immersion.

In 1929 a 'Revival', sometimes called Balokolé, 'the saved ones', began with an English Dr Church and a Muganda Simeon Nsibambi, and it spread from Uganda to Tanzania, Burundi, Kenya and the Sudan. At first the Revival was concerned with a more personal spiritual life, beneath the superficiality of much official Christianity, and it challenged European superiority and made room for African leadership. In the Mau Mau emergency in Kenya the Revival members suffered from both sides, being interned by the government for holding private meetings and refusing to use force in self-defence, and attacked by Mau Mau for not resorting to violence against the European rulers. More recently the Revival has turned its attention to the evangelization of pagans, and by insistence upon hygiene and modern civilization it is helping changes to come into traditional society. By tolerance both from its own members and the church authorities the Revival has been contained within the church, chiefly the Anglican, except in Kenya where a large number of Anglicans left to form the Church of Christ in Africa in 1957. Generally the effect of the Revival, despite pietistic and fundamentalist emphases, has been to strengthen the life of the churches and give expression to Christian African feeling.

Buganda was largely Christian and independent religious movements sought to increase devotion. But in Kenya the churches had come later and were less deeply rooted. There were political difficulties over land and labour, and opposition to foreigners, both governmental and missionary. The government tried to crush political movements by imprisonment and deportation, and in 1952 violence broke out with the Mau Mau rebellion, and a state of emergency was declared which lasted till 1960. How far Mau Mau was a 'religion' has been much debated, it was certainly very different from the prophetic and pietistic movements we have been considering. In fact African resistance to Mau Mau came both from Christians and some leaders of the old traditional religion. Mau Mau has been called a 'synthetic paganism' since it used fearful oaths in the name of the old religion but for political ends. It tried to free the land from foreign occupation and it defended some traditional ways, notably the practice of female circumcision. The Gikuyu and many other peoples practise this excision, which was supposed to be essential to proper child-bearing and was demanded before initiation into the tribe. The missions had opposed this practice, as both useless and dangerous to health, and numbers of Christian girls had refused to accept it. In 1929 the Kenya Missionary Council denounced the practice, and soon some missions forbade parents to allow it to school pupils, under pain of expulsion. The result was schism and the formation of independent churches and schools. Gikuyu independent churches were interested in preserving some traditional customs, notably female circumcision, but they were Christian in intention and some of their leaders opposed Mau Mau and suffered for it. With political independence the churches have continued to progress in African leadership, and the Revival has strengthened Christian life.

Independent church movements have sprung up in Angola and Mozambique, but have often been suppressed as political revolution. In Malawi John Chilembwé founded a Providence Industrial Mission, on the pattern of Baptist missions of the same kind; but during the First World War there was a rising against the government in which Chilembwé and some of his followers were killed and others deported. The Mission was started again in 1926, and from it other independent churches have developed in Malawi. In the struggle for political independence some writers have seen Christian influence in all forms of political organization, but others have pointed out that the dominant force in the political movement was the Presbyterian church of mission origin and not the sectarian groups. The Malawi independents are not Messianic, as are some of the South African churches; they baptize by total immersion but have few of the healing prophets that have characterized the Kimbangist movements in the Congo.*

In Rhodesia and Zambia there have been similar movements. The African Methodist Episcopal Church, found there, in South Africa and in some other parts of the continent, is affiliated to an American church which arose in opposition to the colour bar, and it can be either a mission or an independent church. But particularly well known is the Lumpa Church of Alice Lenshina of the Bemba people. She worked for a time within the older churches, but in 1954, after a serious illness, claimed that she had returned from the dead, said that angels had brought her a new Bible, and sent her agents out to baptize believers. The name Lumpa for her church is explained as the church which 'goes far' or 'excels all others'. The laws of the church are strict, forbidding racial discrimination, immorality, pride, anger, polygamy, and drinking or smoking in church. Sundkler, in his study of South African prophets, said that 'dream and taboo are the two back doors through which the African past enters the church', but others have said of the Lumpa church that 'dream and taboos were the front doors through which Christians went back into the African past'.† Sympathetic observers from other churches spoke highly of Alice, though some of her followers were criticized for excesses. But she came into conflict with the newly independent government of Zambia, largely because Alice had forbidden her followers to engage in politics at all. They revolted against the Independent Party ticket and some five hundred of them were killed in 1964, many believing that the cry of 'Jericho' would save them from bullets. Alice was arrested and sent to another part of the country, she escaped in 1967 but was recaptured. But several thousand people still revere her, and they have been wooed by the other churches.

Southern Africa has been by far the most prolific in producing

* R. L. Wishlade, *Sectarianism in Southern Nyasaland* (1965), p. 136.
† J. V. Taylor and D. Lehmann, *Christians of the Copperbelt* (1961), p. 266 f.

independent churches. In 1872 there was a minor secession from the Paris mission in Lesotho and soon after there was founded a Native Independent Congregational Church in Botswana, a Tembu church, a Bapedi church, and an Africa church in Pretoria, all before the end of the century. But more significant was a separation from the Wesleyan church in Pretoria in 1892, led by Mangena Mokoné, and taking the significant name of 'Ethiopian Church', which meant self-government by African leaders. It was joined by another Wesleyan minister, James Dwané, who was sent to America to seek affiliation with the African Methodist Episcopal Church there. This was achieved and an American bishop, Turner, visited South Africa, ordained sixty-five African ministers, and consecrated Dwané as assistant bishop. This church began to expand all over South Africa and planned to go north to Rhodesia and even to Ethiopia. But Dwané began to doubt the validity of the American orders, and he was received into the Anglican church of South Africa, eventually being ordained priest and became Provincial of an Order of Ethiopia. Most of the Ethiopians did not follow Dwané into the Anglican church, and the Americans sent one of their ablest bishops to lead them.

The African Methodist Episcopals have had some good leaders in South Africa, and they have been active in education, with a Wilberforce Institute that trains teachers and ministers. But some Africans thought this church was too American and in 1904 there was a secession to form the Ethiopian Catholic Church in Zion. A little earlier there had been an important breakaway of Fingo people from the Church of Scotland mission at Lovedale, to form the African Presbyterian Church, and a Zulu Congregational Church was also founded.

In his *Bantu Prophets in South Africa* Bishop Sundkler made one of the first sympathetic yet critical studies of the many South African independents. He distinguished two main types, which he called respectively Ethiopian and Zionist, though this nomenclature has not been followed in most studies of independency in other parts of Africa.* Sundkler classified as Ethiopian those churches which left the missions 'chiefly on racial grounds', and

* B. G. M. Sundkler, *Bantu Prophets in South Africa* (1948), p. 38 f.

later groups which split away from the first independents on similar issues, 'chiefly the struggle for prestige and power'. Not all these churches call themselves Ethiopians, but most of them stress a national outlook. One of the largest secessions was the Bantu Methodist Church on the Rand in 1933, called the Donkey Church because it adopted a donkey as its symbol. This arose from a national spirit, as well as from dissatisfaction with the financial policy of the mother church, and it was followed by further subdivisions.

In the political and social situation of South Africa, with the vote denied to all Africans, Indians and Coloured, it is under-standable that there should be hundreds of churches resolved on governing their own affairs in an area where they can be sure to be free of official interference. But it is noteworthy that such churches have not been very active in political movements, in fact probably less so than members of the mission churches, which have produced such leaders as the late Albert Luthuli. Church independency was national rather than political, though in the latest edition of his book Sundkler notes that some of the inde-pendents now seem to be more closely linked with the chiefs in the Bantustan areas. Many of them, however, depend on the masses in the industrial cities rather than the reserves. As in West Africa, these Ethiopians seek religious independence, and the evangelization of Africa by indigenous agents.

The churches which Sundkler calls Zionist are akin to the prophetic and healing churches of other parts of Africa. They call themselves Zion, Apostolic, Pentecostal, Faith, and so on. They seem to have been first inspired by a Zion church in Illinois, which taught divine healing, triple immersion, and the near second advent of Christ. One of the leaders of this church visited Johannesburg in 1904 and baptized twenty-seven Africans. A number of schisms took place from 1917 to 1920: the Christian Apostolic Church in Zion, the Christian Catholic Apostolic Holy Spirit Church in Zion, and others followed. The many titles, which to outsiders appear fanciful, are important to the members who claim to have received the names in revelations or dreams, designating the character of the church.

The Zionists claim also to come from Mount Zion in Jerusalem, and they emphasize healing by faith, speaking with tongues in ecstasy, rites of purification, and taboos on blood, pork and alcohol in Old Testament and Bantu fashion. Generally they are opposed to traditional African medicines as heathen, but they fight them with their own weapons of holy oils, ashes, water, baptism and prayer. Their churches are modern healing shrines, to replace the shrines of the traditional religion. While the Ethiopians, like the older West African independents, keep close in the main to the pattern of church worship and life of their parent missions, the Zionists are much more African and syncretistic, like prophetic movements elsewhere, even where they make conscious efforts to reject anything 'heathen'. Traditional music, dancing, possession, purification, sacred dress, and ritual avoidance all figure largely in their life. They are modelled unconsciously on African patterns of leadership, and many secessions are due to struggles for control or desire for recognition by a new inspired prophet.

One of the most remarkable South African movements is the Ama Nazaretha Church, which Sundkler classifies with the Zionists though seeing it as 'more deliberately nativistic' than many other churches. The founder and prophet was Isaiah Shembé, who was baptized into the African Native Baptist Church in 1906. This church practised a new sacrament of 'footwashing', perhaps through American influence, and similar purification plays a prominent part in Shembé's system. Shembé had already received visions, put away his four wives at divine command, and practised healing and exorcism. He was ordained a Baptist minister, but seceded in 1911 over the observance of the Sabbath. He called his church Ama Nazaretha, the Nazarites, and he said that all the verses in the Old Testament which referred to the Nazarite ascetics should be applied to his followers (see Numbers 6). In 1916 he established a church village at Ekuphakameni, or the High Place, eighteen miles from Durban, and this is now the Holy Mountain of the Nazarites, the centre for a great festival every July. It is a model settlement, whose members have a high reputation for morality among their neighbours. Since the death of Shembé the church has been led by his sons, Johannes and Amos, more educated men than their father, who have had to struggle for leadership, but the Ama Nazaretha is still a great power among the Zulu.

Shembé died in 1935 and was buried with great honours; he had exercised a wide influence through healing and leading men, and was shown more respect than any Zulu chief. He was recognized as a man of great charm, benevolence and tolerance. Sundkler calls him a 'Black Christ', but considers that the Nazarites are too much under the influence of the Old Testament, speaking of Jehovah and the Spirit, but little of Jesus. There may be some justification for this judgement, though allowance must be made for adulation of a native prophet and the revival of Zulu national pride. Shembé, like some other African prophets, is said to have risen from the dead and to be a present helper to his followers, but it remains to be seen how long this faith can last, and what influence more orthodox Christian Zionists will have upon the Nazarites.

The causes of the rise of African independency are clearly very diverse, and are both social and religious. It is common to stress national feeling, struggles for authority and leadership, disagreements over finance, breaches of church discipline, and the desire to allow polygamy. Not enough attention has been paid to religious experience, dreams and calls to prophesy, and the importance of healing both body and soul in African world views. It will have been noticed that many secessions arose in churches that by loose organization and history encouraged independency, such as Baptists and Congregationalists, or churches which gave a large role to lay leadership, like the Methodists. Few churches have split away from Roman Catholicism, because of its strong power structure and its doctrine of a rigid apostolical succession which allows no salvation outside the church, but there have been a few schisms such as the Children of the Sacred Heart in Zambia and the Legio Maria in Uganda.

Many studies of African independency appear to see it as a judgement upon orthodox Christianity, or they consider it in isolation from similar schisms elsewhere. Certainly the number of separations seems alarming. In the first edition of his book Sundkler listed 800 independent church organizations in South Africa in 1948, of which only seven were recognized officially by the South African government. In his revised edition in 1961 some 2,000 are mentioned, and an estimate in 1968 speaks of over 3,000 secessions.* But is this dissidence much greater than the sectarianism of Europe or America? In these days of movements towards church unity it is easy to forget the great proliferation of sects, which have not only divided the church in the past, but have also been active agents in its spread which is not necessarily best achieved by monolithic organization. The 'fissiparous' tendencies of Protestantism have often been noted, but even in the Middle Ages there was never only one church in western Europe, and there were always the diverse Orthodox churches of the east. In fact diversity is characteristic of Christianity, and indeed of religion as a whole, for most religions have little central organization. One of the few writers who brings this out is the Anglican Welbourn who refers to 'schism as a recurring factor in the historic Church; separatism as a phenomenon of white America.... One is tempted to ask whether division in the Church is not just one aspect of fissiparous tendencies common to human society as a whole.' While persecution and uncharitableness between the churches are to be deplored, and needless overlapping can be eliminated, yet it may be asked 'whether the Church, in becoming a world-wide society, has been too ready to adopt a political structure not merely in the pattern of its leadership but in its whole concept of organization and authority.'†

A further point, which has not received the study that it deserves, is the correspondence between the diverse Christian churches today and the many different shrines of the traditional religion. African independency also stems from the lack of organization of the many temples of the old religion. They had their priests and prophets, healings and purification, and much of this is being baptized into Christianity, so that the independents are agents of the naturalization of Christianity into the African background. There are obvious dangers, of syncretism and relapse into paganism. But there are also powerful forces that hold the independents to Christianity. It has often been noted that they normally keep to the faith of the parent churches, and

* H. W. Coxill and K. Grubb, *World Christian Handbook 1968*, p. 25.
† F. B. Welbourn, *East African Rebels*, pp. 168, 210.

there are few doctrinal heresies. The importance of the Bible in their own language is very great in feeding new life and holding up a pattern of Christian behaviour. There is weakness in lack of international links, which can lead to parochialism and stagnation. Here the Christian Councils can help, and a conference on the subject which was held in Zambia in 1962 recommended the acceptance into these councils of all churches which confess faith in Christ, use the Bible, have a stable life and organization, and Christian home life. As a historical, scriptural and international religion Christianity can lead the independents to a modernization of African life without losing what is valuable in the old culture.

It will have been noted that the independents in the past often came into conflict with governments, even though their aims were principally religious. More recently there have been determined attempts to gain official recognition as legitimate societies, especially in Central, East and West Africa, and through these applications the independents have come to be treated with new respect. Christian Councils have been more hesitant, though four of the many applying churches were accepted into membership of the All-Africa Conference of Churches in 1966, and the World Council of Churches has accepted the application of one of the largest of all African independent churches, the Kimbangist church of three millions called 'l'Église de Jésus-Christ sur la Terre'. Finally, the missionary character of the independents has notably increased, and in at least sixteen African countries their membership is growing faster than those of other Protestant or Roman Catholic churches. In the Muslim areas of West Africa where mission churches have made little headway, independents are now established in many of the major Muslim towns.*

* See *World Christian Handbook 1968*, p. 127 f.

12 Christianity Today

The last two chapters have indicated the varieties of churches in modern Africa and referred to their life and practice. In the present century the church has spread throughout Africa in a manner without parallel before. This is part of a world expansion, and the American church historian Latourette reckons that Christianity has grown, in extent and numbers, more rapidly and successfully in the last fifty years than at any previous period in its long history. This expansion has been particularly noticeable in Africa, where the numbers of Christians were previously so few but where now they are nearly one hundred million and are still increasing.

The churches have benefited by exploration, trade, colonization, new communications, education and international languages. They have put parts of the Bible into more than five hundred African tongues, and this has been one of the most influential ways of naturalizing the religion, both in the older churches and among the independents.

The development of African clergy, lay leaders, teachers, prophets, doctors, healers, and instructed church members has been potent in many ways. Particularly significant, and often unnoticed, is the large part played by women in African church life. This has been stressed by Brandel-Syrier in her *Black Woman in Search of God*.* In South Africa the Methodists adopted the Xhosa word Manyano, 'union', for their women's organizations from 1906, and this term has been used by other language groups and churches for their 'mothers' in many activities. The women play diverse roles: as mothers of the church, class leaders, prayer leaders, wailing women at the houses of the bereaved; running mutual aid societies, home-makers' clubs, youth organ-

* M. Brandel-Syrier, *Black Woman in Search of God* (1962).

izations, missionary societies; and doing community service in schools, crèches, nurseries, kitchens and boys' and girls' clubs. They support themselves and help the needy with cash and service. Many other women, of course, enter such services as are open to them: teaching, nursing, and social service. In independent churches they are prophetesses and prayer leaders, as in the old religion they would have been priestesses, mediums and exorcists.

If Christianity has made great progress in Africa, it also faces problems and challenges. Islam has also spread into tropical Africa in this century, and it is a rival in West and East Africa. Secularism turns young people away from organized religion, and Communism feeds upon political repression. Then, the traditional religions are not dead, and there have been reactions against Christianity in revivals of libations and sacrifices connected with nationalism. Groves concludes his four volume study of the planting of Christianity in Africa by naming three critical factors for the church: polygamy, the fear of witchcraft, and the separatists sects. But the first two are probably declining, both were held in the Old Testament, and educational advance and religious progress will affect them in the future. The independent churches, it has been seen, can be some of the most effective agents for the spread of Christianity and naturalizing it into African life. Far more dangerous to the church are the racial policies of South Africa and Rhodesia, persecution of Christian tribes in the Sudan, and warfare in other places.

The churches must be both African and international, seeking divine inspiration yet guided by the historic scriptures, and aiming at bringing all life within the scope of their faith and morality.

Something of the extent of the churches in modern Africa can be gathered from the figures on page 167. The collection of statistics is difficult. In some countries governmental censuses include questions on religious affiliation, in other lands they do not. Churches have their own methods of estimating the number of members and adherents, and these vary considerably; some keep strictly to the number of full communicants, while others include the whole Christian community, including school children and adherents. Even then there is usually a discrepancy between church and governmental figures, and the latter are the larger. This is because the census figures are the claims of individuals or families, and not just church leaders. Moreover, Christianity, like Islam, has a high prestige in Africa and many people claim to be Christian who rarely if ever go to church, as in England. At least this means that they are potential Christians, within the scope of the church, which has a great opportunity for increasing its size.*

* See T. A. Beetham, *Christianity and the New Africa*, pp. 22, 164.

Statistics of African Christianity

There are Christians in nearly every African country but only those are included here which approximate to at least half a million in number. Orthodox, Roman Catholics, Protestants and Independents are included, reckoned to the nearest half million.

Algeria	500,000	Mauritius	500,000
Angola	3,000,000	Morocco	500,000
Burundi	2,000,000	Mozambique	1,000,000
Cameroon	2,000,000	Nigeria	12,000,000
Central Afr. Rep.	1,000,000	Rhodesia	1,500,000
Congo (Brazzaville)	500,000	Rwanda	1,500,000
Congo (Zaïre)	10,500,000	Senegal	500,000
Dahomey	500,000	Sierra Leone	500,000
Egypt	3,500,000	South Africa	11,000,000
Ethiopia	14,000,000	S.W.Africa (Namibia)	500,000
Gabon	500,000	Sudan	500,000
Ghana	4,000,000	Swaziland	500,000
Ivory Coast	1,000,000	Tanzania	4,000,000
Kenya	3,000,000	Togo	500,000
Lesotho	500,000	Uganda	4,000,000
Liberia	500,000	Upper Volta	500,000
Malagasy	3,000,000	Zambia	2,000,000
Malawi	1,500,000	minorities	2,000,000
		total	**95,000,000**

See *World Christian Handbook 1972*, and Europa publications *The Middle East and North Africa* (1975) and *Africa South of the Sahara* (1975).

Comparative Christian Statistics in Africa, approximately:

Coptic and Orthodox	18,000,000	Protestant	30,000,000
Roman Catholic	37,000,000	Independents	10,000,000
		total	**95,000,000**

Part Three : Islam

13 Egypt and North Africa

Islam is the most recent of the great historical religions of the world and the last to enter Africa, but its success has been astonishing, with rapid military gains and slow consolidation. There is no need to discuss the Arabian origins of Islam or its doctrines, as these are well known and can be studied in many books on the religion. We are concerned with the history and state of Islam in Africa. Islam spread over North Africa from the seventh to the eleventh centuries A.D., and then it turned southwards into the western Sudan of West Africa. It expanded again from the sixteenth century and in the nineteenth it was characterized by Holy Wars. Today the progress of Islam continues into the tropics at the expense of traditional African religions.

After the death of the Prophet Muhammad in A.D. 632 the Arab armies which he had trained secured first of all the loyalty of the Bedouin tribes of Arabia, and then they broke out of the peninsula led by a great general, Khalid. The ancient Near East was ruled by the empires of Byzantium and Persia and the native populations were often glad to see their alien rulers disappear, since even if they were Christian they often had different doctrines from their own. The Arabs conquered Syria, Palestine and Mesopotamia, and then turned to Egypt.

The Copts, as was said before (page 110), disliked the Greek rule and doctrines of Byzantium to which they were subjected, and they welcomed the Arabs as deliverers. The Arab general 'Amr easily captured the frontier towns and the Byzantine fortress of Babylon in 640, near where Cairo was later, while Alexandria surrendered in the following year. There is a story, still sometimes told, which pretends that the Arabs destroyed the great library of Alexandria, and fed the priceless books to the city furnaces, on the grounds that the Koran contained all the wisdom that men needed. This is a complete libel. A great Ptolemaic library at Alexandria had been burnt by Julius Caesar in 48 B.C., and a later one by the Christian emperor Theodosius in A.D. 389. There was no library of any importance in the city when the Arabs arrived, and this lie about them is not found in any writer till the thirteenth century, six hundred years after the event it is supposed to describe. In fact the Arabs respected learning, they were not opposed to Christian or classical culture, and they were to be the preservers of ancient Greek manuscripts and learning throughout the Dark Ages. In Egypt the Arab soldiers were glad to leave public affairs in the hands of Coptic functionaries under their rule. However they were not sailors, at first, and they disliked the Byzantine town of Alexandria; the Arabs built a new capital of Egypt called Fustat, and in the tenth century the Fatimid caliphs built Cairo.

The Arabs sent an expedition southwards into Nubia and bombarded its northern capital of Dongola, but the Negro bowmen resisted and in 652 a treaty was concluded by which Nubia would supply gold and slaves and the Arabs would respect Nubian independence. Nubia was to remain Christian until after the fall of Dongola in the fourteenth century, and it was a barrier to the southerly expansion of Islam.

The Arab leader 'Amr pressed on west and his cavalry occupied Cyrenaica easily, but then they were faced with five hundred miles of Libyan desert before the fertile plains of Tunisia could be reached. The coastal road was narrow and liable to attack from the Byzantine navy, and Berber tribes were more hostile to Arab invasion than the Copts had been. It is said that when 'Amr suggested to the caliph 'Umar that he should advance into Ifriqiya (the Arab version of the classical name Africa), the caliph retorted that it should not be called Ifriqiya but 'the treacherous land beyond the frontier'. He forbade any farther advance during his lifetime, and so it was 'Amr's nephew 'Uqba who conquered Ifriqiya and founded the city of Kairouan (Qayrawan) in southern Tunisia in 670. But when he ventured farther west into Morocco 'Uqba was killed by Berbers and the coastal road was cut by the Byzantine navy. 'Uqba is said to have ridden his horse into the

Atlantic ocean, looking for more worlds to conquer. His tomb is a national shrine near Biskra in modern Algeria.

After the death of 'Uqba the Arabs had to withdraw from Ifriqiya, until the governor Hassan brought Byzantine rule and Berber resistance to an end. The Arabs had now realized the importance of a navy; in 698 Hassan took Carthage and other coastal towns with the help of the fleet, and the new city of Tunis was founded. Then Berber tribes swept down, led by a queen called by the Arabs the Kahina, 'priestess', but she was defeated by treachery and a well still bears her name at the place where she was killed. Hassan and his successor Musa crushed resistance, and Ifriqiya or the Maghrib, 'the west', became the most valuable province of Arab North Africa. It was administered from Kairouan independently of Egypt and directly responsible to the caliph of the Islamic empire in Damascus. The Tunisian plains were settled and prosperous, though the inhabitants of the mountains of Numidia long resisted assimilation. The great Arab historian Ibn Khaldun wrote that the Arab armies captured all the cities and settlements of the Maghrib, but endured a great deal in struggles with the Berbers who 'apostasized twelve times' before Islam finally gripped them. The Arabs were long restricted to the towns because their authority was not strong enough in the open country and it was only in the eleventh century A.D. that 'they migrated in order to colonize it and disperse themselves in tribes'.

Morocco remained 'the far west', al-Maghrib al-Aqsa, and was independent for long periods. Musa extended his province as far as Tangier and his influence reached across to Mauretania. In 711 it was Tariq, a Berber freedman and lieutenant of Musa, who crossed over into Spain and led the Islamic armies into what was for centuries their largest European domain.

Christianity slowly declined before Islam in North Africa, weakened internally by schism and losing its Latin leaders; but its fall was gradual and so was the advance of Islamic religion. There were schisms within Islam which were seized upon by North Africans. The Prophet Muhammad had been succeeded by four caliphs and the last, 'Ali, was superseded by the Umayyad dynasty, named after a Meccan family and ruling from Damascus.

Objectors were the Shi'a, the 'followers' of 'Ali, beginning as a political group among the Arabs but developing as a religious expression of discontented masses against the state in many places. They developed belief in spiritual leaders, Imams, instead of caliphs, and hoped for the coming of a messianic figure, the Mahdi, the 'rightly guided one' who was to give hope to revolutions in many ages. A militant movement of dissent was in the Kharijites, 'those who go out', puritanical fanatics who were often responsible for revolts though weakened by their own internal dissensions.

In the Maghrib of North Africa the divisions within Islam were taken over to express local independency. Many of the Berbers became Kharijites, showing that they were both Muslim and different, as the Donatists had shown that they were Christian yet not Roman. In the eighth and ninth centuries Kharijite communities flourished at Sijilmasa in southern Morocco, in the south of Tunisia and Libya, and especially at Tahert in the central Maghrib. In 785 Idris ibn 'Abdullah fled from Medina to the Maghrib and founded a kingdom that bore his name for two centuries. This was the first Shi'a dynasty and its capital Fez (Fas) was the first capital city of Morocco. The Idrisids were finally destroyed by the Umayyads of Spain but they gave the ideal of a united kingdom to Morocco.

In the east the Umayyad empire was replaced in 750 by the 'Abbasid caliphate which ruled from Baghdad, but although a great Mesopotamian culture developed a political breakup was caused in the west. From 756 Spain had its own Umayyad government, and soon after Morocco and Tunisia had locally independent rulers. Ibn al-Aghlab ruled from 800 over the Maghrib, and although they were nominally subject to the 'Abbasid caliphs the Aghlabids rarely inscribed the caliph's name on their coins. From Kairouan they dominated the central Mediterranean and sent expeditions against Sicily, Italy and France. It was under the Aghlabids that the Maghrib became finally an Arab-speaking and fully Islamic country. The great mosque at Kairouan had been founded by 'Uqba who established the city, and traces of this remain as the oldest mosque in Africa, but it was rebuilt and beautified in 900, adorned with marble from the ruins of Carthage, its portico divided into seventeen aisles and the prayer niche crowned with a dome. Kairouan became one of the most holy cities to the Muslims of Africa, ranking as the fourth gate of paradise, after Mecca, Medina and Jerusalem.

At the end of the ninth century a Shi'a propagandist from the Yemen toured the Maghrib, proclaiming himself as precursor of the Mahdi and gaining particular support among the Kutama, a Berber tribe of the Kabyles which was against the government. With their help the Aghlabids were defeated and the last of their rulers fled to Mesopotamia. A descendant of Fatima, daughter of Muhammad and wife of 'Ali, called 'Ubaidallah, was proclaimed Imam and Mahdi, and founded the Fatimid dynasty in Tunisia in 909, the only major Shi'a dynasty. 'Ubaidallah was an active man, extending his rule from Morocco to Egypt and sending a Kutama tribesman to rule over Sicily. He left Kairouan to live on the Tunisian coastline at a new capital called Mahdiya after himself. He seized Alexandria and ravaged the Delta, and his son strengthened the Egyptian fleet to harry the coast of Spain. Egypt was finally captured by the fourth Fatimid caliph in 969.

Egypt was less fortunate than other parts of North Africa; it was close to the capitals of the eastern caliphs and had a succession of foreign rulers, with its wealth continually drained by the central governments. The rule of Egypt was given as reward to court favourites, but in 868 Ahmad ibn Tulun, son of a Turkish slave from Baghdad, asserted its independence. This was a turning point in Egyptian history, for now money remained in the country to strengthen it and Egypt became a sovereign state for the first time since the Greek Ptolemies long before the birth of Christ. Ibn Tulun built up a strong military organization and soon occupied Syria as well, the great dream of Egyptian rulers, and this rule continued for centuries. Ibn Tulun constructed many splendid buildings, and the mosque which bears his name in Cairo is one of the most remarkable in the Islamic world, with pointed arches, a circular staircase minaret, many Koranic inscriptions, and Shi'a lines in praise of 'Ali which were added later but still remain. Other important rulers followed, building strong armies to repel the Mamluk slave forces from Baghdad.

As soon as the Fatimids conquered Egypt they began to lay

out a new capital, al-Qahira, 'the victorious', known to us as Cairo. This became a royal city, which at its finest period had twenty thousand brick houses. Here in 972 was built the great mosque of al-Azhar, where a great theological school and university developed, which still today is one of the great centres of Islamic authority. The Fatimids ruled for over two hundred years and at their zenith their domains included all North Africa, Arabia and Syria, eclipsing Baghdad. Berber soldiers governed Arabs in many parts of this empire, though the Maghrib was to separate away, and Negro soldiers from the Sudan served in the army. The head of the Fatimid empire was the Imam, an infallible and hereditary ruler from the divinely directed family. Under him were civilian officers and a very powerful order of missionaries, like the Party in modern dictatorships, which sent Isma 'ili Shi'a agents even throughout the empire of the 'Abbasid caliph of Baghdad. These missionaries affected intellectual life and also organized secret religious groups from India to Spain. Fatimid trade was equally important, with the Italian republics such as Venice and Pisa; with Spain and Byzantium, and by controlling the Red Sea, trading with Persia and India. With the traders went Isma 'ili missionaries to stimulate religious life. But being linked with Fatimid rule, when that declined then Shi'a influence also grew weaker.

In the tenth century the Fatimid caliph 'Aziz was one of the most beneficent, beautifying Cairo and giving Christians more toleration than they had known before; his vizier and his own wife were Christians, the latter being sister of the Melkite patriarch of Alexandria. But he was succeeded by his son Hakim, the 'mad caliph', who violently persecuted Christians and Jews, making them wear special dress; many churches were demolished, including the famous and ancient Holy Sepulchre in Jerusalem. Finally Hakim declared himself an incarnation of God, and he has been so regarded ever since by the sect of Druzes who excuse his cruelties as symbolical. Hakim was assassinated and succeeding caliphs were youths who left real power in the hands of viziers. There were revolts in Syria and Palestine, and North Africa broke into open independence. Then there came attacks from the Crusaders from Europe, who battered at the gates of

Cairo in 1167. Four years later Saladin (Salah al-Din) deposed the last Fatimid caliph.

The Crusades were a strange mixture of religious idealism, debased by violence and often extreme cruelty, and backed by commercial and imperialist expansion. The invasion of the Arab empire by the Seljuq Turks brought an end to the Golden Age of Islam, when Baghdad fell to the Turks in 1055. Although the Turks accepted Islam, their capture of the Holy Places in Palestine gave Christian Europe the aim of capturing them for its own faith. Also the Italian city states sought to increase trade with the Levant and disunity in the Islamic world gave them their chance. Pilgrims and soldiers settled in Palestine and for nearly a century Jerusalem was under European rule, though most of the Crusaders lived on the Mediterranean coastal plains. Then Islamic forces recovered and their chief agent was Saladin. He was a Kurd who went to Egypt reluctantly in 1164, but then became fired with two ambitions, to restore the Sunni faith of Egypt against the Shi'a beliefs of the Fatimids, and to expel the Frankish Crusaders. These he succeeded in accomplishing, and in 1171 the name of the 'Abbasid caliph was substituted in the Friday prayer for that of the Shi'a Fatimid caliph, and Saladin declared that the caliphate of the latter was at an end. Saladin became ruler of Egypt, giving formal obedience to the caliph, and within a few years absorbing Syria to create a strong Syro-Egyptian empire with himself as sultan. Then he attacked the Franks, captured Jerusalem in 1187, and by the time of his death six years later the Crusaders only retained a narrow coastal strip of Syria. Saladin built the citadel of Cairo, two hospitals, religious academies, and dervish monasteries.

After Saladin's death Syria broke away again into small states, but Egypt remained the greatest power of the Near East. It protected Africa from invasion by the Mongols of the east and from the efforts of more Crusades to regain the Holy Land. Despite the failure of their armies European merchants continued to flourish under Islamic rule and trade was encouraged since it brought arms into Islamic countries. Saladin founded a short-lived dynasty which was favourable to the Coptic church as well as successfully repelling the Franks. After taking the Egyptian town of Damietta the Crusaders advanced on Cairo, but they were destroyed and the French king Louis IX was captured; later he led another Crusade to Tunisia where he died.

Then the Mamluks ruled Egypt from 1250 for nearly three hundred years. They were slaves of various races, trained in Egypt and building up a remarkable rule. Baybars (1260–77) tried to rival the glory of Saladin and succeeded in uniting Egypt and Syria into one state more permanently. He also ingeniously established a member of the 'Abbasid family as caliph in Cairo, though only as a functionary of the Mamluk sultans. Even more important, he defeated the Mongols who had penetrated into Palestine, and so saved Egypt and Syria and their treasures. These countries remained together until the coming of the Ottoman Turks. Baybars also promoted public works, hospitals and mosques. He appointed four qadis, to represent the four orthodox schools of Islamic laws, and his zeal for Sunni orthodoxy made his name even more popular than that of Saladin. Under the later Mamluks artists gathered in Egypt from areas overrun by the Mongols and helped to beautify its cities. The famous collegiate mosque of sultan Hassan in Cairo is a fine example, in the form of a cross, with open central courtyard and four arms as halls for instruction in the four law schools.

The sixteenth century saw the decline of the Mamluks and Egypt. The Ottomans arose rapidly in Turkey, using new arms, guns and artillery. Constantinople was captured from Europe in 1453, and the last Mamluk sultan was hanged. The Turks absorbed the privileges and powers of both caliphs and sultans, and they ruled most of the Arabic-speaking world for nearly four hundred years. Egypt lost its power and prestige, and these were weakened even more by the Portuguese turning the Cape and landing in India at the end of the fifteenth century. Despite Egyptian attempts to check them, European sailors outflanked the Levant and established trade all over the Far East. The state both of Egypt and Islam was severely influenced by these changes.

Meanwhile, in North Africa when the Fatimids had moved to Egypt, there were declarations of independence, and kingdoms were set up in the Kabyles among important Sanhaja tribes. To enforce their authority the Fatimids sent from Egypt a number of turbulent Arab tribes, notably the Banu Hilal, making them 'a gift of the Maghrib'. This brought about a great change for the new Arabs were not like the old ones of the first Islamic invasions, who had settled in towns as an élite, with their own language and religion, leaving the Berbers still holding their traditional customs and tongues. The historian Ibn Khaldun, a Spanish Arab who was born in Tunis, described the new wave of Bedouin tribesmen as a swarm of locusts that destroyed everything in its path, and he said that the Maghrib was plunged into struggle for three hundred years, during which time the countryside fell into ruin and Mediterranean civilization was destroyed. More and more Arabs arrived and Berber society began to disintegrate, and where it survived in mountains like the Kabyles it was narrowly tribal. The new Arabs were nomads and took long to settle down, and not till the twelfth century were the Moors of Mauretania and Haud arabized. Hope for the Berbers came finally from Morocco, where the Idrisids formerly had a united kingdom, but the inspiration for it arose among the Tuaregs of the Sahara.

In the western Sahara were light-skinned people with muffled faces who were pagans, and Muslim writers speak of them worshipping the sun. Parties of Arabs raided into the desert, and by the ninth century had even made contact with ancient Gana and Kanem, but like the Romans before them they generally found it convenient to leave desert trade in the hands of the muffled Tuaregs. In the tenth century some of the Tuaregs were converted nominally to Islam. About 1020 their chief Tarsina went on pilgrimage to Mecca and got the idea of a Holy War (*jihad*) against the Negroes, and was killed by them for his pains. His successor asked for a teacher and Ibn Yasin came from near Sijilmasa. He was unsuccessful at first, and with some companions Ibn Yasin withdrew to the Atlantic coast to construct a *ribat*, a fortified monastery, where as well as religious teaching there was military training for holy wars, and this soon became popular. His followers became known as al-Murabitun, 'people of the *ribat*', known in Europe as the Almoravids.

When he had trained a thousand followers Ibn Yasin decided that the time was ripe for a *jihad*, and he sent his people home to persuade their villages to become Muslims, peacefully if possible but if not by force. Some of them turned against the Negro kingdom of Gana, which will be mentioned later. Most went north to Morocco and overran it by 1069, since the country was disturbed by the Arab invasions and consequent movements of other tribes. The Almoravids appeared as liberators from alien rule and illegal taxation and they built up a splendid empire in the western Maghrib. In 1086 there was an appeal from Muslims in Spain who were being pressed by Christians trying to recon-quer the country, and the Almoravids responded so successfully that by the beginning of the twelfth century the whole of Muslim Spain was under their control.

The city of Marrakesh from which Morocco took its name was founded in 1062, and became capital of the empire with Seville in Spain as subsidiary capital. There was fresh enthusiasm for Islamic orthodoxy, with recognition of the 'Abbasid caliph instead of the heretical Fatimids, and even the works of the great orthodox theologian al-Ghazali were burnt, because of critical remarks he had made about some teachers of the Maliki school which the Almoravids followed.

The Almoravid dynasty was short-lived in Spain and in the Maghrib its success led to criticism of oppressive ways. A more strongly Berber religious and political movement emerged against it, led by a puritan reformer, Ibn Tumart. He held that it failed to maintain the absolute unity of God, and he attacked the sister of the reigning Almoravid in the streets of Fez because she went unveiled. In 1125 he founded a *ribat* and was proclaimed as Mahdi, supported by his followers called Almohads (al-muwah-hidun, 'monotheists'). His successor 'Abd al-Mu'min became head of the greatest empire of Morocco and Africa, and took the title of caliph with his capital at Marrakesh. The Almohads sent armies into Spain to reaffirm their power, and then pushed on to Algeria, Tunisia and Libya. The Almohad empire became the first united Islamic kingdom which stretched from the frontiers of Egypt to the Atlantic and included Spain. Every Friday throughout this empire prayers were said in the great congrega-tions in the name of the Almohad Mahdi or caliph, instead of the caliphs of Egypt or Baghdad.

In 1170 the Almohad capital was transferred to Seville, where a beautiful mosque was built which was later replaced by a cathedral. But North African cities were also improved; Rabat was built on the model of Alexandria, and at Marrakesh a hospital was constructed which had no equal in the world. To pay for these, and a great civil service that was created, land was taxed on productivity throughout the empire. This caused dissatisfaction and rivalry among Berber groups, and to placate them, as well as give himself time to deal with troubles elsewhere, the caliph al-Nasir gave the command of the empire eastwards from Tunis to a viceroy from the outstanding Hafsid family. Then al-Nasir's army was overwhelmed by the Christians in Spain in 1212, and he fled to Marrakesh where he died two years later; this was the beginning of the end for Islamic rule in Spain. Meanwhile the Hafsids were only too successful and they built up an independent kingdom in Tunisia, cut off from the west. The Almohad empire disintegrated into regions, dominated by powerful tribes, some from Tlemcen dominating Algeria and eastern Morocco, and others finally gaining control of Marrakesh.

The great Berber empires were finished, and the unity of the Maghrib was broken up into the three parts which roughly corresponded to what has remained ever since. Hafsid rulers continued to prosper in Tunisia till 1574, trading with the east, Europe and the Sudan. In the centre what was later called Algeria was divided among various tribes but, lacking central government like that of Tunisia or Morocco, it was at the mercy of Bedouin who destroyed much of the ancient civilization. Morocco in the west under successive dynasties tried to maintain its administration against attacks of tribesmen within and invaders outside.

Most of North Africa eventually came under the power of the Ottoman Turks. First of all Algeria in 1518 was invaded from the sea and became a base for Ottoman raids throughout the Mediterranean. Then Tunisia was invaded and reduced to a Turkish province. Only Morocco remained beyond Ottoman control, but the three centres of Algeria, Tunisia and Libya became seats of Ottoman governors, beys or pashas. These states were often semi-independent, and there were occasional revolts against the exactions of Ottoman agents, until Turkish rule became weak and in the nineteenth century it was broken.

14 West Africa

West Africa was isolated by forest and desert from North Africa and the east. There were difficult routes across the Sahara but they depended on the favour of desert nomads and the maintenance of rare oases. Christianity went up the Nile into Nubia and Ethiopia, but not across the difficult passage into the western Sudan, and it had not had time by the seventh century to penetrate southwards from the Berbers of the Maghrib. Not until the coming of Islam was a strong religious change effected in West Africa and then not for several centuries. Muslim traders followed the major routes, of which the easiest were from Morocco southwards along the western coast and then inland up the valley of the river Senegal. By the eleventh century their faith began to spread among the Negroes.

At that time there were important Negro kingdoms in the West African Sudan, such as Takrur on the Senegal, composed of ancestors of the Tokolor. West of the upper Niger was Gana (far distant from modern Ghana), so named after one of the royal titles and the most powerful Soninké kingdom when the Muslims arrived in North Africa. Then there were smaller chieftaincies eastwards, Songhay, Hausa, and Kanem in the region of lake Chad. In the eleventh century there were Muslim trading quarters in many Sudanese towns; in Gana there were twelve mosques and Muslims were among the court offidials. About this time the ruling family of Takrur accepted Islam and converted neighbouring chiefs. Although small in numbers the Takrur peoples were widely influential, and their language was adopted by the Fulani nomads who took it from the Atlantic to the Nile.*

With the rise of the Almoravid holy wars in Morocco and the north, attention was also turned to the Sudan. Gana was invaded

* J. S. Trimingham, *A History of Islam in West Africa* (1962), p. 45 f.

and after some resistance the capital was sacked in 1076. The fall of Gana reduced its importance and it never managed to rule as widely as before, but it was a large factor in the extension of Islam. The Soninké were forced to accept the new religion and became agents in its propagation. Many of them migrated to other parts and led tribes there to Islam. By the twelfth century Muslim traders had penetrated to the edge of the equatorial forest, where they bought kola nuts, but they rarely went farther south or made converts of the forest peoples.

The place of Gana was taken over by the empire of Mali, of the Mandé people, and before long it was the greatest Negro state of Africa, acting as a buffer between the peoples of the desert and the forest. Its rulers were nominal Muslims, like those of other states in the western Sudan, though the ordinary people generally held to their traditional beliefs. The king of Jenné became a Muslim about 1200; he was sultan Kunburu who assembled all the Muslims in his country, amounting to over four thousand, and in their presence declared his acceptance of Islam. He demolished his palace and replaced it with a mosque.

So far the Arab historians had paid little attention to West Africa for it was overshadowed by the great Islamic empires in the north, but the fame of Mali became known throughout the Islamic world from the time of king Mansa Musa. He made a notorious pilgrimage to Mecca in 1324, passing through Cairo and spending so much gold that it is said the value of gold depreciated considerably in Egypt. The fame of Musa went even to Europe for on the first map of West Africa, in 1375, there is a picture of a king with a nugget of gold in his hand and the inscription, 'This Negro lord is called Musa Mali'.* After his return from pilgrimage, having spent all his gold, Musa conquered Timbuktu, an early Berber settlement on the bend of the Niger and an important religious centre.

Most of the Mandé peoples were not converted to Islam at this time, and two Mossi kingdoms to the east and south impeded the progress of the religion. There was a holy war against the Mossi in 1498 bringing the demand that they should accept Islam, but the Mossi king consulted his ancestors and refused. Islam went

* J. S. Trimingham, *A History of Islam in West Africa*, p. 68 n.

even more slowly into the central Sudan, though Kanem had its first Muslim chief in the twelfth century. The Hausa city-states were affected by Islam even later, and apart from rulers and traders the mass of the Hausa remained attached to their traditional religions until the nineteenth century. But Islam was important to the Sudanese rulers because it gave them sure links with Muslim traders and the kingdoms of North Africa and increased the two-way traffic. Islam also gave the Sudanese rulers a wider claim on the loyalty of their subjects than did family ties; it helped both to provide a bond of allegiance between widely separated peoples and it brought literacy to the western Sudan. The Arabic language was used as a lingua franca – eventually its alphabet was adapted to other languages – and a class of educated men developed that was essential to the maintenance of the administration of large empires.

In the fourteenth century the empire of Mali, from its capital on the upper Niger, extended from the borders of Hausa country in the east to the Atlantic coast in the west. In the fifteenth century its power was replaced by that of Songhay. The founder of this empire, Sonni 'Ali, had no use for Islam, mocked its prayers and objected to its claim to a higher allegiance. But his successor, the Askiya Muhammad, reversed this attitude and used Islam to reinforce his position, with the result that an empire was developed which was even greater than that of Mali, with its capital at Gao on the Niger below Timbuktu. Muhammad adopted the title of 'caliph of the Negroes' and made a pilgrimage to Mecca in 1497, which he tried to make even more magnificent in display than that of Mansa Musa.

These western Sudanese states became part of the Islamic world, and their schools and mosques attracted scholars from many places, especially to Timbuktu. From West Africa also students went far afield and had their own hostels in places like Cairo, where to this day there have been hundreds of African scholars at a time at Al-Azhar. Trade was a powerful link, with the gold of Guinea causing constant traffic, which later the Portuguese from the sea tried to divert to themselves. There was a shift eastwards, to Timbuktu and Gao, which may correspond to the eastward shift of power in North Africa at this time, from the Almohads of Morocco to the Hafsids of Tunisia. The Negro kingdoms were visited by eminent travellers, and Ibn Battuta who had been as far as China visited Mali in 1352. He wrote that its inhabitants had a greater horror of injustice than other people and that its sultans provided complete security for strangers from robbers and violence. The people were careful in the hours of prayer, he said, brought their children to the mosques and made them learn the Koran by heart.*

Ibn Battuta referred to the Hausa and, probably, the Nupé as pagan. Islam was introduced from the west into the Hausa states, and into Kanem from the north. Kano and Katsina, according to the Kano Chronicle, received Islam during the reign of Yaji (1349–85) who accepted ritual prayer and built a mosque under a sacred tree. But there was considerable opposition, his son was a pagan, and Islam did not gain a firm hold until towards the end of the fifteenth century. Then the arrival of Islamic teachers, and the practice of pilgrimage by wealthy people, helped to establish the new religion.

Kanem had interludes of Islamic and pagan rulers from the twelfth century, and some of them went on pilgrimage. Islam was firmly established among the ruling classes by 1240, and there was a Kanem hostel in Cairo for pilgrims and teachers. Ibn Battuta said that the inhabitants were Muslims, and the king never showed himself to the people but spoke to them from behind a curtain, like other West African rulers. There is some confusion with Bornu, and Ibn Khaldun wrote of the two places as being under the same ruler and sending a rich present, including a giraffe, to the Hafsid ruler of Tunisia. In the sixteenth century the chief Imam of Bornu tried to persuade the notables to learn the Koran and regulate their marriages by Islamic law.

Farthest east was Waday beyond Lake Chad and the arrival of Islam here was blocked by nomadic tribes. In the sixteenth century there were invasions by Tunjur tribesmen, probably Nubians, who spoke Arabic but had migrated from Darfur to the east. Some of them were nominal Muslims but did not force religion on their subjects. According to tradition Islam was first

* Ibn Battuta, *Travels in Asia and Africa, 1325–1354*, translated H. A. R. Gibb (1929), p. 329 f.

preached in Waday in the seventeenth century by Jamé, who led a holy war against the Tunjur rulers, overthrew them, and founded his own dynasty which has lasted till modern times. But the Waday rulers continued to pay tribute to Darfur as their predecessors had done. Later preachers came from the eastern Sudan and students from Waday went to the Nile and Egypt for Islamic learning.

In the sixteenth and seventeenth centuries external pressures affected most of West Africa. In 1492 the last Islamic stronghold in Spain, Granada, had fallen and within a few years all Muslims were expelled from Spain, many of them settling in North Africa. Then Algeria and most of the Maghrib came under Turkish rule, and the Portuguese by sailing round the coast began to drain away the gold of the Sudan. Ahmad, sultan of Morocco, tried to break out of these pressures by expeditions into the Sudan, and in 1590 he sent an army of Moroccan and Spanish Muslims across the desert to attack the Songhay empire. After a terrible journey through the Sahara his troops met a large Songhay army, but with superior guns they defeated it and entered Timbuktu without opposition. Moroccan rule dominated parts of Songhay for over a century, under local pashas whose supporters slowly integrated into the Songhay as a ruling class. In 1727 Timbuktu was subjected to the Bambara of Segu, but the power of the Tuaregs was gradually extending over all the Niger bend, and in 1787 the Tuaregs captured Timbuktu.

The fall of the Sudanese Negro empires of Mali and then Songhay brought chaos to West Africa. The Moroccan invasion led to tribes breaking away and preying on one another; the Fulani, Bambara and Tuareg raided their neighbours and with the devastation of the country there were famines and distress. The states west of the Niger fragmented, and the Bambara emerged at this time, but as military leaders rather than steady rulers. They were not Muslims, but they used Muslim officials when convenient and adopted some Islamic customs.

Throughout the western Sudan there were Fulani (Peul) nomads, who were generally pagan. One group of them at Masina on the upper Niger took the opportunity of the Moroccan invasion to assert its independence of Songhay and eventually founded a powerful state of its own. Another Fulani group migrated west-wards to the river Senegal and established a dynasty in Futa Toro. Other Fulani nomads went east and were found in the Hausa states as settlers as well as nomads. Although many of them were pagan they were of great importance when Islam began to spread through Fulani enthusiasts in the nineteenth century.

The greatest expansion of Islam in West Africa is quite recent and began chiefly in the nineteenth century. It was inspired from North Africa and owed much to the religious brotherhoods which had become popular there, and which will be discussed later. Most of the western Berbers had finally become converted to the Arab language and religion, and after the Muslims were expelled from Spain there was a religious revival which saw the emergence of 'marabouts' or holy men with saint cults attached to them. The religious orders of the Qadiriyya and Tijaniyya became potent forces in the dissemination of Islam in West Africa from the eighteenth century. Until this time Islam had been fragmented in the western Sudan, surviving only by fitting into African ways of life, and not penetrating to the tropical coastal kingdoms at all. But now there came great urges towards the formation of Islamic states, ruled by the law of Islam imposed upon older forms of society.

It began in the western highlands of Futa Jalon among the Fulani, and after half a century of struggle an Islamic state was formed in 1776. Schools were opened and provinces placed under the authority of Islamic teachers. At the same time there was a similar revolution to the north in Futa Toro of Senegal, where a state was created under Islamic law and neighbouring peoples, including many Wolof, were converted. These states were headed by chiefs who adopted the title of Almami or Imam.

Then in the Fulani kingdom of Masina there arose a new power, led by Hamadu who had seen something of holy war elsewhere but returned to settle at Jenné. He proclaimed a *jihad* against the Bambara and delivered Masina from their rule by 1810. He took the title of emir of the faithful, and claimed to be the last of the imams or spiritual leaders. Hamadu organized the state on military lines and under Islamic law, and imposed Islam on those

Religion in Africa

Fulani who had remained pagan. He died in 1844, but his Islamic state did not end till the French arrived in 1893.

A more fearsome conqueror was al-Hajj 'Umar, who was born in Senegalese Futa. His title came from his pilgrimage to Mecca, where he became a member of the Tijaniyya order, and claimed that he had been appointed caliph for the Sudan. 'Umar came back by way of Bornu and Sokoto, taking part in wars and slave-trading. Then he settled near Futa Jalon, and tried to persuade people to join his order. After nearly forty days spent in retreat, 'Umar proclaimed the holy war among the people to the north in 1854. His way was blocked by the French, and he turned east to carve out a kingdom among the Bambara where people were forced to accept Islam, though later many lapsed. Then he made a fatal mistake in turning against the already Islamic state of Masina and was killed. 'Umar had sought to spread Islam by force and his slave-raiding upset many areas. He opposed the French conquest of the Sudan and for a time tried to boycott their trade, but he bartered slaves for European firearms. The nucleus of his army was drawn from the Tokolor who regarded him as the Mahdi, and many still believe that he will come again.

A less extensive rule was created among the Mandinka of the region of the upper Niger and its tributaries by Samori (1830–1900). He tried to carve out a kingdom south of the zone ruled by the successors of 'Umar, and though not an Islamic teacher he used Islam to forward his conquests and assumed the title of Almami. Then Samori came into conflict with the French and had to retire to the upper Ivory Coast, and finally he was exiled by the French for the last two years of his life.

Between the river Niger and lake Chad there were many small kingdoms, but in the nineteenth century some of these were united into an Islamic empire through the holy wars of 'Uthman dan Fodio (or Usuman dan Fedio, 'dan' means 'son of'). A Fulani born at Gobir, he was an enthusiastic Muslim teacher who was disgusted at the compromises that his fellows made with traditional religion. He began as a wandering preacher and gathered disciples about him, and when he heard of the Islamic revolution that had taken place in Senegal and Guinea, 'Uthman resolved to start a similar holy war among the Hausa. In 1804 his followers defeated the army of Gobir and proclaimed 'Uthman as emir of the faithful, or Sarkin Musulmi in the Hausa language, a title that the ruler of Sokoto still bears. The chiefs of the Hausa towns were alarmed at this militant Islam and oppressed the local Fulani, who were then aroused to fight for 'Uthman. He blessed flags and sent them out to the Fulani to proclaim the *jihad* and Hausaland was plunged into war. The Hausa states were divided, and despite strong resistance they fell to the Muslim armies, Zaria in 1805 and Kano in 1809. Bornu was invaded but repelled the army as it had its own military religious leader.

The Fulani *jihad* was both racial and religious, though not entirely either. Islam was imposed on the Hausa and traditional rituals were suppressed, as far as possible; at the time of the British occupation at the end of the century probably half the Hausa still followed the old religions. Fulani control was established over the Hausa kingdoms, and then went further to dominate Adamawa, Nupé and invade Yorubaland as far as Ilorin and Old Oyo. Here the forest saved the Yoruba who grouped themselves on Ibadan and repelled the Muslim invaders. But due to its foothold at Ilorin, Islam now began to spread among the Yoruba and was aided by modern communications to reach right down to the coast.

'Uthman retired from political life, perhaps overwhelmed by the success of his armies, and unable to control the deputies who were carving out personal domains for themselves. His son Muhammad Belo was given charge of the domains east from Sokoto and his brother ruled the west. 'Uthman died in 1817 and his tomb at Sokoto came to be visited by pilgrims. The empire gradually broke into separate states which only loosely accepted the leadership of Sokoto. They were in full decline when the coming of the British gave new importance to Sokoto and the emirs.

Bornu had been more stable than the states to the west under its leader al-Kanemi, and when the Fulani were repelled they recognized each other's spheres of influence. Al-Kanemi was succeeded by his son, Shehu 'Umar, whose power and centralized administration impressed European visitors to the kingdom. Islam was the state religion, though vassal tribes were often pagan.

The tropical coastal states of West Africa remained generally attached to their traditional religions, but modern times saw the infiltration of Islam from the north and the arrival of Christianity from the sea in the south.

15 East Sudan and Eastern Africa

The energy of Islamic expansion in North Africa was much slower in the south than to the west. South of Egypt the country was difficult and there were kingdoms where Christianity was well established. A Muslim expedition besieged Dongola in Nubia in 652, but made a treaty of non-aggression and mutual trade, in the name of God, the Prophet Muhammad, the Messiah and the Apostles. As long as Egypt was under Arab rule this treaty was respected, but Ibn Tulun in 869 sent further expeditions against Nubia and the country became attractive to those who found the Tulunids and Fatimids oppressive. There was Islamic infiltration from the Red Sea ports, some influence from Darfur to the west, but a much stronger tide of Arab immigrants from the north which increased as Egypt grew in strength and Nubia declined.

Only with the coming of the Mamluks in the thirteenth century were there determined efforts from Egypt to attack Nubia; Baybars sent two expeditions and others followed, in which the country was devastated and churches were destroyed. The kingdom of Dongola fell about 1320, and though many people were still Christian the Arab tribes now flooded the country towards the richer lands to the south which Nubia had blocked. Ibn Khaldun says that as the Nubian kingdom disintegrated the Arabs spread rapine and disorder, showing no statesmanship because they were still nomads. There remained a Christian bastion at 'Alwa, north of modern Khartoum. The Mamluks still did not think of establishing regular government, but Arab tribesmen kept on advancing and the country was overrun. It is said that 'Alwa fell in 1504 to combined forces of Arabs and a Negro tribe called the Funj, perhaps the Shilluk. This alliance has been questioned, but the Funj were soon present in force and Christianity disappeared from the Sudan till its establishment among Negro tribes in the south in modern times. Remains of ancient Sudanese churches are still to be seen.

Islam had entered the Sudan also by traders, and there were mosques in Dongola and 'Alwa before they fell as political kingdoms. But even after the establishment of Egyptian rule this government was loose; when Egypt fell to the Ottoman Turks the new overlordship extended into Nubia, but local governors were often independent except for sending tribute to Cairo. In the Sudan proper the Funj founded the kingdom of Sennar, known as the Black Sultanate. Despite their pagan origins they encouraged Muslim holy men from Arabia to settle in their midst, and they dominated most of the Sudan with their seat of power between the White and Blue Niles.

The end of Funj power came in 1820, when the vigorous Ottoman ruler of Egypt Muhammad 'Ali invaded the Sudan, deposed the Funj sultans of Sennar, and established an Egyptian governor in a new capital at Khartoum. The Ottoman armies attacked Darfur in the west but had to withdraw, and Egyptian rule was not established there till later. Meanwhile Khartoum became a vast centre for slave-trading and raiders pressed farther south into other African territories.

This provided the setting for the rise to power of Muhammad Ahmad of Dongola, a teaching shaikh who gathered pupils round him on an island in the White Nile. Disturbed by his people's sufferings he came to see himself as Mahdi, and from 1881 he bound others to God through himself and vowed a holy war against the 'infidel Turk'. From Kordofan the Mahdi sent letters to world rulers, declaring the arrival of a new world order, and a general revolt followed in the Sudan. The British had taken formal control of Egypt and its southern domains, and now decided to abandon the Sudan, sending General Gordon to Khartoum to withdraw the garrison and leave an orderly government behind. Gordon was killed by Mahdist troops in 1885, but the Mahdi himself died of typhus in the following year. He was succeeded by a caliph, who was defeated by the British, and the Anglo-Egyptian Sudan was created which lasted till independence in 1956.

The spread of Islam in the Sudan continued over centuries, but became a flood after the fall of the Christian Nubian kingdoms. Even then it was blocked by pagan tribes further south, and by the Christian kingdom of Ethiopia. To the west Islam linked up with Darfur, Wadai and the West African Muslims though, as has been shown, these latter states were Islamized from the west. The Sudan, of course, is not far from Arabia and pilgrimage to Mecca is easier than for other African peoples. So there came teachers, religious orders, and cults of saints which are powerful in the Sudan and have allowed for the incorporation of pagan practices that are otherwise foreign to Islam. In the nineteenth century the Wahhabi puritan revival in Arabia, and the awakening of dervish orders, brought missionary zeal over to the Sudan and began the evangelization of African tribes which had been impervious to Islam down the centuries.

Neighbouring countries, Ethiopia and Eritrea, were not influenced so deeply, and many tribes were only indirectly affected by the influx of Muslim Arabs into the Sudan. Hamitic peoples like the Somali accepted Islam, but Semitic populations like the Christian Amhara of Ethiopia rejected it. Until the fourteenth century the kingdom of Ethiopia was small and surrounded by warring tribes, but then there was a great extension of its power under early Solomonid rulers and Islam was even less able to gain control. With a centralized Ethiopian state, ruled by a Christian king of kings, and dominating mountains and plains, Muslims were inadequately organized for conquest. The diffusion of Islam was mainly peaceful, with Arab traders coming over the Red Sea, intermarrying with coastal peoples, and even adopting their language instead of Arabic.

At the south of the Red Sea trade from Arabia spread Islam slowly among the coastal peoples and nomadic Somali. From the tenth century there arose a series of Islamic states, organized by small Somali dynasties, chiefly concerned with trade in gold, ivory and slaves with the inland pagan states south of Ethiopia. They did not immediately threaten the Christian kingdom, but when Ethiopia had recovered from struggling with other peoples it turned against the Islamic kingdoms and exacted tribute from them. There was no religious war till the Muslim kingdom of

Ifat used Islam as a rallying cry and was incorporated into Ethiopia in 1415.

Zaila on the coast and Harar inland were Islamic centres, and from Harar Islam was diffused among the Galla people. In Eritrea pagan tribes were converted in the fifteenth century, and some Christians were Islamized under Egyptian domination in the nineteenth; but modern times have seen an intensification of Ethiopian Christian missions in Eritrea and considerable successes are claimed. In Ethiopia itself Islam claims about a third of the population, chiefly on the plains, reckoned at two to four million out of a total population variously estimated at between seven and fourteen million. Less than half the Eritreans are Muslim, but practically all the Somali. By the sixteenth century Islam had been adopted in the commercial centres of Somalia, but the southern part of the Horn of Africa was held by Bantu who followed their traditional religion. Somali expansion began there in the sixteenth century, conquering and infiltrating the southern lands and taking Islam with them. In the nineteenth century a Mahdist movement began at Ogaden with Muhammad ibn 'Abdullah Hasan, who after pilgrimage to Mecca sought to improve the piety of his fellows and, from 1899, proclaimed himself Mahdi and led military expeditions against neighbouring tribes. Called the 'mad Mullah' by the British, he was pursued for two decades and died in Ogaden in 1920 and his dervish order declined. The Somali today are fervent and orthodox Sunni Muslims, attached to one or other of the two principal orders.

The spread of Islam in East Africa was remarkably slow, in view of the nearness of Arabia, and until modern times it was virtually confined to the coast. The coherence of traditional African societies effectively prevented penetration of the interior. It is notable that Islamic traders were Persians as well as Arabs, for the winds blow from the Persian Gulf towards Africa during four months of the year, and then in the reverse direction, and sailing ships traded between South Arabia and the Persian Gulf to Africa, and even to India and China. This is shown by Asian coins and pottery and other remains in East Africa.

The Persians called East Africa the land of Zanj, a term vaguely applied to the country south of the Horn of Africa. Writers speak of kings of Zanj, its language, and of a belief in a creator called 'the great Lord'. The first Muslims in East Africa are said to have been Shi'a refugees who in the eighth century arrived from southern Arabia, and they were followed in the next century by orthodox Sunni Muslims from Shiraz in Persia. The Chronicle of Kilwa says that colonizers founded Mogadishu, and much later settled at Kilwa and coastal islands, where they found a Muslim family settled and a mosque. Excavations have revealed a rich palace at Kilwa, dating from the twelfth century, in Persian architectural style. There is an inscription in a mosque in Zanzibar which is dated from 1107.

Another writer in the twelfth century said that the king of the Zanj lived in Mombasa, and he mentions medicine men who charmed snakes and other people who worshipped stones anointed with fish oil. Ibn Battuta in 1329 visited the 'shaikh' of Mogadishu who spoke Arabic as well as his own language. He stayed a night at Mombasa and saw orthodox Sunni Muslims who had well-built mosques. Then he went south to Kilwa where most of the Muslims were Negroes and said that they had wooden mosques, though archaeologists think that the chief mosque there at this time must have been made of stone. The trade in gold, ivory and slaves was in full force, but it seems to have been in African hands and Muslims did not penetrate far inland at this time.

The Persian and Arab settlers married Bantu women and formed a new people, the Swahili or 'coasters', whose language became used along the coast and later over much of East Africa. Unlike the Arab families that settled in North Africa, these traders came as individuals and so adopted African languages and customs. Other settlers came across from Malagasy and Indonesia but were absorbed into their new environment. A tradition of the Shirazi Muslims from Persia says that a Persian king and his six sons founded colonies at Zanzibar, the Comoro islands, Malagasy and several other places in all of which a Shirazi prince ruled; by the fourteenth century there was strong Shirazi influence which lasted till the Portuguese arrived. Kilwa was in this sphere of influence and became one of the principal ports, as is shown by many copper coins minted there. It controlled much of the coast to Sofala in the south.

The kings of Zanj who ruled in Mombasa were replaced by Shirazi rulers in the thirteenth century, till they were deposed by the Portuguese. Muslim traders liked to settle on islands, like Zanzibar, Pemba and the Comoros, as that gave them freedom of movement from the pressures of African peoples on the mainland and an exit to their homes in time of need. In the sixteenth century Bantu warriors came from south of the Zambezi and destroyed Islamic and Portuguese colonies, sacking Kilwa so that it never regained its former prominence.

When Vasco da Gama visited the East African coastal towns in 1498 he saw prosperous trading centres, and shops which sold products from India and farther afield. From the tribute that he levied it seems that Mombasa and Kilwa were more important at this date than Zanzibar. The Portuguese arrival changed the balance of power. They sacked both Kilwa and Mombasa and by 1530 they controlled all the coast. This led to the downfall of Persian influence, and its later replacement by Arab dominance. Mombasa was often attacked but kept returning to prominence. In 1592 the Portuguese deposed the shaikh of Mombasa, replaced him with their own nominee, and built Fort Jesus which still stands. Then the Arabs of Oman expelled the Portuguese from the north, and in 1698 Mombasa fell to them. Shortly afterwards Arab garrisons were placed at Zanzibar and Kilwa and the Portuguese lost control.

After the Portuguese interlude, the Arabs continued to dominate the coast but were split by factional struggles. Some of the Persians returned and revived smaller towns, but now entire Arab families settled in East Africa and made a strong impression on Swahili culture that has lasted till now.

The nineteenth century saw an acceleration of the slave trade, for reasons which are not clear. The Arabs penetrated the forest by rivers up to the great lakes, seeking principally for ivory but needing slaves for its transportation, and though they did not introduce slavery which was current among the indigenous populations they greatly increased it. By 1840 they had established permanent trading posts, with a busy route from Lake Nyasa to Kilwa. The traders stuck to their work and did not intervene in tribal life or attempt to introduce Islam. Yet Islam spread through the example of the traders and by Islamic toleration of raiding expeditions under the guise of religion. The Christian missionary Krapf in 1850 noted that the chief of Usambara had Swahili secretaries and that two of his sons had become Muslims, though the father remained in the old faith.

Arabs arrived in Buganda in 1844 and made converts slowly but then were involved in conflict. King Mwanga killed Christians in 1884 and supported the Muslims, but he was deposed by Muslims and Christians in alliance. The Muslims were strengthened by the entry of Sudanese troops, used by Lugard, but there was a mutiny in 1897 in which the Muslims suffered a severe reverse. Another rising in Tanganyika led to Germany taking full control of that country.

Although European rule led to suppression of the slave trade, Islam began to expand under the new colonial orders as never before in the East African hinterland. Imperialist peace and new communications enabled Muslim traders to penetrate to areas that they had never before visited. The governments used Swahilis as officials, soldiers and school-teachers. Although African chiefs disliked the Arabs who had engaged in slavery, they came into close contact with Swahili officials and were impressed by their ways. In Kenya Muslim influence was limited chiefly to the coastline. In Uganda there is a strong Muslim minority, principally to the north of Lake Victoria. In Tanzania there is Islamic dominance on the coast and areas of strong influence inland, especially since the influx of Muslims from Mozambique. The north of Mozambique up to Lake Nyasa is predominantly Muslim, along the old trade route and in Malawi, particularly among the Yao people who have taken to Islam more than other peoples in these parts. The Yao are an inland people but their trade with the coast not only brought them into competition with the Arabs but subjected them to Islamic influences from the late nineteenth century and they became the chief agents of the spread of Islam.

In South Africa the situation was different, for Arab advance was checked by the persistent Portuguese hold on Mozambique. The small Muslim groups of South Africa arrived in a different manner, to provide labour for European farms. There are Indian

Muslims in Natal and Malay Muslims at the Cape. In 1960 there were 79,000 Muslims among the Asiatics in South Africa and 62,000 among the Coloured population. Only 5,000 Bantu were said to be Muslims.

Similarly in Malagasy, but on a much larger scale, there was colonization from Indonesia from an early period. With the spread of Islam throughout Indonesia, the northern part of Malagasy in particular became Muslim eventually, with about half a million Muslims now in the whole island.

16 Modern Times

North Africa, like most of the world, entered a new period in the nineteenth century through European expansion. In the Middle Ages the Arabs thought of Europe, if they considered it at all, as a place of dark barbarism and the Crusades reinforced that opinion. Even Ibn Khaldun in the fourteenth century said that God alone knew what went on in those parts.

Trade between Europe and the east increased from the sixteenth century, and the French and British in particular established consular posts in Egyptian and other ports. But when Napoleon landed with an army at Alexandria in 1798 things changed rapidly. This was the first armed attack from Europe since the Crusades and the power of the Mamluk viceroys was broken. Napoleon in a proclamation said that he was a better Muslim than the Mamluks and that he was restoring the rightful power of the Ottoman Turks. Although British and Turkish forces obliged the French to withdraw, Egypt was in a state of anarchy till the brilliant Muhammad 'Ali became master of Egypt by 1806. He was a Turk, and held Egypt for the Ottomans, but he was a great reformer and has been called the founder of modern Egypt. Cairo and Alexandria were embellished, and the latter linked to the Nile by a canal. Cotton was introduced from the Sudan and a great programme of educational progress was instituted. Western teachers, Western books printed in Cairo, a school of medicine, missions invited from Europe, and students sent there, all brought in new ideas.

There were reactions against westernism, but it continued. The Suez canal was opened in 1869, and new roads and railways developed the economy of Egypt and opened it to a wider world. But weak government and a revolt against Turkey led to intervention from Britain to defend traders. Egypt remained nominally under Turkey, with a Khedive as governor, but a British garrison with a consul-general was the effective power. It was not till 1922 that Egypt became independent, for the first time for many centuries. In nationalist movements a powerful role was played by the Ikhwan al-Muslimun, the Muslim Brotherhood, which has sought to sweep away corruption and return to pure Islamic principles. Unfortunately it has not seen clearly what are the real problems of a modern state, and being led into conservatism and secrecy has lately been in conflict with Jamal 'Abd al-Nasir, President Nasser.

Political and religious history have been closely entwined in Islam and religious movements have reflected and influenced public affairs. The religious orders will be mentioned later, but mention can be made of a few modern Egyptian writers. New ideas found expression in Muhammad 'Abduh (1849–1905) who rose to the highest religious position in Egypt, that of mufti. Exiled to Syria for taking part in a revolt, he was depressed by the decadent state of Islam and the accretions to its original purity. Muhammad 'Abduh wrote and spoke for reform, and also sought to reconcile Islamic teaching with modern science, interpreting some passages of the Koran rationally. He aimed at religious revival rather than political revolution and tried to break through the barrier of Muslim scholasticism. Although he reads today like a very moderate reformer, his influence was great. Some of his followers went further. Qasim Amin attacked polygamy, divorce and the veiling of women, and Rashid Rida went from Syria to Egypt to edit the works of Muhammad 'Abduh and continue his efforts at reform. In recent years writers like Taha Husain and Kamel Husain have gone even further in reinterpretation of traditional religious teachings.

Throughout the Islamic world there have been tensions brought about by the effect of Western ways of life, religion, science, democracy and nationalism. Reformation has been attempted by purifying Islam from corrupting influences and practices, by reforming Islamic teaching in the light of modern thought, by changes in higher education, and by the defence of Islam against European influence and Christian criticism. At one extreme there is the complete refusal of any compromise by the puritanical Wahhabi of Arabia, who forbid many practices that are accepted throughout the Islamic world. At the other, there is the secular state established in Turkey, with rejection of Islamic law in favour of the Swiss code and prohibition of dervish orders, though a great deal of Islamic faith and practice remains in Turkey. Other Islamic countries vary between these extremes, and in Africa Tunisia and Egypt are among the most progressive.

Islamic education was based on the Koran and Traditions, with four law schools dealing with problems that seemed out of touch with modern life. Al-Azhar University in Cairo was nearly a thousand years old, but was moribund, and was by-passed as a centre of modern learning by the higher schools founded by French and English-speaking missions, and by the American University and the State University in Cairo. In 1937 Azhar was reorganized into three faculties, Islamic law, religious sciences, and Arabic language. But this was not enough, and in 1962 it enlarged its courses of study to add colleges of medicine, agriculture, engineering, industry, management and administration. Women students were admitted for the first time. Arabic was the medium of instruction but other languages were used as well, and non-Egyptian Muslims served on the faculty. Similar reforms were inaugurated or prepared at Kairouan, Fez and other Islamic cultural centres in Africa.

From the sixteenth century Libya, Tunisia and Algeria were all ruled by Ottoman governors. Britain and France had an interest in Libya after Napoleon left Egypt and supported rival pashas of Tripoli in 1835; only with difficulty did the Turks restore their hold on the country. Then Italy, looking belatedly for a colonial empire, and ousted from Tunisia by France, landed troops in Libya in 1911 and despite strong Berber and Arab resistance they seized political power from the Turks. The Italians had to face the power of the Sanusi, a Sufi order which they called fanatical but which had been peaceful till its country was invaded and its land seized (see p. 212). Finally in the Second World War Libya became independent with British help. Sayyid Idris, grandson of the founder of the Sanusi order, became not only head of the religious community but king of the state of Libya in 1951.

France had been in relationship with Algeria from the end of the eighteenth century, and was helped by grain from there during her Egyptian campaign. But difficulties arose over French trade and in 1830 a French army occupied Algiers, Oran and Bone, and planned to colonize the country. In Oran a holy man, 'Abd al-Qadir, who had twice been on pilgrimage to Mecca, and was only twenty-two years old, declared war against the French in 1832, taking the title of Commander of the Faithful. The French had a bloody struggle, forced 'Abd al-Qadir into the mountains, but later had to concede to him Oran and much of the west, while he also advanced into the Sahara. Then further attacks were made against him and he fled into Morocco, where a small French force defeated a large Moroccan army, but did not capture the holy man. Not till 1845 was he seized and taken to Toulon, finally being permitted to settle in Damascus where earlier he had rescued Christians from massacre by Druzes. 'Abd al-Qadir died there in 1883.

The religious brotherhoods of the Maghrib were bitterly opposed to the French. The Derkawa continued guerrilla warfare, and in 1857 from the Yenni tribe emerged a prophetess, Lallah Fatmah, who roused all the surrounding tribes, till after several bloody battles she was captured. The tribesmen retreated farther and farther into the Sahara and French rule was not firmly established till 1884. The defeat of France by Germany in 1870, and the wars of 1914 and 1939, which absorbed much energy, gave further opportunities for Algerian struggles towards independence; which was not achieved however till after the harsh fighting which ended in 1962.

French rule was imposed later over Tunisia and Morocco, and was relinquished earlier. The beys of Tunis maintained their independence for long, began to westernize their government, and granted a constitution in 1857. But financial difficulties that followed gave the French a chance of intervention, and in 1881 they landed troops to disarm the bey and declare a protectorate over Tunisia. The bey remained, but without real power, and independence did not come till 1956.

Morocco had remained outside Turkish rule, under a dynasty that was 'Alid, claiming descent from the son-in-law of the

Prophet, but strictly orthodox Sunni; the rulers took the title of caliph, and Commander of the Faithful. In the sixteenth century the Moroccans were attacked by Turks in the north and Portuguese in the south, but managed to force them back and by the end of the century sent an army across the Sahara to subdue the Negro empire of Songhay. Andalusian Moors who had been driven out of Spain settled at Rabat and Sale and formed wealthy republics. There were also holy men (Murabits, marabouts), who had monastic colonies and exercised considerable temporal power. The authority of the sultan was challenged by claimants to the title of Mahdi. Morocco came to be divided into conflicting parties and was only protected from colonization by European powers by their jealousy of each other, owing to the strategic position of the country at the entrance to the Mediterranean. Britain was in Egypt, Spain in parts of Morocco, and finally France was allowed to extend her zone of influence, though with some challenges from the Germans. Casablanca was occupied and a revolt followed, but by 1912 a French protectorate was established with the sultan as titular head. There were further revolts after the First World War, but independence came only in 1956. Mauretania became an Islamic republic in 1960.

North African intellectual life did not begin to stir out of medieval bondage till after the modern revival of Egypt. Moroccan scholars continued in the old manner, but in Tunisia and Algeria reform parties were founded. Marriage laws slowly came under criticism, and the traditional Islamic permission for a man to take up to four legal wives was attacked as out of date, suited only to medieval conditions and only dubiously supported by the Koran. In 1958 new laws in Morocco gave women the right to choose their own husbands, sue for divorce, and refuse their husbands permission to take a second wife. Similar laws were enacted the following year in Algeria; polygamy was not forbidden but was said to be practised by less than two per cent of the population. But Tunisia went farther and made bigamy a punishable offence. Also in Tunisia the month's fast of Ramadan was said to be responsible for much backwardness in the Islamic world, leading to sleep by day and indulgence at night. Traditionally children, pregnant women, the sick and travellers had been exempt from the Ramadan fast, and this exemption was now extended to include students, soldiers, and such factory workers as wished to avoid it in the interests of a real holy war against poverty and ignorance.

Modern times also brought great changes in Islamic communities in East and West Africa, and enough has been said about the former area to indicate that while European imperial rule replaced or dominated Islamic communities, it also brought great opportunities for Islamic expansion under peaceful and easy communications. From the time of the first Portuguese traders Muslims in East Africa had been in contact with Europeans. But in West Africa European trade had been on the coast, among mainly non-Islamic peoples, and the Muslims in the interior have only come into direct contact with European ways during the last century or so.

The nineteenth century saw both the great extension of Islam in the western Sudan by the holy wars of the militant Fulani, and the 'scramble for Africa' by the European powers. The double tension caused great upsets, which were only partially and temporarily settled by European conquest, and whose results can still be seen, notably in Nigeria. French invasion developed from Senegal, advancing up the river into the western Sudan, subduing Fulani kingdoms, occupying Timbuktu, and then descending into the forest and coastal lands of the Bight of Benin through Dahomey and the Ivory Coast. French territories were unified and much larger than British. The British had no pattern, but to protect trade they advanced slowly inland from different places, like Gambia, Sierra Leone and Ghana, coming almost by accident to form the most populous country in all West Africa, Nigeria. Going up the rivers Niger and Benué they occupied the Fulani emirates, and proclaimed protectorates of northern and southern Nigeria by 1900.

Along with the political and trading enterprises of the European powers went Christian missions, often preceding the foreign governments and living closer to the people. They were warned off the Muslim areas, forbidden to enter certain towns, such as Kano, and so opened no schools there. Muslim regions were preserved from the full blast of colonization, but were also deprived of the advantages of cheap and widespread education. Later some of them saw the dilemma, missions and education, or no missions and little education. Belatedly some Muslims accepted Christian education, and found that their children usually remained Muslim.

As in East Africa so in the West, Islam was often helped by European rule. The new governors, who did not understand much of African life, rarely realized that Islam was only practised by the rulers in many states. They put their authority behind the emirs, took it for granted that their subjects must come under Islamic law, and even extended their power over some peoples who had not been ruled by Muslims before. Further, the disintegrating effect of European ways upon traditional African customs and religions helped both Islam and Christianity to extend their scope and engage in a religious 'scramble for Africa. The formation of new towns weakened village life and religion, new roads and railways made travel easy for Muslim traders and missionaries, and few of the towns are now without Muslim quarters. Islam has spread continuously for the last fifty years in Senegal, Guinea, Sierra Leone, the western Sudan, and north and western Nigeria. It has had little success so far in eastern Nigeria, and southern Dahomey, Ghana and the Ivory Coast.

In Senegal the Wolof people had been in contact with Muslims from Morocco and the Sudan for centuries, but only a minority had accepted the religion and the chiefs were against it. The spread of Islam has been largely due to the work of Ahmad Bamba who died in 1927. From 1886 he felt impelled to propagate his religion by a holy war, but colonial conditions prevented that. He was exiled by the French several times, and then undertook peaceful missions as head of a religious order, the Murid movement. Ahmad Bamba was regarded as a saint and the Wolof in large numbers accepted his teaching and leadership. This led them to expand into Fulani and other territories, to cultivate the land, and found colonies throughout Senegal and into Gambia.

In Guinea, both independent and Portuguese, and the western Sudan, Islam has extended its influence among people who before this century had resisted it, and even the Bambara who were for long a barrier against Islam have a strong Muslim minority. In

Sierra Leone many of the two largest groups, Mende and Temne, have accepted Islam and perhaps a third of the population of the whole country follow this religion.

Nigeria was one of the areas of most considerable Islamic advance under colonial rule. The dominant position of the Fulani after the holy wars was recognized by Britain, recent gains such as that over the Yoruba of Ilorin were consolidated; Islam was accepted as the official religion; even tribes where a majority followed traditional religion were subjected to Islamic rule; and Christian missions were forbidden or discouraged. It is said that half the Hausa were pagan when British rule began but eighty per cent are Muslims today. In Ilorin province censuses of villages near the city gave forty-eight per cent of Muslims in 1930 and eighty per cent in 1954. But just as striking is the advance of Islam among the Yoruba who were beyond Fulani rule in western Nigeria. In the city of Ibadan there were no mosques before the end of the last century, but the census of 1953 gave sixty per cent of the inhabitants as Muslims or sympathizers. In Lagos the number of Muslims was returned as 61,000 at the 1931 census and 95,000 in 1950. But here the increase in numbers of Christians was even larger, perhaps because this cosmopolitan town included many easterners.

Eastern Nigeria has few Muslims, the Fulani did not succeed in entering there, and Islamic influence will hardly be enhanced by modern wars. In southern Dahomey the strong organization of the traditional religion in the old kingdom of Abomey has given little foothold to either Islam or Christianity, though they flourish among the Yorubas of middle Dahomey and across into Togo. In the south of Ghana, the Ivory Coast and Liberia the old tradition was long dominant and is now being mostly affected by Christianity, especially through prophetic movements. In Upper Volta the Mossi were long resistant to Islam, but they were subjected to *jihads*, and proselytized by refugees and traders, and today Islam is growing among the Mossi though the secular government contains people of all religions.

Throughout Africa, especially in the north and the tropics, Islam is adjusting itself to the changes of modern times. In the north it has the field virtually to itself but has to face the insidious influences of modernism. In the east and west it faces these, but also encounters a missionary Christianity and deeply rooted traditional religious attitudes. But the power of Islam is great and its international links are vital. No student of African affairs, and no politician, can afford to ignore Islam, and in North Africa, the Near East, and much of the tropics no part of life can be understood without it.

17 Religious Movements

Since the first century of Islam there have been movements which have served to deepen personal faith and extend the influence of the religion. The Prophet Muhammad himself was a man of devout life, and the Koran contains verses of intense devotion that were later much cherished. Early contacts with Christian monks, who are mentioned in the Koran, brought Muslims into touch with ascetic life and in the first two centuries they often entered Christian monasteries, and for much longer studied Christian books. From the monks the Muslim ascetics adopted robes of simple wool (*suf*) and were called Sufis. Wars and the worldliness of the times drove devout souls to withdraw from the world, first by themselves and then in communities.

The teachings of these mystics became Gnostic and panthe-istic, emphasizing knowledge and identifying all things with God. This was strange for Islam, and there was probably some Indian influence; but orthodox teaching, that there is no god but God, led mystics to say that there is nothing else but God and that man finds himself by absorption in the divine being. Efforts were made to reconcile Sufism with orthodoxy, but it has often been regarded as heretical, or encouraging superstitions, though the Sufi orders have done much to give Islam a deeper hold on the people.

The mystics grouped themselves round a shaikh and followed his 'path' (*tariqa*), which could be centred in a communal retreat-house, though members of the order often wandered to other towns and villages. In the later Maghrib these houses be-came fortified monasteries (*ribat*, see p. 179) where men were trained in religion and prepared for holy war. Elsewhere the monastery was peaceful and open to visitors. The *tariqa* came to mean a system of spiritual doctrine and practice, given by the founder of the order, and the bond between the shaikh and the novice (*murid*) is strong. A member of such a fraternity may be called a dervish (Persian) or fakir (Arabic), both terms meaning 'poor' or beggar, and in North Africa such people are known as 'brethren' (*ikhwan*). These are not sectarian movements, though they may act as a sort of inner church. By alliance with popular cults of saints, they have great influence with the masses, as well as with more intellectual mystics. Muslims believe in an invisible order of saints, under God, who direct the affairs of the world. Holy men work miracles and exercise a great power or 'benediction' (*baraka*) which can be passed on to other people and transmitted to their successors. All the saints are connected with religious orders, and pilgrimages are made to the tombs of past saints throughout North Africa and the eastern Sudan.

Popular Orders

The earliest order that still exists is the Qadiriyya which was founded by 'Abd al-Qadir (1077–1166), whose school in Baghdad became so popular that during his lifetime the teachings spread to Egypt. His doctrine was fairly orthodox, but he gave mystical interpretations of the Koran and recommended repetition of words and texts fifty or a hundred times, a method that became very popular to induce a devotional frame of mind. 'Abd al-Qadir is the most popular saint in Islam and is called Sultan of the Saints, Emir of God, Light of God, and so on. The looseness of his system allowed it to be varied in every country and guaranteed its success. It was introduced into Morocco in the twelfth century, and into the Sudan in the seventeenth where it became the most numerous of the Sufi orders, especially in the Jezira, with successor caliphs of the founder becoming heads of families. It is strong in southern Ethiopia and Eritrea. The Qadiriyya is said to be 'more African' than other orders. Arab tribes took it to North Africa, founding *zawiyas* or monasteries. One branch spread from Mauretania in the nineteenth century and so influenced Ahmad Bamba of the Wolof that the Qadiriyya is the most powerful religious force in Senegal. Ahmad made his own form of the order, the Muridiyya, which is affiliated to the Qadiriyya, and this has been called a genuine Negro *tariqa*, adapted to life in changing Africa. The spiritual centre of the Muridiyya is a great mosque at Touba, one of the biggest in Africa, which is a place of pilgrimage and of the cult of Ahmad. The order has developed a system of collective farms in the service of God, in the fashion of African religious communities. The Qadiriyya spread to Timbuktu and the central Sudan as far as Waday, but at first its effect was limited to religious leaders and it was not till the *jihad* of 'Uthman dan Fodio that it became widely influential in the Fulani emirates. However in the present century the Qadiriyya has lost ground in Nigeria to the Tijaniyya.

The most popular order in Egypt is the Badawiyya or Ahmadiyya (not to be confused with the Indian order of that name which is found in West Africa, see below). It was founded by Ahmad al-Badawi (1200–1276) who was born in Fez and claimed descent from 'Ali. As a child Ahmad went with his family to Mecca and stayed there for some years, studying the Koran and having visions. He visited Iraq and tombs of saints, and then settled in Egypt at Tanta till his death. Badawi lived an ascetic life, had visions, worked miracles, and wore a face veil like African Tuareg Bedouin, hence he was called al-Badawi (the Bedouin). The teachings of Badawi do not appear remarkable, but it seems that he crystallized the needs of his time for an ideal of asceticism and holiness. His followers wear red turbans and are found all over Egypt, the Sudan and beyond. Three festivals are celebrated in his honour every year, not only at the very popular shrine in Tanta, but in Cairo and elsewhere. Under the Mamluk sultans the caliph of the Badawiyya ranked with the chief religious heads, and although the Ottomans did not favour his order like their own yet Ahmad al-Badawi remains the favourite saint of Egypt. The Turkish Bektashi order of dervishes also still has a famous and beautiful centre on the Mukattam on the east slope of Cairo; they are extreme Shi'a in secret doctrines, and teach the appearance of God in many emanations.

One of the most active of African religious orders is the Tijaniyya, founded by Ahmad al-Tijani (1737–1815), whose name came from an Algerian Berber tribe called Tijana. Born in an oasis in southern Algeria, he felt the call to the Sufi life when he was twenty-one and travelled to Fez to meet Sufi shaikhs in that important centre of learning. Later he went to Tlemcen, Cairo and Mecca, where he is said to have received occult learning from an Indian teacher. He was initiated into the Qadiriyya and other orders but finally founded his own movement, returned to Algeria, was expelled, and settled in Fez. Tijani believed that the Prophet Muhammad had appeared to him in daylight, given him litanies to use, and told him to propagate a new order. He travelled to many places, but Fez was his headquarters and he was buried in his monastery in that city. The Tijaniyya teach simple devotions with the founder as central figure. They allow worldly comforts and these, with philosophical liberalism, provide an attraction for modern educated people, since Tijaniyya scholars reject the asceticism and sadness of other Sufis. An important teaching has been submission to established authority and this put the order on good terms with colonial rulers in North and West Africa, and allowed it to spread easily in modern times. There are Tijaniyya centres in Egypt and the Sudan, but it was attacked by Rashid Rida and other leaders of Islamic reform movements for superstition and acceptance of foreign rule and culture. There are Tijanis throughout the Maghrib, but the most significant modern expansion has been in West Africa. Going south through Mauretania, where some tribes were converted to the Tijani way, al-Hajj 'Umar was converted to it (see p. 188). He claimed that in Mecca he had been appointed caliph for the Sudan, and opposed Qadiriyya teachers by saying that their way was like iron compared with the Tijaniyya gold. The Tijaniyya spread across the western Sudan to Nigeria, forming powerful groups even where the leaders were Qadiriyya. It has become the dominant order, claiming many teachers in Senegal, half the Mandé and Hausa, a third of the Fulani, and a number of the Yoruba and Nupé. The Qadiriyya have managed to hold their own in some of the Fulani centres and in Waday. But the appeal of the Tijaniyya in West Africa, as in the Maghrib, is in its simple devotions, its recognition of worldly comforts, and its peacefulness. It is attractive to educated West African Muslims who tend to look on the Qadiriyya as reactionary.

One of the most conservative African orders is the Sanusiyya, which is conventional in its Sufism, follows the Maliki law school and has never been convicted of heresy. The founder, 'Ali al-Sanusi (1787–1859) called the Grand Sanusi, was born at Mustaghanim in Algeria and studied at the famous mosque school at Fez. He went on a preaching tour by way of southern Tunisia and Cairo to Mecca and stayed there some years. On returning he settled in Cyrenaica in Libya, finally building a monastery in 1856 at Jaghbub, about a hundred miles from the sea, which became an Islamic university centre second only to al-Azhar. One reason for choosing this semi-desert place was that at the time it was beyond the encroachments of Turks, Italians and French who held or were invading the North African coast-line and had already wrought havoc in Algeria. The Grand Sanusi had founded a missionary order in 1837 and this won over some of the Bedouin peoples of Libya and Egypt, but it was less successful in the towns and the Nile valley, and so poured its energies south to the Fezzan, Sudan and Sahara trade routes. The Grand Sanusi was an outstanding scholar, with a library of eight thousand volumes, and he gathered other scholars round him. He aimed at returning to the purity of original Islam, though not in such extreme ways as the Wahhabi of Arabia; his followers ate and dressed well and sought to bring the peoples of the desert and Sudan to the knowledge of true Islam by peaceful missionary work. When the Grand Sanusi died, a magnificent tomb was erected whose white dome shines over the desert. He was succeeded by his eldest son and then by other relatives.

The Sanusiyya became involved in struggles against France and Italy when their lands were stolen. They were a peaceful order, but fought to defend their rights. For this some foreign writers called them secretive and puritanical zealots, but Islamic visitors commented on their cheerfulness and benevolence. Italy was involved in several Libyan wars and in 1922 the Arabs of Tripoli, who had often opposed the Sanusiyya, invited the present head of the order, Sayyid Idris, to become emir of all Libya. This he did after some hesitation and consultation with the Bedouin, and then had to flee to Egypt. Sayyid Idris was thirty-three, and he did not return to Libya till victory came in

1943. It is remarkable that the Grand Sanusi, who came from outside, was able to establish himself as head of the divided Bedouin of Cyrenaica; but the identification of the Sanusiyya with the Bedouin forged a national unity which survived different rulers, from the Turks to the Italians. Down in the desert Sanusi missionaries went to Fezzan, Air, and as far as Waday, but their domination of the central Sahara was checked by French colonial rule and today their chief influences are at Air and Waday.

An example of a modern movement may be seen in the 'Alawiyya, founded in 1920 in Mustaghanim in Algeria by Mustafa al-'Alawi (1869–1934). He was first attracted by the asceticism of fire-eating sects, and travelled all over North Africa founding monasteries and sending missionaries far afield. His centre was at Mustaghanim where he died. 'Alawi regarded himself as the renewer of Islam for this century, as the Prophet Muhammad is said to have promised that there would come a renewer in every century. Like Tijani he believed in peaceful submission to authority, and some of his followers were so closely associated with the French that critics said the order was a French creation. But this cooperation allowed the order to spread in North Africa and among Africans resident in Europe.

Very different is the Ahmadiyya from India and Pakistan, which has been a prominent factor in Islamic proselytization in West Africa and to a smaller degree in East Africa. This sect was founded in Qadian in the Punjab by Ghulam Ahmad (1839–1908), who sought to provide a movement that would attract Muslims, Christians and Hindus. He announced himself as the expected Mahdi of Islam, the Christian returned Messiah, and the Avatar of Krishna of the Hindus, and this led to estrangement from orthodox Muslims. He also taught, contrary to orthodox Islam, that Jesus had really been crucified but had been taken down alive from the Cross and wandered off to Kashmir where his grave was still to be seen; a claim that has been refuted by Christian and Muslim scholars but is still held by the Ahmadiyya. A further difficulty was that Ghulam Ahmad was called a prophet after Muhammad, and there was division after his death when, in 1914, a group based on Lahore called him only a 'reformer' and drew nearer to Islamic orthodoxy. The headquarters of the majority group is now at Rabwah in Pakistan. Ahmadiyya literature found its way to West Africa; in 1916 a group was formed in Lagos and a missionary called Nayyar visited Ghana and Nigeria in 1921. The movement spread particularly among the Fanti and Yoruba, and also in Sierra Leone, but it was not well received by Islamic leaders in Kano and Sokoto. Its chief headquarters became fixed at Saltpond in Ghana, and here Ahmadiyya still has its largest African following and principal centre of propaganda. The Pakistan missionaries were welcomed at first, but when they refused to pray behind orthodox prayer leaders something of their different teachings appeared, divisions occurred and litigation took place for possession of mosques.

The Ahmadiyya is different from other West African Islamic movements in coming from the sea, like Christian missions, and being less rooted in African life. But on the other hand its leaders have devoted great attention to literature and education, and have brought some liberalism to West African Islam. Its numbers are small: about 3,000 in Sierra Leone, 7,000 in Nigeria and 25,000 in Ghana. The future of Ahmadiyya in Africa is uncertain, for it has hardly come into contact yet with orthodox Islamic teachers, has attacked Christianity more openly than other African Muslims do, and appears to have few direct converts from traditional religions.

In East Africa the first Ahmadiyya missionary came in response to requests from Asian immigrants belonging to the sect. He was Mubarak Ahmad, who landed at Mombasa in 1934, and is still called the emir of Ahmadiyya for all East Africa. Finding the coast too difficult he went inland to Tabora in Tanzania, where a school was opened but closed again after opposition from orthodox Muslims. There are still a few schools and several mosques in Tanzania, Kenya and Uganda, chiefly in large towns where there is an unsettled population that is little or only superficially Muslim. But, as in West Africa, the Ahmadiyya here has considerable influence through literature in English and Swahili, and it publishes a Swahili translation of the Koran.

The Ahmadiyya is an example of extreme Shi'a Islam, virtually a modernist syncretism, but small numbers of more regular Shi'a are found in East Africa, chiefly among Asian immigrants.

For the Shi'a the supreme authority is the Imam, the spiritual leader, whereas for most Muslims, the Sunni to which nearly all African Muslims belong, the infallible law, the Shari'a, is the basis of authority. The Shi'a are divided into a number of groups, of which the two principal ones are the Twelvers and the Seveners. The Twelvers follow twelve Imams of whom the last, who vanished in 878, is expected to return in triumph one day; this sect is said to have about 17,000 followers in East Africa, especially in southern Tanzania. The Seveners or Isma'ilis follow the seventh Imam, Isma'il, who went into concealment; they are subdivided among themselves, and the Mustalis are particularly strong in Zanzibar. The other group, Khoja or Nizari, is the best organized Islamic community in East Africa. Its head is the Aga Khan, who has most of his followers in Asia, and in 1944 he formed five East African territorial councils with a centre at Mombasa. The whole community is taxed, not just for the Aga Khan, but for general welfare; the Khoja Isma'ilis are noted for their large community centres, libraries, schools and clinics. Most of the Isma'ilis are Asians, but a few Africans have been attracted to them and Arabic prayers have been introduced to form a bond with African Muslims, though the emphasis is still upon 'Ali and the Imam.

Modern Islamic Life in Africa

Pilgrims can go from Casablanca or Senegal to Mecca, by bus or on foot, passing through Islamic countries all the way, seeing the extent and brotherhood of Islam, and also many differences of race and custom. There is a marked uniformity in Islamic faith and external practice, but there are different cultures and traditions, local saints and orders, and varying responses to the tensions of modern times. Egypt is closely linked with Arabia, Syria and the Middle East, but also has ties with the eastern Sudan, Ethiopia and the Maghrib. North Africa belongs to the Mediterranean world and Tunisia, for example, probably has more affinities with Europe than with Senegal and certainly more than with Tanzania. Africa south of the Sahara, or Negro Africa, has appeared to modern writers a more coherent unity; yet there are many differences between West, East and South, and many links between West and North Africa, and between East Africa and Arabia, Persia and India.

Islamic life is regulated by different interpretations of the law according to the four major schools which go back to the early centuries of Islam. Egypt follows the school of Shafi'i, which is said to allow a limited exercise of common sense, and since this dominates in South Arabia, which was largely responsible for the Islamization of East Africa, the Shafi'i teaching rules there also, as in Somalia and Ethiopia. But Indian Muslims in East Africa follow the Hanafi school which is preponderant in India. Over most of Africa, that is Upper Egypt, the Maghrib, West Africa, the Sudan, Eritrea and Equatorial Africa, it is the Maliki school that is followed, which places great emphasis on tradition. Maliki teaching has allowed for adaptation to African custom, since it permits the application of customary law which is not based on the Shari'a, and the local *qadi* or judge can use this extensively or even exclusively for his decisions. On the other hand Maliki teaching tends to resist efforts to modify Islamic law to fit in with modern conditions. In African Islamic courts the Shari'a dominates, in theory, but it may be modified in practice by local custom which is not in conflict with it. Frequently African custom is continued in Islamic society and Maliki regulations are added to it. In matters of religious practice, of course, the Shari'a is followed, but in questions of land, inheritance and family, legislators have to take much account of local traditions.

There are no priests in Islam, it is a lay religion. But Koranic teachers, lawyers and professors are sometimes called clergy in the sense of religious 'clerks'. Because it is diffused by trading laymen, and also by holy men who are leaders of brotherhoods, Islam extends principally through towns and takes much longer to get hold of rural areas. Buildings for worship are mosques, but in villages and nomad camps the 'place of prostration' may be simply a marked out square, thus giving the religion considerable mobility. Prayers in the mosque are led by the local imam, the prayer leader, especially the communal prayer at midday on

Friday for men. But prayers are usually said at home or wherever the Muslim may be, facing towards the Ka'ba in Mecca and using a prayer mat. Ritual prayers, which take up most of the devotion, are always in Arabic all over the Islamic world. In Egypt and North Africa and the eastern Sudan Arabic is the language of the people, but to other East and West Africans it is a foreign tongue of which most people know nothing except the formulas of prayer. Sermons and exhortations are given in mosques on Fridays and during the fast of Ramadan, expounding the Koran in the language of the people.

Almsgiving, which is a religious duty in Islam, has sometimes been imposed as a state levy, but that has disappeared under modern forms of government, and almsgiving is a charity which helps to fill the place of social insurance. With no priesthood to support the upkeep of the mosque is inexpensive, till some major repair is needed and then appeals are made for large and small donations. Koranic teachers are paid by the parents of their pupils and rich patrons, and pupils often pay for instruction by work in the teacher's field.

In new Islamic lands, and some old ones, observance of the prescribed five times of prayer each day is often slack. The fast of Ramadan is more strictly observed, since it is a social matter that can be watched in communities where there is little privacy. The two great festivals of the Islamic year, the Great Festival of sheep sacrifice during the month of pilgrimage, and the Little Festival at the end of Ramadan are popularly observed. The birthday of the Prophet is commemorated nowadays, with differing popularity in various places, and there are also local and agricultural festivals. The religious orders, with cults of founding saints, provide many devotions. Pilgrimages, prayers and votive gifts are offered at tombs throughout North Africa and the eastern Sudan, but little as yet in West or East Africa where the traditional religions still provide outlets for popular worship. Laymen and leaders of religious orders meet for 'remembrance' (*dhikr*) of God and the saints. The ninety-nine Beautiful Names of God are recited on prayer beads and the chanting, with physical movement and breathing techniques, often accompanied by vocal or instrumental music, may lead to trance states and ecstasy.

Pilgrimage to Mecca is a religious duty to be performed by every adult Muslim at least once in a lifetime. About a million people go to Mecca every year, though three quarters of this number are from Arabia and near-by countries. From Egypt, the Maghrib, the Sudan and East Africa the pilgrimage is fairly easy, but for those who live farther away it is an expensive and arduous journey. In modern times there are pilgrimage ships and aeroplanes that take the wealthy to Arabia, but poorer people go by bus, lorry or even on foot. Since the pilgrimage is often left till old age many men and women take months or years to perform it, and may never return home. In 1956 2,483 pilgrims were given travel certificates to Mecca from Northern Nigeria and of these all but sixty were going by lorry or on foot. But 1,500 richer Muslims from Western Nigeria booked air flights to Mecca that year. In Senegal a survey found that only twenty Islamic teachers out of 1,385 had been on pilgrimage.

The role of Islam in personal and family life varies considerably in Africa. It is most dominant, of course, in North Africa, where it has been established for over thirteen hundred years. But some of the modern reforms that have appeared in North Africa have had little effect yet on Islam in tropical Africa. Polygamy is legal and common in African customary laws, and the permission for four wives in the Koran provides one of the attractions of Islam for a pagan African. There is little knowledge in the tropics of the divorce reforms and restrictions on plural marriages which have been effected in North Africa. Women are being freed from the veil in Egypt and North Africa, but in the eastern Sudan and interior villages veiling is still the rule. In tropical Africa women have traditionally often had considerable independence, trading on their own account, and the fortunate ones amassing large sums of money. Few of the newly converted Nupé and Yoruba women cover their faces in public, though in the western Sudan some women pull their head cloths down if there are men present. The Fulani are more strict in Nigeria and insist on the veiling and seclusion of women; at least the rich do so though many of the poorer women work unveiled on the land. But in the west, Futa Jalon and Senegal, women are more free.

Education provides further stimulus to change. Traditionally

Islamic education has been instruction in the Koran and law, with some Arabic language. But Western education is popular all over Africa, and children often go to the Koranic school for a year or two, and then transfer to the nearest primary or secondary school where they learn the ways and thoughts of the West. Higher education in the tropical countries is in English or French, though there are schools of higher Arabic studies, for example at Zaria in Nigeria, and students also go to al-Azhar in Cairo. Some tropical African languages have been reduced to Arabic characters, Wolof, Tokolor, Fulani, Hausa and Songhay, but far more have been written in the European alphabet and this makes transition to English and French easier.

In his study of Islam in East Africa, Trimingham says that the outlook is not bright; leaders are out of touch with modern ways and unlikely to make progress against the forces of Christianity, education and secularism. In West Africa Islam is making wide-spread advances and, like Christianity, is profiting from the break-down of the traditional religions. In North Africa and Egypt it is the sole or dominant religion and must be always taken into account. Christians and Communists are apt to ignore the determinative effect of Islamic faith and practice upon all aspects of life, political as well as others – to their own loss.

Statistics of African Islam

These figures are all approximate, as there are varying estimates of religious allegiance. Recent census returns, for example in Nigeria and Ethiopia, show considerably higher general populations than earlier counts and if they are correct the proportions of Muslims would be higher. Even in lands where the Islamic population may be counted as the same as the whole population a worldwide growth in numbers must be recognized, and it may be assumed that Muslims in Africa number about 125 millions, well over a third of the total number of inhabitants of this continent.

Algeria	11,500,000	Morocco	14,000,000
Cameroon	1,000,000	Mozambique	1,000,000
Chad	2,000,000	Niger	3,500,000
Dahomey	500,000	Nigeria	19,000,000
Egypt	26,500,000	Senegal	3,000,000
Ethiopia	9,000,000	Sierra Leone	1,000,000
Gambia	500,000	Somalia	2,500,000
Ghana	1,500,000	Sudan	10,000,000
Guinea	2,500,000	Tunisia	4,500,000
Ivory Coast	1,000,000	Uganda	500,000
Kenya	1,000,000	Upper Volta	1,000,000
Libya	2,000,000	minorities	1,500,000
Malagasy	500,000		
Mali	3,000,000		
Mauretania	1,000,000	**total**	**125,000,000**

See *A Concise History of Islam* (1957), *The Statesman's Year Book* (1966), and Europa publications *The Middle East and North Africa* (1975) and *Africa South of the Sahara* (1975).

Part Four : Conclusion

18 Other Religions

Judaism

The oldest of the historical living religions of Africa is Judaism; but it is one of the smallest and perhaps on the verge of temporary extinction in some northern parts of the continent and unrepresented in many other African countries. Some of the Hebrew tribes were captives in Egypt under the Pharaohs and were led out by Moses at the Exodus about 1300 B.C. In the Assyrian and Babylonian invasions of Palestine many Jews fled to Egypt, and at least by the time of the fall of Jerusalem in 586 B.C. there were considerable Jewish settlements in Egypt. The prophet Jeremiah was taken there with others and denounced the worship of the queen of heaven by Jews. Papyri discovered at Elephantiné, at the First Cataract, show that there was a settlement of Jews at this place in the fifth century B.C. who had a temple of their own, which was destroyed; some of them may have travelled south to Ethiopia, and the prophet Zephaniah said that the children of the dispersed would bring offerings from beyond the rivers of Cush (Nubia; Zeph. 3, 10). When the city of Alexandria was founded, Jews were among the first colonists; the Jewish historian Josephus lived there for a time and said that special quarters of the city were assigned to Jews, though some lived in other quarters as well. The Greek translation of the Old Testament, the Septuagint made by 'seventy' scholars, was prepared in Alexandria, and the great Jewish philosopher Philo lived there, seeking to reconcile Jewish and Greek thought. Since most of the first Christians were Jews Christianity soon spread in Alexandria and other Jewish centres in Africa, and soon outstripped its mother religion.

Under Islam, and down to the modern period, Jewish communities have continued to exist in North Africa. As People of the Book, like Christians, they were tolerated by Islam since the Prophet Muhammad regarded them as true believers in God.

223

They seem to have fared rather better than Christians, for they were much smaller in numbers and did not present such a problem to an Islamic state. Jews were well treated under the first Umayyad caliphs, but 'Umar II (717–20) made both Jews and Christians wear special dress and excluded them from positions in the government. But pressures relaxed and a synagogue built in Cairo in the ninth century guarded valuable manuscripts, which were discovered seventy years ago in its Geniza or old manuscript chamber. An Arabic translation of the Old Testament was made in Egypt, which has remained the standard version for Arabic-speaking Jews. There were heavy persecutions later under the Fatimids and Almohads. The 'mad caliph' Hakim forced Jews and Christians to wear black robes and ride on donkeys, and Jews to carry a yoke with bells; but other Fatimids were more tolerant. The Almohads in North Africa and Spain were fired with the belief that they were the only true Unitarians and spread this faith by the sword, against fellow Muslims as well as Jews and Christians. Many Jews then left Spain for the Maghrib and Egypt. The most famous Jewish philosopher, Moses Maimonides, was born in Cordova in 1135 but was driven out with his family, settling first at Fez. Then impelled by continuing pressures they made their home in Egypt, at Alexandria and then at Cairo where he died in 1204. Maimonides came to be called Moses Egyptius and wrote his great works in Arabic. His son introduced prostrations into the synagogue service, following the Muslim pattern. Other waves of Jewish immigrants entered Africa in the sixteenth and seventeenth centuries.

In 1829 there were 5,000 Jewish families in each of Algiers, Tripoli and Cairo, and 30,000 in Tunis. Some of these were European, but most were native African. There has been considerable debate about their origins. It used to be thought that they were Judaized Berbers, children of old converts, but some recent writers stress their national integrity, as descendants of old immigrant families which have preserved their identity down the ages.

No doubt conditions would have remained quiet, with the Jews a tiny tolerated minority in North Africa. But the great flood of immigrants to Palestine due to the mass persecutions by the

Nazis, the establishment of Israel and the ensuing wars with Arab countries have changed the situation entirely. Immigrant Jews in Africa have been under pressure, and the existence of Israel has provided a refuge to which even native African Jews have gone. There were anti-Semitic riots in Morocco in 1961 but Jews were forbidden to emigrate to Israel since its existence was not recognized and thousands left the country illegally. Later 37,000 Jews left Libya. Tunisia was more tolerant, and until the 1967 war Egypt claimed that native Jews had freedom and were distinguished from Israelis. But then further difficulties arose and it was reported that the last remaining synagogues had been closed. In 1966 there were 3,000 Jews in Libya, 2,500 in Algeria and 3,000 in Egypt, with large communities of 20,000 in Tunisia and 30,000 in Morocco.

There is evidence of Jewish communities at oases in the Sahara from the ninth century, and some seem to have reached the western Sudan but were absorbed in time so that no traces of them remain today; some Saharan Jews were converted to Islam. Suggestions have been made of Jewish influence on West African traditional religion, in monotheistic belief or in the decorated breast plates of Ashanti priests, but these are highly unlikely to be Jewish influences and there is no sign of any of their missionary activity to compare with the huge efforts of Muslims and Christians. There are tiny communities of European Jews engaged in trade in the African tropics today.

The traditions of Ethiopia claim that their royal family is descended from Menelik I, the son of King Solomon and the Queen of Sheba. It is also said that other Jews arrived there after the Babylonian Captivity, and this is not impossible though not certain. From the Elephantiné papyri it appears that the Jews did not observe the reforms instituted in Judah and even worshipped other gods, and their mixed customs might explain some of the practices of Judaized tribes in Ethiopia today. But there were probably several Jewish immigrations into Ethiopia across the Red Sea from Arabia, though they were not organized communities. The Jewish dispersion over the centuries went up the Nile to the ancient kingdoms of Meroé and Axum, and there is an Ethiopian tradition that this kingdom was converted to Christianity from Judaism, which means perhaps that some of the tribes under the Axumite kingdom followed a form of Judaism. In A.D. 883 a Jewish writer Eldad wrote to his fellows in Spain of adventures in Ethiopia and of the Jews there who saved him.

Members of the Agao people in Ethiopia follow religious practices which are mixed Jewish and pagan, and are called Falashas or Esra'el by the Ethiopians though they are fully indigenous. Their places of worship (called *masjid* or mosque) have stone altars for sacrifice and they are the only Jews who have retained sacrifice. They practise circumcision, observe the Sabbath and the festivals of Passover, Harvest, Tabernacles, Covenant and Abraham. They know little Hebrew, but their priests have borrowed the Old Testament books in Ge'ez from Christians. The Falashas are monogamous and have high moral standards, and they have followed Christians in establishing monasteries where monks and nuns live strict lives. Mostly they are farmers, but some live in towns as depressed minorities. Estimates of their numbers vary between 15,000 and 60,000.

In South Africa Jews are numerous and are all immigrants from Europe and America. They have formed a wealthy and generally liberal minority and have naturally been opposed to racial prejudice. Largely with Jewish support in 1966 Mrs Helen Suzman was the only member of the multi-racial Progressive Party to retain her parliamentary seat in the general election. There were Jewish pilots for the Portuguese navigators in their early explorations round Africa, and over the centuries Jewish traders established themselves, particularly in South Africa. But the first organized community was not established at Cape Town till 1841. Today there are 116,000 Jews in South Africa with two hundred synagogues.

Indian Religions

Indian traders have long been settled all down the coast of East Africa and by 1860 there were thousands in Zanzibar and Mombasa. In that year indentured Indian labourers were introduced to Natal to work on sugar plantations, and more than

100,000, mostly Hindus, were said to be 'welcomed as permanent settlers in the colony'. In 1892 18,000 men were recruited in India to build the Uganda railway; most of these were chosen among Muslims for fear of trouble with Hindu customs and food laws.

Indians brought to Africa their religious beliefs and customs, of which the two dominant religions were Islam and Hinduism. The Hanafi law school followed by the Muslims has been mentioned. Hindu temples were built and Hindu ceremonies and festivals observed. Despite pressures against them Hindus remained active in East and South Africa, and generally kept to their religion. Many of them prospered through hard work, rising from manual labour to trade, and migrating to other parts from Natal, with their numbers increasing by natural growth. As Hinduism is not a missionary religion they have not sought to propagate their faith among Africans and it remains a purely Indian cult. In 1960 the Indians in Natal were mainly Hindus, and those in Transvaal rural areas generally Muslims. Over seventy per cent of South African Indians were Hindus, a number reckoned at 246,000. In 1960 in Kenya there were 46,000 Hindus, and 28,000 in Tanzania.

Some of the Indians follow minority Indian religions, such as the Parsis and Sikhs. The Parsis (originally Persians) are descendants of the old Zoroastrians of Persia and mostly come from their centre in Bombay, chiefly to Kenya and Tanzania where they are reckoned to number 500. Sacred fire burns always in their temples but there are no images. Their dead are not exposed to the vultures as in India, but are buried in lead coffins. As a tiny national minority the Parsis are not missionaries, but the Sikhs on the contrary are often energetic propagandists. The Sikh religion, a monotheism which combines elements from Islam and Hinduism, is most powerful in the Punjab but has centres in many Indian towns. It is open to all races, but while Sikhs have temples in Africa where their scriptures are chanted they do not yet appear to have organized regular missions among Africans, and their numbers are small, about 16,000 in 1960, mostly in Kenya. There were also about 6,000 Jains in Kenya, followers of a small but ancient Indian religion.

19 Relationships of African Religions

In his study of Islam in West Africa, J. S. Trimingham gives a diagram to illustrate six ways in which the different religious forces interact on one another.* In the tropics writers have often spoken of the mutual influences of Christianity and traditional religion and have ignored Islam, but nowadays all three major religions must be taken into account. Christianity in Africa influences traditional religion, but is itself modified by it. Islam affects traditional religion, but is also affected by it. And Islam is touched by Christianity, and exerts influences on it. Trimingham suggests thirty-two sub-sections, but the major portions can be considered more broadly.

The impact of Christianity upon African traditional religion is apparent in the breakdown or decay of ancient practices. There have been many direct conversions to the Christian faith, increasing over the years, but many African Christians in the tropics are descendants of three or four generations of Christian life, and have been moulded in Biblical and Christian thinking. The Christian effect upon the old religion can be seen in ruined temples, neglected festivals and initiations, and some revivals which are almost pathological, such as Mau Mau. In daily life a money economy has changed the forms of marriage dowry, and European legal fashions have changed procedures in customary courts. The popularity of European education, in every African country, has made an immense change in outlook. Despite some reactions, it seems likely that the outward forms of the old religion will continue to decay, and the pressures of an educated, historical and international faith are very great.

On the other hand there is undoubted influence from traditional religions upon the forms of Christianity in Africa. It must not be

* J. S. Trimingham, *Islam in West Africa*, p. 22 f.

supposed that the convert leaves all his beliefs behind and comes to Christianity with a blank mind. Sometimes the first generation convert makes a great break with the past, but his successors conform more to the pattern of life around them. Even when objects of worship are changed, images broken, charms (sometimes) thrown away, it is difficult to adopt a completely different world view. Moreover the European world view, not to mention many social customs, is not necessarily always Christian or Biblical. Early missionaries were shocked at bare breasts and introduced dresses with high necks and long skirts, which were not only absurd in the tropics but were not even better aesthetically. Today some Africanization of music, liturgy and costume is at work in the churches, and there is need for reinterpretation of doctrines into African forms without reverting to ideas that contradict a monotheistic faith. The effect of traditional religion may be seen in the independent churches, which are often most successful in proselytization by joining Christian and African practices. African law also affects Christian life, as seen in the many debates on polygamy.

Islam has had varying effects upon African life, of which the most upsetting were the holy wars of the seventh and the nineteenth centuries. But almost as drastic has been the colonial imposition of Islamic law upon pagan or only nominally Muslim peoples. Otherwise Islam has extended itself slowly, and has taken much longer to strike root than to establish a formal dominance. The points of contact between Islamic doctrine and traditional beliefs are not many but practice is more accommodating. Faith in one God and abhorrence of idols means that Islam is iconoclastic. But there is some compensation in the clearer ideas that Islam has about faith and conduct, reward and punishment, and life after death. Saint cults in North Africa and the eastern Sudan are popular attempts to fill gaps left after the decline of the old religion. Islamic law is imposed, but it often allows room for local custom that is not forbidden by authority. In family life, such as naming children, Islam enters more fully when a teacher comes to the home and utters sacred verses and prayers.

In reverse the traditional religion has affected Islam. This is seen in many elements that remain or even revive under long established Islamic dominance, not only in rites of circumcision, marriage and funerals, but dances and possessions. The Songhay have been under official Islam for centuries, and their men mostly go to the mosque for Friday communal prayers, but on Sundays there are dances in which people go into ecstasy under the belief in the age-old river spirits. Many Muslim traders are the chief salesmen of magical charms; some are verses from the Koran wrapped in leather amulets, and others are preparations of leaves, bones or skin. There is little difference in principle between this magic and that of the old medicine men. Local customs and laws manage to survive despite official action to replace them by Islamic laws, and African life has put up strong resistance against Islamic changes for centuries. The saint cults of the north and east have shrines which are thinly disguised holy places of the old religion, with sacred trees, wells and rocks. One of the most powerful modern Sufi orders is the Tijaniyya, which allows considerable laxity and gives important concessions to the comforts of modern times, so suiting African desires for life-affirmation.

Less studied but also important are the mutual influences of Christianity and Islam. Under imperialism there was some protection of Islam by colonial governments that tried to keep the peace by various modifications of indirect rule. But today there are Christian missions in many Muslim areas in the tropics, and smaller ones in the Islamic north. Converts from Islam to Christianity have been very few in North Africa, because conversion goes against the whole community, from which an individual can hardly be separated. But much indirect influence has come with Western education and government in the last hundred years. Economic and social changes have been forced upon Islamic society, for example by the abolition of slavery or the growth of industrialism. These changes have produced Islamic rulers who have partly or largely assimilated the outlook of the West, and therefore they have moved away in varying degrees from old Islamic ways, for example in legal, social or marital concerns.

The influence of Islam upon Christianity is less obvious and has been disputed. But it is clear that Western imperial governments imposed a change of policy upon Christian missions, and often adopted a role of 'protectors of Islam', needless to say for political and not religious reasons. The effect of Islam upon the ancient Christianity of Egypt was to drive it in upon itself for centuries, but the Arabic language largely replaced the old Coptic, even if there was little inter-religious dialogue. In modern times there have been serious attempts at dialogue between Christians and Muslims, retreats have been shared and common festivals observed. Although fundamentalist Christian missions still try a frontal attack on Islam, the clear failure of this method has made the larger missions, Roman Catholic and Protestant, give more attention to study and discussion (see p. 145).

Trimingham's six major sections do not distinguish between Christianity and secularism, and the two are identified as Western-ism. While it is true that Christianity, like Islam or any other religion, cannot travel devoid of cultural dress and for Chris-tianity that dress is chiefly Western, yet there are large areas of Western life that are commonly separated from Christian religion. Christianity is not just a religion, in the narrow sense of creeds and cultic practices, but education, industry and politics may pass beyond the point where they are recognizably Christian. If this were not so then China would have to be regarded as a Christian country, since it has adopted politics, industry and education from the West. And so have Islamic countries.

Moreover in many lands there are people who reject religion, either openly as in Russia and China, or by implication in Western and African cities. Mention has been made of some of the effects of modernism upon Islamic countries, and they lead not only to reformation within Islam but sometimes to rejection of religion altogether. The elders often fear European education because the young come back from school mocking the gods or Allah, just like the godless Nazarenes. Whether it is possible to live without any faith, or ever to break completely free from one's religious background, is debatable. The loosening of religious ties is evident in Africa as elsewhere, yet the small appeal of Commun-ism in Africa is remarkable. Egypt and other North and East African countries have received massive Russian help, but this has not made them Marxists in the sense of becoming atheists. Not only is atheism repulsive to Muslims, but the Communist world view is foreign to Africa and has been resisted. It is likely that Communism is strongest in those countries, like South Africa, where oppression is greatest, and where it challenges other faiths that have failed to practise the brotherhood demanded by their own creed.

20 Characteristics of Religion in Africa

Is it possible to distinguish national or continental emphases in religion ? Are the English really practical and the French logical ? Plenty has been written about French illogicality and the long traditions of English mysticism and romantic poetry. Nevertheless apart from caricature and exaggeration there are probably some attitudes that are formed by long tradition, and certain of these can be considered for Africa.

The African world view is life-affirming; a philosophy of vitalism or dynamism lies behind many attitudes and actions. This view clearly differs from the Indian, Hindu or Buddhist, tradition of world-denial, the exaltation of celibacy and monastic life, and the abnegation of material pleasures for an indefinable nirvana. The Indian belief in a painful rebirth, in human or animal form, into this sad life contrasts strongly with African belief that rebirth strengthens the family and is a desired return to this sunlit world.

This world-affirmation is behind arguments on polygamy, healing shrines which minister to the health of both body and soul, and dances and fertility cults. There is frank acceptance of the importance of sex, erotic dances, phallic symbols, vivid portrayal of sexual acts in art, and occasional saturnalia. This shocked the early missionaries, but Victorian Europe was only beginning to emerge from that medieval monastic attitude, perhaps itself an infection from India, which is now giving way to a more Hebrew or ancient Greek recognition of sex and material things as good. Egypt, of course, began the monastic movement, but that was because of its links with the east and in this respect it was out of tune with the rest of Africa.

'Africa, your gods are sex', wrote a European visitor after a short trip to South Africa. No doubt he had learned this notion from his European hosts there, but it could be said even more truly of Europe in South Africa which produced a 'coloured' population of over a million and now tries in vain to repress its sexual energies by laws against miscegenation. Yet it is remarkable in African religion that not only does it recognize the power of sex but it has its own strong ascetic tendency, in proper ways and times. Much African art is not sensual but highly formal. Many African religious leaders have been ascetic in their lives, from Algeria to Nigeria or Natal. Most religious movements have their times of retreat, prayer, fasting and chastity. The enclosed convents of Dahomey, which the ignorant used to suspect of sexual abuses, have long been shown to be places of rigid training where unchastity receives the severest punishment since it could bring danger from the gods. But African asceticism does not imply celibacy. Some people are naturally celibate, homosexual by constitution though not necessarily in practice. Yet marriage is the norm for society and it is honoured in religion. African priests and holy men are usually married and in this they follow the practice of most religions. Even Hindu and Buddhist priests marry and celibacy is only imposed on monks in community, and even then not always for life. The Roman Catholic church, alone among world religions, has imposed celibacy on clergy that was originally intended only for monks and this has been a great handicap to training priests in Africa. It is possible that there may be some change as an after-effect of the second Vatican Council. But Orthodox and Coptic priests are married, and only their bishops are celibate and are chosen from the monasteries.

Because of this life-affirming character African religion covers the whole of life. It has often been regarded as purely social, and although this is an exaggeration, there is a large social element in rituals, festivals, societies and brotherhoods. There is a personal and private element, in daily life and in the retreats and meditations of religious reformers; but this is manifested in social action. Religion plays an important part in the hierarchy of society, the choice of chiefs or the actions of politicians, and the association of chiefs with Islam or with independent churches is significant. Africans have been called 'incurably religious', but this they share with all mankind in needing an ideology that affects life and conduct.

A further characteristic of African religion is general tolerance. There have been outstanding exceptions: the Almohads in the Maghrib, the Fulani *jihads* in the western Sudan or the Mahdi in the east, and the Anglican–Roman war in Uganda. But other inter-religious battles have been too closely associated with imperial or commercial interests to be called purely religious. Africa today is a field of multi-religious activity that induces tolerance of different ways and beliefs. In the same family in the tropics it is possible to find Christians, Muslims and pagans. There has been traditional toleration of Christians and Jews by Muslims, with exceptions due to personal or political aberrations. The many divisions of the churches flourish in such a plural society, which allows for variety and did not organize the ancient shrines into one monolithic system. The many brotherhoods and saint cults of the Islamic areas permit variations within a general uniformity.

Some writers have suggested that Africans are too tolerant, conservative of their own interests and not bothered to evangelize. This impression arises partly because studies of African churches were generally concentrated upon the efforts of foreign missionaries, and there is very little literature on the life of African churches. But William Wadé Harris in the Ivory Coast, Samuel Crowther in the Niger Delta, Simon Kimbangu in the Congo, Reuben Spartas in Uganda, Alice Lenshina in Zambia, and Isaiah Shembé in Natal are all examples of people who have not only been inspired by individual religious experience, but have felt impelled to call others to the truth as they saw it, and they built communities that are impressive. Similarly in Islam Ahmad al-Badawi in Morocco and Egypt, Tijani and Sanusi from Algeria, Ahmad Bamba in Senegal and Dan Fodio in Nigeria were all fired by personal religion and set out to bring others into their way. The role of foreign missionaries must be fairly recognized, but also the role of their converts like the martyrs in Uganda and the Sudan. The naturalization of Islam and Christianity in the African continent is now being accomplished by

Africans themselves, even when they employ outside specialists for a time to do particular work.

Looking towards the future is a difficult, almost an impossible task. Prevalent tendencies can be noted and they may continue, but new factors may emerge within the African continent or invade it from the outside. There is no doubt that most of North and Sudanese Africa will remain Muslim. Movements of reform are taking place and there are closer links than for many centuries, both with Europe to the north and with the rest of Africa to the south. Barring accidents the Coptic church in Egypt will continue to play a minority but not insignificant part and keep firm links with Ethiopia. Ethiopia itself has found rather surprising ties with tropical Africa, much of which has become Christian without its help. There is an Orthodox church in Uganda which is directly connected with the Melkite Orthodox in Egypt. Christians in tropical and southern Africa are fragmented, but they have growing consultations through Christian Councils, and this may extend to some of the Independents and perhaps also to Roman Catholics. Roman Catholicism is the largest religious organization in Africa, despite its many different orders, and it is but a part of the whole Roman communion, which is the biggest religious organization in the world. Links with Europe are strong despite local naturalization.

There is no doubt that the old traditional African religion is declining in outward manifestations. Islam and Christianity have enormous advantages in superior organization, education, social prestige and international power. But while old clay temples vanish into dust, many traditional beliefs will no doubt persist for centuries. They have already done so under North African Islam or Ethiopian Christianity. Superficially Islam and Christianity will probably come to dominate the whole of Africa, and in some people and places their effect will be profound. Islam may gain the uncommitted more easily than the churches in West Africa or the coast of East Africa, because it appears less alien and has had centuries to adapt itself to a tropical African environment. But so far Islam has made little advance in central and southern Africa, as Christianity has little influence in North or Sudanese Africa apart from Egypt.

A complicating factor is the spread of Westernism which is not specifically, though perhaps by implication, Christian. This affects the Islamic north as much as the tropical and southern regions. Western culture and ideas of the state are different from the Islamic but are influential. Some newly independent African states, such as Mauretania, have declared themselves Islamic and this has been written into their constitutions. But others, after early professions of the same ideal, have quietly dropped it, because the demands of the *'ulama* teachers or Muslim brotherhoods were too much for the effective rulers of the state. Most African governments proclaim themselves impartial in religion, but this need not mean that they are secular. Ethiopia is a Christian state but has Muslim, pagan and Jewish minorities. What the absorption of Western ideas means is that educated people of different faiths often have more in common with each other than with illiterates of their own religion.

A general tolerance allows people of different religions to live side by side, to learn from one another, and prepare the way for a religious dialogue that was difficult or impossible in earlier centuries. The closer understanding of all religions, Christian, Muslim and traditional, can help towards a better adjustment of all African life to the many problems of modern times.

Bibliography

Traditional Religion and General

ABIMBOLA, W., *Ifa*, 1976.

ASHTON, H., *The Basuto*, 1952.

BEIER, U., *African Mud Sculpture*, 1963.

BUSIA, K. A., *The Position of the Chief in the Modern Political System of Ashanti*, 1951.

CARROLL, K., *Yoruba Religious Carving*, 1967.

COLIN, P., *Aspects de l' Âme Malgache*, 1959.

DANQUAH, J. B., *The Akan Doctrine of God*, 1944.

DIETERLEN, G., *Les Âmes des Dogons*, 1941.
  Essai sur la Religion Bambara, 1951.

EVANS-PRITCHARD, E. E., *Witchcraft, Oracles and Magic among the Azande*, 1937.
  Nuer Religion, 1956.

FAGG, W. and PLASS, M., *African Sculpture*, 1964.

FIELD, M. J., *Religion and Medicine of the Gã People*, 1937.
  Search for Security, 1960.

FORTES, M. and DIETERLEN, G., eds., *African Systems of Thought*, 1965.

GRIAULE, M., *Conversations with Ogotemmêli*, 1965.

IDOWU, E. B., *Olódùmarè, God in Yoruba Belief*, 1962.

JAHN, J., *Muntu*, 1961.

KAGAME, A., *La Philosophie bantu-rwandaise de l'Être*, 1956.

KENYATTA, J., *Facing Mount Kenya*, 1938.

KUPER, H., *An African Aristocracy*, 1947.

LIENHARDT, G., *Divinity and Experience*, 1961.

LITTLE, K. L., *The Mende of Sierra Leone*, 1951.

MBITI, J. S., *Concepts of God in Africa*, 1970.
  The Prayers of African Religion, 1975.

MIDDLETON, J., *Lugbara Religion*, 1960.

NADEL, S. F., *Nupe Religion*, 1954.

NKETIA, J. H., *Funeral Dirges of the Akan People*, 1955.

PARRINDER, E. G., *African Traditional Religion*, 3rd edn 1974.
   Witchcraft, European and African, 1963.
   African Mythology, 1968.

PARSONS, R. T., *Religion in an African Society*, 1964.

PAUW, B. A., *Religion in a Tswana Chiefdom*, 1960.

RATTRAY, R. S., *Ashanti*, 1923.
   Religion and Art in Ashanti, 1927.

ROUCH, J., *La Religion et la Magie Songhay*, 1960.

SCHEBESTA., *Les Pygmées du Congo Belge*, 1952.

SMITH, E. W., *The Ila-speaking Peoples of Northern Rhodesia*, 1920.
   ed., *African Ideas of God*, 1950.

TAYLOR, J. V., *The Primal Vision*, 1963.

TEMPELS, P., *Bantu Philosophy*, 1959.

TURNER, V. W., *The Drums of Affliction*, 1968.

UCHENDU, V. C., *The Igbo of Southeast Nigeria*, 1965.

VERGER, P., *Dieux d'Afrique*, 1954.

WILSON, M., *Communal Rituals of the Nyakyusa*, 1959.

ZAHAN, D., *Sociétés d'Initiation Bambara*, 1960.
   ed., *Réincarnation et vie mystique en Afrique Noire*, 1965.

Christianity

AJAYI, J. F. A., *Christian Missions in Nigeria, 1841–1891*, 1965.

ATIYA, A. S., *A History of Eastern Christianity*, 1968.

ATTWATER, D., *The Dissident Eastern Churches*, 1937.

BAËTA, C. G., *Prophetism in Ghana*, 1962.

BEETHAM, T. A., *Christianity and the New Africa*, 1967.

BRANDEL-SYRIER, M., *Black Woman in Search of God*, 1962.

CROSS, F. L., ed., *The Oxford Dictionary of the Christian Church*, 1958.

DAVIES, H., and SHEPHERD, R. H. W., *South African Missions*, 1954.

FOSTER, R. S., *The Sierra Leone Church*, 1961.

FREND, W. H. C., *The Donatist Church*, 1952.

GROVES, C. P., *The Planting of Christianity in Africa*, 4 vols., 1948–58.

HALIBURTON, G. M., *The Prophet Harris*, 1971.

ILOGU, E., *Christianity and Ibo Culture*, 1974.

LATOURETTE, K. S., *A History of the Expansion of Christianity*, 7 vols., 1937–45.

MARTIN, M. L., *Kimbangu*, 1975.

NEILL, S., *A History of Christian Missions*, 1964.

OLIVER, R., *The Missionary Factor in East Africa*, 1952.

PEEL, J. D. Y., *Aladura*, 1968.

PHILLIPS, A., ed., *Survey of African Marriage and Family Life*, 1953.

SUNDKLER, B. G. M., *Bantu Prophets in South Africa*, 1948.
The Christian Ministry in Africa, 1960.

TAYLOR, J. V., and LEHMANN, D., *Christians of the Copperbelt*, 1961.

TRIMINGHAM, J. S., *The Christian Church and Mission in Ethiopia*, 1950.

TURNER, H. W., *African Independent Church*, 2 vols., 1967.

WEBSTER. J. B., *The African Churches among the Yoruba*, 1964.

WELBOURN, F. B., *East African Rebels*, 1961.
and OGOT, B. A., *A Place to Feel at Home*, 1966.

WILLIAMSON, S. G., *Akan Religion and Christian Faith*, 1965.

WISHLADE, R. L., *Sectarianism in Southern Nyasaland*, 1965.

Islam

ABUN-NASR, J. M., *The Tijaniyya*, 1965.

ANDERSON, J. N. D., *Islamic Law in Africa*, 1954.

BEHRMAN, L. C., *Muslim Brotherhood and Politics in Senegal*, 1970.

BOVILL, E. W., *The Golden Trade of the Moors*, 1958.

EVANS-PRITCHARD, E. E., *The Sanusi of Cyrenaica*, 1949.

FISHER, H. J., *Ahmadiyya*, 1963.

GILSENAN, M., *Saint and Sufi in Modern Egypt*, 1973.

GREENBERG, J., *The Influence of Islam on a Sudanese Religion*, 1946.

HITTI, P. K., *History of the Arabs*, 1937.

HOLT, P. M., *The Mahdist State in the Sudan*, 1958.

IBN BATTUTA, *Travels in Asia and Africa*, trs. 1929.

LEWIS, I. M., ed., *Islam in Tropical Africa*, 1966.
A Pastoral Democracy, 1961.

LHOTE, H., *Les Touaregs du Hoggar*, 1944.

MINER, H., *The Primitive City of Timbuctoo*, 1953.

MITCHELL, R. P., *The Society of the Muslim Brothers*, 1969.

MONTEIL, C., *Djenné*, 1932.

NADEL, S. F., *A Black Byzantium*, 1942.

OLIVER, and FAGE, J. D., *A Short History of Africa*, 1962.

PRINS, A. H. J., *The Swahili-speaking Peoples of Zanzibar and the East African Coast*, 1961.

ROUCH, J., *Les Songhay*, 1954.

SMITH, M. F., *Baba of Karo*, 1954.

SMITH, W. C., *Islam in Modern History*, 1957.

TRIMINGHAM, J. S., *Islam in the Sudan*, 1949.

   Islam in Ethiopia, 1952.

   Islam in West Africa, 1959.

   A History of Islam in West Africa, 1962.

   Islam in East Africa, 1964.

   The Sufi Orders in Islam, 1971.

WESTERMARCK, E., *Ritual and Belief in Morocco*, 2 vols., 1926.

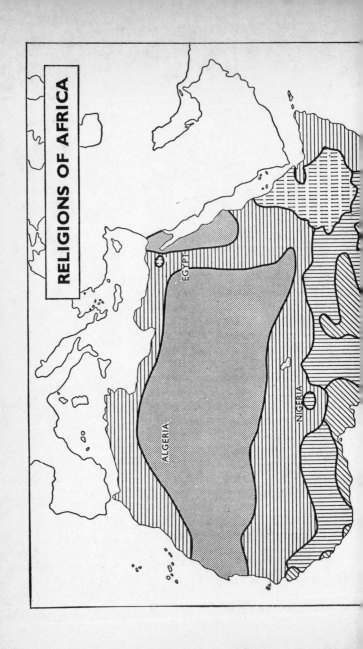

RELIGIONS OF AFRICA

ALGERIA

EGYPT

NIGERIA

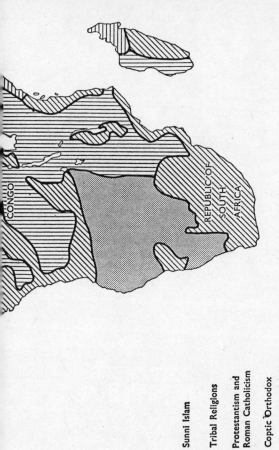

CONGO

REPUBLIC OF
SOUTH
AFRICA

Sunni Islam

Tribal Religions

Protestantism and
Roman Catholicism

Coptic Orthodox

Scattered Tribal and
Missionary Religions

Index

247

Index

Index

Also published by Sheldon Press

African Traditional Religion

GEOFFREY PARRINDER

Third edition, with a new preface by the Author

This book is now the standard work on religion in Africa. The third edition has been thoroughly revised and updated.

'It seems almost incredible that so much can be set down so clearly and with such precision in so little space. The book makes clear not only the homogeneity of a great deal of negro African traditional belief and practice, but also that this indeed cannot be understood without it.'

Methodist Recorder

'This book fills an important role, giving so much information in such a compendious form. It is also refreshing to find a writer who is able to write broadly without getting bogged down in tribal detail. I regard him [Parrinder] as the leading authority on African religions in general.'

Professor J. C. Carothers

'Dr Geoffrey Parrinder is the doyen of scholars on African Traditional Religion. In fact one might almost say that it was he who in the 1950s put the subject on the academic and university map ... Dr Parrinder's book, succinct, tightly packed and flowing over in an inimitable way which no one else has so successfully achieved.'

Noel King, Professor of History and Comparative Religion,
University of California

Also published by Sheldon Press

Asian Religions

GEOFFREY PARRINDER

This clear, concise guide gives brief histories and backgrounds of Asia's living religions: Islam, Hinduism and the other Indian faiths, Buddhism, the Chinese religions and Japanese Shinto. The scriptures, religious life and present-day position of these religions is also discussed. The author seeks to dispel the myth that all religions are essentially the same and to show the amazing variety of beliefs and practices in Asia.

'. . . is exactly what it claims to be and excellently so.'

Theology

'Behind the simple style there is obviously wide and up-to-date knowledge of the Asian religious situation.'

Baptist Times

If you would like a complete list of books published by Sheldon Press, please write to the Editorial Department, Sheldon Press, Marylebone Road, London NW1 4DU.

CHESTER COLLEGE LIBRARY